T0285267

THE JOY OF CONSENT

A Philosophy of Good Sex

MANON GARCIA

The Belknap Press of Harvard University Press

CAMBRIDGE, MASSACHUSETTS   LONDON, ENGLAND   2023

First printing

LIBRARY OF CONGRESS CATALOGING-IN-PUBLICATION DATA

Names: Garcia, Manon, 1985– author.
Title: The joy of consent : a philosophy of good sex / Manon Garcia.
Other titles: Conversation des sexes. English
Description: Cambridge, Massachusetts ; London, England : The Belknap Press
of Harvard University Press, 2023. | First French edition published as La
Conversation des sexes: philosophie du consentement by Climats, a department
of éditions Flammarion, 2021. | Includes bibliographical references and index.
Identifiers: LCCN 2022061129 | ISBN 9780674279131 (cloth)
Subjects: LCSH: Sexual consent. | Sexual ethics. | Sexual harassment. |
Women—Violence against. | Sexism.
Classification: LCC HQ32 .G36513 2023 | DDC 176/.4—dc23/eng/20230223
LC record available at https://lccn.loc.gov/2022061129

To Norah and Éliane, in the hope that your world
will be freer than ours

To Tamer

Contents

Why do you consult their mouths, when it is not they who should speak? Consult their eyes, their complexion, their breathing, their fearful air, their soft resistance: this is the language that nature gives them to answer you. The mouth always says no, and must say it; but the accent it adds to it is not always the same, and this accent cannot lie. Does not the woman have the same needs as the man, without having the same right to express them?

—JEAN-JACQUES ROUSSEAU

The major distinction between intercourse (normal) and rape (abnormal) is that the normal happens so often that one cannot get anyone to see anything wrong with it.

—CATHARINE MACKINNON

INTRODUCTION

WHO IS RUINING SEX? American puritanism? Feminist college students? Macho men? In newspapers as well as in academic research, a worry is looming: What if people were to stop having sex? Many grown-ups prefer a thrilling TV show to a good time with a partner, and we are told college students do not know how to become intimate without dating apps or a lot of alcohol. Although many agree that there is a problem, its exact nature divides deeply. For some, there is no doubt that it is the consent culture developed on American college campuses that ruined our sex lives. Nowadays, a reasonable young man should not have sex with a lady without making her sign a contract or, better, talking first to his dad's lawyer. For others, the consent culture is the cure rather than the disease—a response to the way sex has served as a pretense and an occasion for male sexist violence. The reason people are having less sex is that women are finally strong enough to say they do not want what has historically been forced on them. Either as the guilty party or the solution, consent is at the core of the reorganization of our sex lives.

Misleading Intuitions

We think we know what consent means. There is, after all, a great deal of discourse in which consent is taken as an excellent criterion to distinguish between good and bad—between good and bad government, good and bad contract, good sex and rape. We also know what consent is because we consent all the time, whether we are accessing a website, signing up for a credit card, or voting. And we know that the vocabulary of consent is useful in thinking about amorous and sexual relationships in a (hopefully) egalitarian context between men and women.

But we don't actually have a clear understanding of consent. Our apparent understanding rests on mistaken intuitions that conceive of consent as self-evident. Regarding the definition of consent, it is commonly held that sex is consensual when two (or more) people agree to have sex with each other. This makes some sense. Of course, establishing sexual consent in court can be difficult, especially given the usually private context of sex, but in ordinary contexts consent is taken to be given when people agree. Besides this intuition that to consent is to agree, the common view on consent consists of two more intuitions: consensual sex is permissible and permissible sex is consensual; nonconsensual sex is rare, and it is rape. (As I discuss below, although there is much evidence that rape is not rare, and although this evidence is widely reported, most people behave as though rape is highly aberrational.)

Yet none of these intuitions is as simple as it seems, calling into question whether consent itself is really so straightforward as both its proponents and doubters presume. First, the definition of consent is not self-evident. What is it, indeed, to "agree" to have sex? The rosy picture that comes to mind is that of two people who love each other, have sexual desire for each other, and have sex on the basis of this reciprocal love and desire. Another increasingly popular representation is that of "Tinder sex"—nearly immediate sexual interactions between strangers, in which the act amounts to a mutual provision of bodies with the object of all partners' sexual pleasure. In that context, the agreement appears almost contractual. Indeed, in some cases, users of dating and hook-up apps agree ahead of time on the exact sexual services they will exchange.

But the range of situations in which one can agree to sex is much larger than these images convey. You may agree to sex because you have an urge to have sex with a given person, but you may also agree to sex because you know that your partner will lengthily insist and you have to wake up early the next day so you would rather say yes, get it over with, and go to bed. You may agree because it's your job, because you need money and the sex will be paid for, because you're scared to anger your partner, or because you hope to get or keep a job by agreeing. You may also agree because you feel lonely, because you are in need of physical contact, or because, after all, why not? You may agree because the other person seems lonely, because they seem to really want it, because you don't have the courage to say no, or because it would seem impolite or confrontational to do so.

The terms by which one agrees to have sex may be vague. When one agrees to go into another's hotel room, does one agree to have sex with the occupant, as defenders of disgraced former Hollywood mogul Harvey Weinstein implied as woman after woman accused him of rape? Does an agreement to have nonpenetrative sex (like oral sex or sexual petting) mean, or signal, an agreement to penetrative sex? If you agreed to have sex with someone, but this person lied about their identity to seduce you, did you really agree to the sexual encounter? It is easy to imagine that the response to this question will differ depending on the status of the liar—their age, marital circumstances, and so on.

Here's an even trickier question: What should we think of situations in which a partner's behavior changes radically once sex starts? Many news articles and testimonies on social media recount cases of women who agreed to have sex with a sweet and loving man who, as soon as sex started, seemed to turn into someone else completely—someone domineering or even violent. Does an agreement to have sex with someone imply an agreement to have whatever kind of sex that person wants?

This list of questions, purposely inspired by mundane situations as well as morally troubling ones, challenges the apparent simplicity of consent. The definition of consent as a simple agreement to have sex is obviously insufficient.

It is precisely this insufficient equation between consent and agreement that undergirds the current moral consensus and legal mechanics surrounding sexual relations in liberal societies. Sex is viewed as a matter of privacy that is morally permissible as long as the participants are consenting adults, an intuition that has for several decades and in many countries grounded changes in the legal definition of rape and inspired the adoption of a minimal age for consent. Yet when we go through the above nonexhaustive lists of reasons for which one might agree to sex, it is clear that agreement is not consent's twin: agreement may be more or less free, more or less constrained, and it does not always reflect a choice that is free enough to be considered consent in the sense that philosophers and lawyers give this word. To agree to sex when you can refuse it without incurring risk is not the same as agreeing to sex when your safety or your job depends on it. In law, which I will return to in detail, there are limits to the power of consent: the consent of the parties does not always suffice to make an agreement valid (for instance, in most jurisdictions it is forbidden to kill someone even if they freely agree to be killed), and most legal systems establish conditions that must obtain lest even an apparently free agreement be invalid. For instance, labor law often deems certain work conditions unlawful—and society deems them wrong—even if the worker accepts them. Thus a work contract that stipulates a salary below the minimum wage would not be valid; the contract would not bind the people who sign it.

It seems therefore that if sexual consent is to render sex permissible, then it cannot be just any type of agreement, for whatever reason. We think consent is self-evident because we think it is equivalent to agreement, yet agreement on its own is not always the same thing as consent. And so we must think harder about what consent actually involves.

Mores and the Law

The above examples of agreement's inadequacy show us two things. First, they demonstrate that our intuitions about consent are simplistic and wrong. Second, they reveal a tension between a legal approach to consent and a moral one. One can readily imagine situations in which the partners' consent would be invalid on a legal level yet valid on a moral one, and the other way around. For example, in France, the purchase of sexual services is illegal, so it is forbidden to consent to sex in exchange for money. Thus a prostitute cannot be considered as consenting in the context of their job, as the sex they provide is prohibited. However, sex workers who choose this activity and who are not the victims of pimps and human trafficking consent to the sex they sell, at least according to some sense of consent. In the same way, until very recently, willing participants in BDSM play (a term referring to bondage, discipline, dominance, submission, sadism, and masochism) could not be considered consenting because BDSM practices constituted offenses of assault and battery. The legal prohibition of this type of sex appears to many observers as a form of state puritanism and paternalism.[1] Conversely, until the 1970s in the United States, 1990 in France, and 1997 in Germany, it was considered impossible to rape one's spouse: any sex that took place between spouses was deemed consensual and permissible, including sex obtained through threat, coercion, and violence. In such a context, sex could be morally nonconsensual and still be legal. Moral and legal definitions of consent can, therefore, be in conflict. Some sex can be consensual and unlawful, and some nonconsensual yet lawful.

These examples show that consent is not only a tool we might use to prosecute or otherwise punish bad sex, whether that means putting a person in prison, kicking them out of school, or firing them from a job. Consent is also a concept at the heart of a moral problem—the problem of knowing how we *ought* to have sex. The intuition that consent is a legal term, raising mainly legal issues, oversimplifies the problem. When we use the vocabulary of consent in the prosecution of bad sex, we in fact take for granted two views from which morality is inextricable: first, consent is morally necessary for a sexual encounter to be good; second, the state, thus the law, should protect us against the moral wrong of bad sex.

The Parking Lot Scenario and Other Myths

The intuition that any sex is permissible if it is consensual is wrong, and so is its correlate—that any lawful sex is consensual. This second intuition, that any lawful sex is consensual, is linked to the idea that people largely consent to the sex they have, so that rape is an exceptional phenomenon. As analyses of rape culture confirm, rape is commonly understood to be a crime committed by a stranger, at night, in a parking lot, with a knife or a gun. In this scenario, the rapist is perceived as a misfit, often mentally ill, like a serial killer in a TV show. The rapist is not held to be an ordinary man. Of course, a rapist could be a deranged stranger opportunistically assaulting people, but, in contrast to myth, this is not at all a typical scenario. In most cases, the rape victim knows the perpetrator, and the crime happens in a familiar place. According to the Rape, Abuse & Incest National Network, in about 75 percent of US rape cases, the victim is acquainted with the perpetrator; in 33 percent of rape cases, the perpetrator is the partner or ex-partner of the victim. In France, the figures are even more striking. In 2016, 91 percent of actual or attempted rapes were perpetrated by a person known to the victim. In 47 percent of cases, the perpetrator was the partner or ex-partner of the victim.[2]

More importantly, rape happens far more often than the parking lot scenario leads us to believe. This scenario rests on the idea that rapists are sick, out-of-control people and that if such people are simply put away from society, then we can eliminate rape. But profiles of rapists show that they are not monsters, and they are not extraordinary. For the most part, they are the guys next door. They belong to all social classes. They are not lashing out in desperation because they are unable to find willing partners; in fact, they often have more active sex lives than the average man in their respective societies. And there are very many of them. In 2021 alone the FBI reported that 149,724 men committed sex offenses in the United States. This number is surely low; consider that only about 35 percent of sexual offenses were reported to the authorities in 2013.[3]

It is because people hold the intuition that rapists are crazy and abnormal that we have a tendency to exonerate rapists who do not fit this imaginary profile. The philosopher Kate Manne calls this "himpathy"—the sympathy that men accused of rape and sexual assault receive in courts and in the media. Manne takes the example of Brock Turner, a Stanford University student who was caught in the act of raping an unconscious fellow student, Chanel Miller. Turner received widespread support from the public and enjoyed a lenient judicial hearing. The judge in the case sentenced him to six months in jail—he served only three—because, the judge said, the conviction itself would have a "serious impact" on the young man's life.[4] This kind of sympathy, born of the false intuition that "real" rapists are sick and that "normal" men therefore cannot be rapists, perpetuates rape culture—that is, a culture in which sexual violence is constantly minimized and hidden and thus rendered socially acceptable.

Our intuitions concerning rapists' profiles are false and so are our intuitions about the experience of rape. Contrary to what many people think, rapes and sexual assaults make up a considerable portion of people's sexual experiences. In the United States, there are, on average, 463,634 rape and sexual assault victims, age twelve or older, each year.[5] One in five US women has experienced completed or attempted rape in her lifetime.[6] On average almost 130,000 rapes were reported to authorities each year between 2013 and 2020, according to the FBI.[7] Again, it is commonly recognized by researchers that rapes and sexual assaults are underreported, so it is very likely that the actual figures are much higher. In any case, these numbers make clear that the experience of rape and sexual assault is common, especially among women.

Is Nonconsensual Sex Rape?

This short analysis of myths about rape, rapists, and their victims aims to challenge one of our primary intuitions about consent: viewing consent as a self-evident criterion to distinguish (good) sex and rape is inextricably linked to the idea that, overall, people's experience of sex is an experience of consent. Despite our tendency to think of nonconsent as extraordinary, studies on sex and sexual violence show a very different situation: both the experience of rape and the experience of less-than-fully consensual sex are widely shared. Studies on these issues are still scarce, but recent research highlights the frequency of nonconsensual sex in heterosexual as well as nonheterosexual relationships, not only in the form of legally recognized marital rape but also in subtler forms that a court may not recognize as rape—such as sex obtained through threats, coercion, intimidation, and blackmail.[8] Taken together, the statistics concerning sexual violence and the studies of nonconsent in stable relationships draw a picture that is resolutely different than the simplistic view of self-evident consent. Consent is neither self-evident in the sense that it is present in the large majority of sexual encounters, nor in the sense that we know exactly what we are talking about when we speak of consent.

That consent is in fact nuanced and ambiguous becomes obvious when we assess the claim that all nonconsensual sex is rape. This claim is grounded in our intuitive understanding of rape, and at first glance it seems clearly to be true: obviously, where consent is absent, rape has occurred. This is not only what we intuit but also what lawmakers have in mind when they define rape: a rape occurs when one of the partners does not agree to have sex with the other(s), yet sex—usually meaning penetrative sex—takes place. Yet there are cases when a person claims they had sex against their will, but a court finds they were not raped, because the alleged perpetrator had no intention to rape. According to French criminal law, for instance, it is not enough that the facts show a defendant broke the law; every crime must also have a moral element. That is, the author of the facts must have intended to break the law when they did so. Thus there cannot be rape if the instigator of penetrative sex obtained by violence, coercion, threat, or surprise had no intention to rape. (US criminal law also incorporates a requirement of criminal intent, known by the Latin term *mens rea*.) One might argue that this is simply a failure of law to accord with common understanding, yet sociologists who study consent in action find that when people give accounts of their experiences of nonconsent, they very frequently refuse the use of the term "rape." Study respondents tend to feel that this term refers to an unbearable violent act, whereas their experience is rather of situations that are deeply unpleasant but ordinary and livable. Nicola Gavey's important book *Just Sex?* overflows with examples of women who reluctantly acquiesce to undesired sex with insisting husbands—husbands who know full well that their wives do not want sex—but also reject the notion that they have been raped.[9]

More broadly, the question of whether all nonconsensual sex is rape is an invitation to wonder what it is to *not* consent. Not agreeing to do something can take many forms. Is it saying no? Must one struggle frantically? Is it enough to not say yes? Is it not really being in the mood, or need one be strongly opposed? Consider that members of many couples have the experience of not feeling sexual desire at the same time. When you have sex with your spouse to please them, even though you don't feel like having sex, do you consent to sex? It is probable that the response to this question depends on the details of the scenario. In the context of a relationship that is generally going well and in which sex is not a subject of haggling, one can easily conceive of a sexual encounter in which one partner joyfully accepts sex initiated by the other, even though the accepting partner is not experiencing sexual desire in the moment but only wishes to please the other. One has, in other words, little trouble imagining a nondesiring person agreeing to sex with their partner out of a sense of love for them. But let us imagine another scenario, one in which a partner insists on having sex every night, even when their partner has had an exhausting day, is physically unwell, or is feeling depressed. Now, let us imagine that the undesiring partner gives in, not out of love but in order to "have some peace." In this second scenario, the evidence of consent is far less tangible than in the first one.

Let us imagine a third scenario, in which a man and a woman meet at a party. They don't know each other. They chat, they have fun. They dance, they kiss, they have a great time. At the end of the evening, the man offers to walk the woman home. She would be happy to leave it at that for the night, but she already told the man where she lives, and he insists that it is not a big detour for him. She tells herself that it is late and she will probably feel safer on the street if she walks with him. She accepts. When they reach her building, the man insists on coming up to her apartment. He promises he won't stay long. She would rather go to sleep, but he went out of his way, and it's cold outside, so she accepts. They go up, he kisses her, she lets him, but she doesn't want to go further. His hand finds its way under her shirt; he insists. She gently pushes him away, but she is worried that if she says no, she'll be seen as a tease. And he seems to really want her. Maybe it won't be that bad after all. And, let's be honest, it's probably going to be over fast. She is less and less in the mood, though. But what if he takes a rejection badly? What if he gets angry? What if he were to force her? She lets him proceed. They have sex.

In this scenario, the influence of social norms is clear: the woman does not want to be a tease, male desire is conceived as irrepressible, and the woman feels like she owes the man for the favor of walking her home. These norms lead the woman to have a sexual relationship she did not want. Meanwhile the man may well go home believing he has not just had nonconsensual sex. It is unlikely that he feels he was in the wrong, even if he may know, more or less consciously, that the woman did not seem really excited.

These three scenarios—agreeing to sex in order to please a loved one, agreeing to sex in order to "get some peace," and agreeing to sex because one feels obligated by social norms—are all plausible. Indeed, many adults have experienced situations like these. In all three scenarios, a person agrees to sex, but have they consented? Have they been raped? The context matters a great deal, compelling us to recognize the complexities of consent. When we consider the many reasons that people agree to sex, we cannot escape the conclusion that consent—construed as agreement—isn't a sufficient condition for good sex. And the testimonies of our peers make clear that the absence of consent isn't equivalent to rape.

Consent and Patriarchy

To better understand what is going on in these scenarios, and to grasp the relationship between consent and good sex, it is essential to clarify the role consent plays in patriarchy, understood as the sociopolitical system that organizes the social oppression of women by men. Consent is a key term of contemporary feminist discourse because it is implicitly understood as referring to women's sexual consent, especially in their relations with men. For most people, when we talk about sexual consent, we talk about women's consent to sex in the context of a heterosexual relationship. Yet, as I will explain later, I disagree with this (sexist) assumption. I therefore consider not only what patriarchy does to the consent and desires of women but also of men and nonbinary people, in the context of heterosexual as well as nonheterosexual relationships. True, the problem of consent is particularly acute in heterosexual relationships, and this justifies particular attention to these relationships. But people in nonheterosexual relationships are also stakeholders in the patriarchal system, and that system shapes their intimate lives.

Just as I refuse the notion that sexual consent refers solely to women's consent to heterosexual intercourse, I reject a neutral analysis of consent, which argues that men and women can consent to sex in exactly the same way. To the contrary, I show that such an analysis, oblivious to the effects of male domination not only on society but also on our pleasures and our desires, misses precisely the nuances that make consent such a fetching but also inadequate solution to the problem of bad sex. The discourse of consent reflects women's liberation: historically, women haven't been considered autonomous people; the capacity to consent highlights the autonomy that women have gained. But consent is also a risk, given how its vocabulary can be used to conceal gender injustice.

How so, you might ask—what is the risk? One risk is that, under patriarchal conditions, a consent regime may actually respond only to nonconsent. That is, having sex with a person who says no will be understood as rape, but the same will not be true of having sex with a person who says nothing at all. The French have an adage: "who does not say a word consents"—in France as elsewhere, silence has traditionally been seen as a sign of consent. If one's concern is to identify physically violent rape, then only nonconsent is considered worthy of attention.

Decades of feminist work, some of which crystallized in debates surrounding sexual consent in the context of the #MeToo movement, have complicated this picture in at least two ways. First, thinkers and activists have highlighted experiences in which people did not necessarily say no or otherwise clearly manifest nonconsent, yet in which they claimed they did not consent. Attention has thus shifted to the "gray zone" between sex that is fully consensual and sex that is fully nonconsensual and identified as rape. And we now have the resources to think about consent in affirmative terms: consent's conditions of validity and expression have become a topic of investigation because eschewing the traditionally recognized manifestations of nonconsent is no longer viewed as sufficient to identify consent itself. In other words, people are beginning to wonder if we can use the idea of consent not only to discern impermissible sex but also to figure out what constitutes good sex. Second, feminist debates about consent have made it possible to wonder whether consent is the right tool to evaluate the permissibility of sexual experiences. On the one hand, consent is more and more firmly embedded in our psyches as the only framework through which it is possible to conceive and practice nonoppressive sexual and amorous relationships. On the other hand, the rise of consent has made it a target of criticisms, as opponents decry it as worse than useless—indeed, harmful to those who want to have freer and more egalitarian sex and love.

It is not my goal to defend any of the commonly held positions but instead to take seriously the impact of gender norms and patriarchy on our sexual lives. The moral and political questions are urgent: How can we reimagine sex and love so that they are not based on sexist and inegalitarian social norms? How can we conceive of amorous relations that would be, if not joyful, at least harmless? How does gender inequality manifest itself in love and sex? How can we fight against the perpetuation of oppressive and unjust norms in our intimate lives? And, finally, how can the concept of consent help us to address these issues?

For a Philosophy of Sexual Consent

Here, then, is the departure point of this book. Consent, we are made to understand, is at the heart of living a good sexual life and a good life more broadly. Consent orients us in our action toward each other and in constructing our sense of self. Yet, despite its wide use, the notion of consent produces overlooked moral inferences—first among them, that consent is the criterion for permissible sex. If we are to affirm that consent is the key to egalitarian and free intimacy, then we must go beyond our simplistic intuitions and propose a more rigorous analysis. Consent must be precisely defined, its functioning must be analyzed in a way that gives an account of its power of legitimation, and the conditions for a valid exercise of consent must be established.

This book argues for a moral analysis of consent. I am convinced of the importance of legal debates on how to prosecute rape and adjudicate harassment and assault allegations on campuses. I believe the law should be committed to sexual justice without exacerbating mass incarceration and racial injustice—a fraught terrain, as the prosecution of sexual violence and harassment often becomes a means for selectively punishing people of color. But law is not the topic of this book. Law can be built only on the basis of moral and political views, which are too rarely articulated with clarity. Therefore, I want here to discuss the moral and political views of consent, on the basis of which legal debates—and perhaps policymaking—can then unfold.

Because my goal is not to supply legal language but to pursue justice, I aim not only to analyze what consent is but also to determine whether, and under which conditions, it can effectively be an emancipatory tool. To do so I will rely on what the anthropologist Clifford Geertz called "thick descriptions"—detailed examples and hypotheticals like those above, which not only describe the actions of agents but also the contexts in which these actions take place and the meanings that these contexts can confer on them.[10] To put the matter bluntly, my overarching claim is that a moral and political analysis of consent reveals two problems we must solve, only one of which is addressed—usually unsatisfyingly—in the mainstream consent discourse. The first problem, the one that we can't stop talking about, is to establish which kinds of sexual relations are wrong and therefore ought to be impermissible. The second problem is that of knowing what good sex looks like—something we cannot know by adopting only the perspective of those who can or do impose their desires and their sexual practices on others. My goal, then, is not simply to describe consent but to show how it can contribute to the normative and emancipatory enterprise that sex can and should be.[11]

A French American Perspective

Why hold onto consent to promote sexual emancipation and why write about it? Probably at least partly for biographical reasons. I was born, raised, and trained as a philosopher in France but had been living and teaching in the United States for seven years when I started writing this book. My French colleagues and the French media (which pays attention to philosophers) see me as deeply influenced by American thought and values. When, in 2017, I was interviewed by a French newspaper about affirmative consent policies, several French writers published critical responses.[12] They worried that I would endanger the French art of love by importing American puritanism. In the United States, meanwhile, I am often perceived as *very* French, especially when it comes to talking freely about sex. The French seem convinced that Americans talk about consent all the time but rarely have sex. Americans, for their part, seem concerned that French people have a lot of sex but do not care enough about consent. According to these clichés, Americans' obsession with consent is ruining sex, while the French are obsessed with sex at the expense of gender equality. Like most clichés, these are both exaggerated and truthful.

In my first book, I argued that women are not naturally submissive but are made to submit to men by the gender norms of femininity. A consequence of this thesis is that these norms make it harder for women to reject men's sexual advances than for men to reject women's. Another consequence is that women are taught by society that they should prioritize other people's desires, pleasures, and well-being over their own. It therefore seemed logical to me to shift attention to our intimate lives: surely, if all of this is true—if women are made to submit—then it must be very difficult not only to successfully contest sexual violence but also, simply, to have a joyful sex life. How can women have a fulfilling intimate life if patriarchy prevents them from seeking their own pleasure?

I decided to write a book on sex through the prism of consent both because I am interested in the question of what women can choose in a patriarchal context and because consent is the most popular framework through which to think about women's choices in the context of sex. Consent has indeed triumphed; no other concept is so central to the practice of sex equality today. The importance of consent has been widely discussed in the United States at least since the adoption of an affirmative consent policy at Antioch College in 1991. In the aftermath of #MeToo, consent has also become the foundation of the mainstream discourse on love and sex in Continental Europe and in many other places where it was, until just a few years ago, the special province of academics and feminist activists.

Writing a philosophy book on sex and consent means trying to make the most of this French American position in which I find myself, not only regarding sex and consent, but also on the question of what it is to do philosophy. Indeed, not only sexual obsessions but also philosophical methods differ between France and the Anglophone world in general. In broad strokes, French philosophy is notorious for tackling very large issues and trying to make sense of them through interdisciplinary work and references to past philosophers. Anglophone philosophy—insofar as it overlaps with what is usually called analytic philosophy—is probably less ambitious in its scope and more ambitious in its quest for precision, logical consistency, and clarity. While the French constantly refer to past philosophers, sometimes to the point of hiding behind them to advance their own ideas, analytic philosophers often seem to focus exclusively on their contemporaries. Historically, French philosophy addressed a general audience—think of how widely Sartre, Beauvoir, Camus, and Foucault were read—while the Anglophones built philosophical truth in specialized academic journals. This last distinction, it should be said, has faded somewhat in the last decade or so, with a growing commitment to "public philosophy"—philosophical writing addressing a general audience—in the Anglophone world.

This sketch of differences simplifies complex and diverse ways of doing philosophy. Yet it suffices to hint at what a philosophy taking the best of both traditions should endeavor to do: embrace the broad ambition of the French, take interest in neighboring disciplines, and use the philosophers of the past, while committing to the precision, clarity, and argumentative efficiency of the Anglophone philosophical world. And speak not only to other philosophers but also to a general audience. This last commitment is particularly important for me. I love philosophy insofar as it intends to make sense of the world and of our lives, but I dislike the tendency of some philosophers—Anglophone and French—to write in a way that very few people can understand. *Ce que l'on conçoit bien s'énonce clairement,* as the French saying goes: "what is well conceived can be clearly stated." At the same time, I have always been skeptical of the view, held by some publishers and journalists, that nonacademics cannot read "real philosophy"—that the uninitiated can at most imbibe simplified arguments, made agreeable by references to popular culture or current politics. (To be clear, I am not averse to these references as such, only to the idea that the general public cannot understand any theoretical position unaccompanied by them.) I believe that one can write philosophy in a way that does not presuppose a specific knowledge of philosophy but which still uses references to the past and some technical analyses as long as they are justified. This is my methodological horizon.

My French American situation gave me yet another insight: very often, Anglophone humanities and social sciences—here again, broad strokes—cite primarily works in English and examples from the Anglophone world, thus narrowing their analyses and their arguments. But my specific subjects—sex, intimacy, love, and consent—are of course also subjects of French scholarship, literature, and jurisprudence. I believe that these sources address the issues of interest in ways that have not been acknowledged by contemporary Anglophone philosophy. The reverse is also true, as French philosophers ignore or trivialize Anglophone arguments about the politics and morality of sex. That is why I wrote this book in French and now I am writing a version of it in English. In both cases, my ambition is to respond to a pressing question: Can consent help us achieve good sex lives?

1

SAYING YES TO SEX IS NOT LIKE
SAYING YES TO A CUP OF TEA

WHAT IS CONSENT? Is consent a legal issue? A moral one? Are we talking about the same thing when we talk about sexual consent and consent in general? To understand and evaluate the contemporary debates on consent in intimate relationships, these are the first questions to address. And in so doing, we will need to address a further important question: Why are we intuitively convinced that there is something about sex that makes it different from other activities we do with other people, like going on a hike, or drinking tea together?

This is not a purely theoretical question. We are trying to figure out what elements of philosophical, legal, and historical thought about consent in general we can use in order to understand sexual consent. It seems self-evident that sexual consent is a subcategory of consent; that it is the phenomenon of consent as it appears in sexual encounters. Knowing if that is indeed the case has important practical consequences: if we understand sexual consent as a particular case of general consent, then we can draw lessons about our sex lives from analyses of political and legal consent, and from moral consent to mundane actions like lending one's bike or agreeing to join another person for a cup of tea. But if sexual consent is radically different from these other types of consent, then analyzing sexual consent on the basis of thought experiments about our nonsexual lives—as some analytic moral philosophers do—is likely to lead us astray.

In this chapter, I consider the meaning, traditional uses, and ambiguities of the notion of consent in law, politics, and ordinary life to show that the consent at work in sexual relations is not the consent of contract law, of citizens to political power, or of mundane interactions. The very specific place given to sex in society means that we cannot simply apply a general analysis of consent to the sexual realm to understand what sexual consent does, how it works, or how it should work.

A General Definition of Consent

When we talk about consent, we refer either to the *action* of consenting or to the *result* of this action. To consent is an action that consists in giving one's agreement. For instance, I consent to buy something from someone when I enter a sales contract with that person. Consent is also the agreement that results from this action—for instance, the consents exchanged during a wedding.

These examples emphasize that consent is social: to consent is to give *somebody* one's agreement on something. One cannot consent alone; there is always another person involved in the action of consenting.

Moreover, it is generally admitted by lawyers and philosophers that consenting consists in granting someone a right that they would not have in the absence of consent. When I consent to lend my car to a friend, I give them the right to take my car, whereas they would be trespassing my property right if they were to take my car without my consent. To consent is therefore to give someone one's agreement over some claim, such that one grants through that agreement a right to oneself or one's possessions.

Three Domains of Consent

Although consent is initially a legal term, it is nowadays a core notion in three different domains: law, politics, and intimate interpersonal relationships, in particular those of marriage and sex.

In law, consent refers to the agreement through which someone contracts with someone else. It is central in legal systems grounded heavily in precedents or judicial rulings—usually called common law systems, like the United States and the United Kingdom—as well as in legal systems in which jurisprudence has less influence on codified statutes and ordinances, called civil law systems, like the French one. Consent is "at the essence of contract law."[1] The centrality of consent is most easily identified in civil law systems, as consent figures directly in the definition of contract. Contract is defined in the official English translation of Article 1101 of the French Code civil as "a concordance of wills of two or more people intended to create, modify, transfer, or extinguish obligations." As an agreement between individuals that creates reciprocal obligations, contracts are different from unilateral legal acts, such as wills and testaments. Obligation, here, is to be understood in its technical legal sense, meaning the legal bond by which one or several people (debtors) are required to provide goods or services to one or several other persons (creditors). Consent is one of the fundamental notions of contract law, as it is a necessary condition for the validity of a contract: a contract cannot be legally valid if the parties do not consent to it. Article 1128 of the French Code civil thus states that the first condition of the validity of a contract is "the consent of the parties." The consent of the parties is so central to the contract that there are, in French law, contracts that exist only through the exchange of consents and do not need to be legally formalized. This is what law calls a consensual contract, defined as follows: "A contract is consensual when it is formed by the mere exchange of consents, in whatever way they may be expressed."[2] The notion of consent is therefore at the foundation of contract law and of individuals' ability to contract with one another.

In the political realm, the vocabulary of consent is a response to the problem of so-called political obligation. One of the main challenges of any political philosophy is to know why subjects obey laws. If state power is not received from God, and if subjects are naturally free and equal, then only obligation—understood as an individual's freely accepted duty toward others—can explain the functioning of political power. As the political theorist Hannah Pitkin shows, there are at least four problems embedded within the problem of political obligation:

(1) The limits of obligation ("*When* are you obligated to obey, and when not?")
(2) The locus of sovereignty ("*Whom* are you obligated to obey?")
(3) The difference between legitimate authority and mere coercion ("Is there *really* any difference; are you ever *really* obligated?")
(4) The justification of obligation ("*Why* are you ever obligated to obey even a legitimate authority?")

Social contract theories ground political obligation in consent: one has to obey if and only if one consents. Pitkin shows that consent thus is a solution to the four problems of political obligation:

> Your consent defines the limits of your obligation as well as the person or persons to whom it is owed. Legitimate authority is distinguished from mere coercive power precisely by the consent of those subject to it. And the justification for your obligation to obey is your own consent to it; because you have agreed, it is right for you to have an obligation.[3]

Social contract theories assume that subjects' obedience to the laws of the state is established by the contractual origin of the state: because the state is the result of an original pact—or contract— in which each person commits to obey political power, its laws are obligatory, just like any other contract. In return for obedience to the law, the state grants citizens its protection. Since the functioning of the contract is grounded on the idea that an exchange of consents creates an obligation, the notion of consent becomes, in the social contract tradition, the unique source of political obligation and political legitimacy.

It is, in an analogous manner, from law and from the contractual form that the vocabulary of consent became established in intimate relationships. The vocabulary of consent appears first in the context of marriage because marriage is conceived as a contract. The exchange of the betrothed's consent is the necessary condition for the marriage bond to be formed. In Christianity, for instance, the public consent of the betrothed was deemed by the Fourth Council of the Lateran (1215) a necessary condition of the validity of marriage. A whole lexical field related to consent has developed around marriage, from the parental consent sometimes necessary to authorize a marriage to divorce by mutual consent.

By extension of this conjugal use, the vocabulary of consent has progressively emerged in two other contexts: in a literature on love and desire, where consent appears as the virtuous woman's way of loving, and as a norm in discussions about sexual violence. Many countries now use consent as part of the legal definition of rape. In the United States, for instance, the FBI in 2013 adopted a new definition of rape as "penetration, no matter how slight, of the vagina or anus with any body part or object, or oral penetration by a sex organ of another person, without the consent of the victim."[4] In France, however, the definition of rape is different in a key way. According to Article 222–23 of the French Code pénal, rape is "any act of sexual penetration, whatever its nature, or any act of oral sex committed on someone else or on the author by violence, coercion, threat, or surprise."[5] In France it is therefore only in everyday language and not in court that the norm of consent is used to delineate between rape and normal sex.

The Ambiguities of Sexual Consent

When we focus solely on differentiating the three spheres of consent, we risk missing one of the important problems raised by consent: it is polysemic—it means different things in different contexts and to different people. There is, in other words, nothing simple about the nature of the agreement that consent is supposed to be. Consider the definition of consent adopted by Georgia Southern University: "a voluntary, sober, imaginative, enthusiastic, creative, wanted, informed, mutual, honest, and verbal agreement."[6] If so many qualifications are needed, then agreement in itself is probably too ambiguous to constitute consent.

This ambiguity is evident as well in the legal discourse from which ideas of sexual consent have been imported, which might give us pause. Law rarely defines consent in a straightforward way. In common law systems, consent is not defined once and for all by legal codes; jurisprudence can redefine consent. In civil law, meanwhile, the definition is often taken for granted. For instance, the term "consent" appears more than a hundred times throughout the French Code civil but is never positively defined.

Moreover, consent can refer either to the agreement itself (to the mental state of giving assent to something) or the manifestation of the agreement (for instance, shaking hands to seal a deal).[7] As renowned legal scholar Jean Carbonnier put it, "Consent is both the will of each contracting party and the agreement of their wills."[8] Thus, in legal contexts, consent is both a mental state that an individual can have regarding a decision they make and a social phenomenon of reaching agreement with someone. But when we think of sex, does consent reflect both of these realms—those of intention and of action? Do we care what each partner *thinks,* or are we focused on something else—what partners communicate, how they reach agreement, how they manifest agreement? The consequences will vary greatly should we establish that consent to sex is the fact of agreeing, mentally, to a sexual encounter; that it is the fact of manifesting (verbally or tacitly) one's agreement to the sexual encounter; or that it is the fact of deciding together to have sex and signal this decision.

Besides this ambiguity between agreement of will and manifestation of will, consent includes a second ambiguity, between choice and acceptance. When consent is an encounter of wills in order to form a contract, consent manifests a *positive* choice and a positive agreement. Yet consent can also refer to the fact of accepting an offer or a request made by someone else. In that case, consent is in some sense *passive.* This is a common sense of consent in everyday usage: to consent is to accept something that is suggested to us or even to not refuse something that is offered. To consent, therefore, can be to choose (positive) or to accept (passive), and there is considerable difference between the two. For instance, on the normative level—that is, on the level of moral evaluation—choosing to have sex is not the same thing as not refusing sex.

Law needs this polysemy surrounding consent to account for the wide range of behaviors that can generate lawful transactions. For instance, the concept of consent enables law to consider that there is a contract, and therefore an obligation, both when a landlord and a tenant sign a written rental contract and when a person jumps in a taxi. In one case, the parties can come to a careful, negotiated arrangement, affirmed by both through their signatures; in the other case, the contract is tacit and made in haste. Both of these are legally binding contracts based in consent of very different kinds. But the same polysemy that allows for useful flexibility in contracting is likely to muddy our understanding of sexual consent.

Sexual Consent Is Not about Contract

Now we understand the different uses of the word consent and the problems raised by its polysemy, yet a further question persists: Do we use "consent" in all these contexts because we are referring to similar phenomena, or is there something specific in the meaning of consent as applied to the sexual domain?

That we use the same word in the contexts of contracts and of sex leads to the intuition that we are talking about the same thing. And this intuition is no doubt at the root of the belief held by many people that, if we are going to approach sex through the lens of consent, then we should all sign contracts before having sex with anyone. After all, and as we'll see in later chapters, BDSM practices often involve contracts, as popularly depicted in the novel and film *Fifty Shades of Grey*.

Here is the issue: when we talk about sexual consent, and in particular when we advocate that rape be defined in law as sex without consent, we conceive of consent as a legal norm. (Germany, Belgium, Canada, Greece, Iceland, Ireland, the United Kingdom, and the United States all now define rape as sex without consent.) More specifically, in this case, we consider that consent is a legal notion that allows people to distinguish between criminal and noncriminal behaviors. So it is tempting to think that the "consent" of sexual consent is the same as the "consent" of legal consent.

But this view is false, and understanding why it is false requires a somewhat technical legal explanation. Distinguishing between criminal and noncriminal behaviors in fact is *not* the function of consent in the legal domain most concerned with consent—that is, contract law. In contract law, consent creates an *obligation*, not an authorization. Consent determines not what others can do to someone but what one must do. When you enter a contract, you consent to the necessary consequences of your act, meaning you are morally and legally obligated to do what you agreed to according to the contract. This conception of consent is not—and cannot be—the one that grounds the understanding of consent as the criterion to distinguish between rape and sex. Indeed, no one conceives of sexual consent as creating an obligation to have sex. As the judge and legal theorist Richard Posner writes:

> The law of rape is not a part of the law of contracts. If on Friday you manifest consent to have sex on Saturday, and on Saturday you change your mind but the man forces you to have sex with him anyway, he cannot use your Friday expression to interpose, to a charge of rape, a defense of consent or of reasonable mistake as to consent. You are privileged to change your mind at the last moment.[9]

This hypothetical illustrates vividly the distinction between consent in contract and in criminal law. According to both civil and common law, there is a contract if and only if there is an agreement of will *and* the creation of an obligation. This means that, absent an obligation, there is no contract. And in contract law, by definition, one cannot legally go back on one's consent as long as it is valid. The possibility of revoking one's consent at any time—what legal scholar Evan Raschel calls a "unilateral and discretionary right of withdrawal"—is contrary to the existence of an obligation.[10] Wherever such a right of withdrawal prevails, there is no obligation. So unless one views sexual consent as binding on the consenting individual—consent that cannot be withdrawn—sexual consent cannot be understood as having the same meaning and function as legal consent.

And, indeed, no one advocates such a view of sexual consent. Even in legal discussions on the use of consent to distinguish criminal from noncriminal sexual conduct, there is never any consideration of sexual intercourse as the subject of a contract in the literal sense. It is never the case that consent to sex is understood in the sense that consent is understood in contract law—the sense in which consent is the criterion of legitimacy.

This does not mean, however, that consent in contract law and consent in criminal law are two entirely different notions. In both fields, the role assigned to consent is based on the theory of the autonomy of the will. Every individual is recognized as autonomous—that is, as literally capable of giving themselves their own law. But this principle of autonomy of the will has distinct consequences in the cases of contract law and of criminal law. Under contract law, to be autonomous is to be free to generate *obligations*. In the case of criminal law, to be autonomous is to have the capacity to generate *authorizations*. The increasing role of consent in criminal law—in particular in adjudications of rape—follows from criminal law's invocation of autonomy.[11]

An authorization is "an irrevocable unilateral act, which suspends an incrimination protecting an available interest, either as an obstacle to its material constitution, or as an element of justification." This means that consent can be used in criminal law either to prevent an act from being considered a crime (for instance, consent could be used to distinguish rape from authorized sex) or to justify an action (for example, consent could constitute a mitigating circumstance in the commission of a crime). Nevertheless, in the majority of cases, the victim's consent is not relevant to criminal law: "Since criminal protection is primarily directed at defending the social order, it is beyond the reach of any private permission."[12] In other words, even if one agrees by contract to be murdered, therefore giving an authorization to one's killer, the killer could still be prosecuted for murder. With this in mind, we can appreciate why it is wrong to argue that affirmative-consent rules mean one would be wise to sign a contract before having sex, as some claim in response to campus policies: in fact there is no contract that can ensure that sex is not rape. Consent is linked to the contract in civil law only and, within this framework, creates obligations. In criminal law, consent can create authorizations and is not linked to the contract.[13] Sexual consent belongs to criminal law and therefore has not much to do with what we usually think about when we think of legal consent and contracts.

The question then arises as to how sexual consent can be established in criminal proceedings and thus what counts as proof of consent. One might answer that, in this context, a signed piece of paper authorizing another's actions could, in some cases, be considered proof of consent. And it does seem plausible that, in a rape trial, the existence of a piece of paper on which the alleged victim has signed a written agreement to have sex with the accused would play a significant role in an acquittal. But it is not reasonable to infer from this hypothetical, as consent opponents routinely pretend in the media, that applying the notion of consent in criminal law means that personal interactions can be lawful only if organized by contracts.[14] Objections to the use of the vocabulary of consent in the legal definition of sexual violence on the grounds that such use would imply signing contracts—or thinking of intimate relationships as though they were commercial relationships, subject to contracts—are wrong and are based on the error of reading consent in criminal law as identical to consent in civil law.

Political and Sexual Consent

What is called consent in the sexual domain is also not the same thing as consent in the political domain. As we have seen above, consent in politics is primarily intended as an answer to the question of why one is obligated to obey the law. According to social contract theories, political obligation is the consequence of a contract between citizens and the state or between citizens and each other. Here again, consent creates obligation. In the philosophy of John Locke in particular, the concept of consent makes it possible to understand how individuals born into an already-structured society come to be obliged by the law in place. The individual in this situation cannot distinguish their adherence to the social pact proper from their adherence to the regime chosen by the majority of the civil society resulting from this pact.[15] They are thus in a situation where they cannot choose anything other than adherence or nonadherence.

In the political realm, consent is used in the two senses of choice and agreement previously established, without distinguishing between their different meanings. The individual consents to the social pact, in that they express their will through the establishment of a contract—consent here is a legal synonym of will—or they consent to it in the broader and less technical sense that the regime has already been installed and that they therefore have no option but to consent or else refuse membership in civil society.

At this point, you may be wondering just how political consent is articulated. After all, even if you consider yourself a party to the social contract, no one ever asked you to sign a document expressing your agreement. Locke wondered about this. What, he asked, constitutes "a *sufficient declaration* of a man's *consent, to make himself the subject* of the laws of any government"?[16] Insofar as not all subjects explicitly consent to be members of the society in which they live, Locke argues that "tacit consent" is sufficient to make a free man born under a government a member of the republic. According to Locke, anyone within the territory of a government can be taken as having given their tacit consent.[17]

This shift from active consent—which is the consent of the contract—to passive or tacit consent explains other political uses of the notion of consent, notably the idea of "manufacturing consent" proposed in 1922 by Walter Lippmann and reused by Noam Chomsky and Edward Herman in their 1988 book *Manufacturing Consent: The Political Economy of the Mass Media.*[18] Chomsky and Herman analyze propaganda as the means of manufacturing mass political consent, where consent is a form of passive adherence. This notion of consent is far from the voluntary and active conception at the heart of sexual consent. Sexual consent has the function of ensuring that the person *wants* to have sex, that they have not been forced to do so in any way, and that their autonomy is fully expressed in the sexual act in question. By contrast, to speak of consent in the political domain refers to the adherence, often passive, of citizens to the regime in which they live. Sexual consent is therefore essentially different from political consent.

Sex Is Special: Why Saying Yes to Sex Isn't like Saying Yes to Tea

Sexual consent is neither the consent of contract law nor that of political theory. It is also not the same as consenting to a trivial everyday act. Sexual consent is not, as a recent UK campaign against sexual violence asserts, like agreeing to someone's offer of a cup of tea.[19] If only it were that straightforward.

Not only media campaigns but also philosophers, especially contemporary analytic philosophers, analyze complex issues using simplified cases considered analogous. The problem with such analyses is that they rest on the presupposition that the two actions to which one consents are comparable. In the case of sex, that presupposition goes against our intuitions: at first sight, having sex and agreeing to a cup of tea are utterly different actions. One might infer that we should instead use a tighter analogy. I recall a discussion on consent between two philosophers in which one offered the following example: he was often busy or tired at night when his children asked that he kiss them before they went to bed. This philosopher explained that he sometimes had no desire to kiss his children under these circumstances but did so anyway and that he did not think he was deeply affected by giving these kisses despite not having, in some sense, consented to doing so. Would matters necessarily be different if, instead of not-quite-consensually kissing his children, he was having not-quite-consensual sex with his wife?

The question underlying the suspicion that such a comparison is bad (and maybe wrong) is whether there is something exceptional about sex: Is there some special quality of sex that would make it impossible to reason about sexual consent from other kinds of consent? The philosopher Martha Nussbaum asks this question in an article on prostitution.[20] Nussbaum's argument is motivated by Adam Smith's observation, in *The Wealth of Nations,* that "some very agreeable and beautiful talents" are admirable so long as no pay is taken for them. "The exercise" of such talents "for the sake of gain is considered, whether from reason or prejudice, as a sort of publick prostitution."[21] Nussbaum asks whether a commonly held intuition—that it is wrong to receive money or to contract for the use of our sexual or reproductive capacities—proceeds from rationally defensible emotions (that is, from reason) or else from irrational emotions based on prejudice. Her thesis is that the condemnation of prostitution is the result of prejudice and not of rationally defensible intuitions. One of the ways she shows this is through a thought experiment: imagine a person who is paid to have their colon examined with the latest medical instruments, in order to test their capacities. According to Nussbaum, we have no moral problem with this "colonoscopy artist," though they are paid in exchange for being penetrated by medical equipment with their consent. According to Nussbaum, then, the condemnation of prostitution derives from a moralistic view of sexuality in which a prostitute is seen as an evil and dangerous woman whose activities are at odds with the morally valid sex that occurs between married heterosexual partners.

But another intuition may be at work here. Is it not the case—whether rightly or on the basis of prejudice—that we think there is something specific about sex that makes payment for sexual penetration different from payment for nonsexual penetration, even where the same body parts are involved? This separate intuition is at work in the definition of rape in French criminal law, which specifies "sexual penetration." French jurisprudence, constructed over a series of cases, has interpreted "sexual penetration" as a matter of intention: what makes penetration by a foreign object sexual is not the body part penetrated or the object employed but the aims and mindset of the penetrator. Consider the case of Theo L., who in February 2017 was attacked by police in a Paris suburb. An officer anally penetrated Theo L. using his telescoping baton and was charged with rape. However, the investigating authority eventually decided that the officer should be tried not for rape but for "deliberate violence resulting in permanent mutilation or disability," a lesser charge.[22] In the French legal system, unwanted anal penetration with a baton could be rape, but in this instance it was deemed something else—something less serious because the intent, violent though it was, was not sexual. This idea that a given material act may or may not be sexual in scope, depending on the intent of the perpetrator, implies that sexual acts are not like other acts. Sexual acts have a specific kind of meaning to which is attached particular importance—a meaning essentially different from other meanings we attribute to things we do with our bodies.

It is difficult to say whether this view—that sex is special in some way that both makes sexual violence more serious than other violence and justifies special protection against sexual violation—is legitimate. People's determinations on this score will depend on their values and belief systems: some people believe sex is sacred, while others consider the very notion of the sacred to be meaningless. But one pragmatic way of resolving this issue is to recognize that, to the extent that our laws, institutions, norms, and practices give sex a particular importance and make sex a sphere of activity that engages one's autonomy and vulnerability in a particularly acute way, sex occupies a specific moral position—whether or not that position is justified by reason. In other words, the fact that rape is considered legally and morally different from torture or battery, or that prostitution is the subject of specific debates that do not attend other practices of selling physical labor power, means at the very least that sex is not conceived of as an activity like any other. This specificity must be accounted for in analyses of sexual consent, if these analyses are to be relevant to the way people actually feel and live.

This is not to say that nothing can be learned from comparisons to innocuous, everyday forms of consent, but simply that it is a mistake to proceed by analogy without also questioning how the special moral valuation of sexuality in our societies shapes sexual consent. Moreover, sexual consent often takes place in the context of affective and intimate relationships that are not necessarily well analyzed when examined without taking into account their specificity: the role of feelings, the duration of a relationship, and other factors often involved in sex plausibly make sex qualitatively different from other sorts of acts to which one might consent.

The above analysis reaches no conclusions regarding the usefulness of sexual consent or the wisdom of particular moral or legal regimes concerning sex. Instead, this is a starting point. If we are to make sense, and good use, of sexual consent, then we must begin by understanding that the consent at work in sexual relations is neither the consent of the law of obligations, nor that of citizens to political power, nor that of anodyne interactions between individuals in daily life. That those who make use of sexual consent do not agree on its definition, its function, or the role it can play in an emancipatory agenda makes it a true philosophical *concept*—not a self-evident notion or just a term of media discourse, but a subject of debate in which strong moral and political disagreements are at stake. With these complications in mind, we can proceed to a fuller appreciation of how consent might guide the specific area of human lives that is intimacy and sex and to decide how one ought and ought not behave in that sphere.

2

HOW DOES CONSENT MAKE
THINGS "GOOD"?

CONSENT, broadly understood as valid agreement, has evolved over the past few decades. What was once a concept primarily of interest to philosophers and political theorists is now a basis of law and organizational rules. And particularly in the wake of the #MeToo movement, consent has become the key term in public debates about sexuality and gender equality. Today consent carries such weight that it is, according to countless millions of people, the only criterion for distinguishing good sex from bad sex, sex from rape.

Americans were pioneers in this evolution, thanks to their advocacy for affirmative consent on college campuses. In 1990 young female students from Antioch College—including L. A. Paul, who is now a well-known philosopher—created the first affirmative-consent sex policy. It made headlines and was ridiculed by many media outlets, including in an unfortunate skit on *Saturday Night Live*. The policy even made waves abroad, galvanizing French critics who saw Americans as antisex and undone by political correctness, even as Americans of course were not unified behind Antioch's decision. Indeed, the US debate about affirmative consent was sparked anew in 2014 when California passed a law conditioning public funding of colleges on the adoption of a demanding affirmative-consent policy.[1]

But while controversy remains, consent has continued to pick up supporters, resulting in important legislation. For example, in 2016 Germany amended Articles 177 and 178 of the *Strafgesetzbuch,* the penal code: rape is no longer defined as a sexual act involving violence, threats, or a victim unable to defend herself, but as a sexual act perpetrated against the recognizable will of the victim (*gegen den erkennbaren Willen*). Sweden's 2018 Rape Act, as I detail elsewhere in this book, has gone even further by defining as rape any form of sex without consent. The new law introduced a crime of "negligent rape" for cases in which the courts recognize that, even as consent has not been established, the perpetrator did not intend to rape and so is merely culpable on the basis of negligence.

As momentous as these developments are, they do not fully capture the evolution of consent in popular discourse. Consent increasingly is the hinge that will open the door not just to non-violent sex but also to women's freedom from sexual domination generally. Across diverse arenas of public life, consent is perceived as a silver bullet: it is the only way to prevent rape *and,* not unrelatedly, it is the key for challenging the many ways in which patriarchy has shaped our sexualities. Why is it that we attribute such power to the concept of consent?

In this chapter, I respond to this question by exploring the two major traditions in thinking about consent: a liberal tradition, inherited from John Stuart Mill, and a Kantian tradition. These traditions, each in their own ways, view consent as enabling individuals to express autonomy. And the Kantian conception, which is more demanding than the liberal one, also invests consent with the capacity to justify actions. As I will show, one of the major deficits of contemporary consent discourse is that we are mostly trying to use a liberal conception of consent, but we want consent also to have the justificatory power of its Kantian form. We are trying to eat the whole cake, even as our arguments merit only a slice.

The Right and the Good

Consent has wonderful powers. Legal theorist Heidi Hurd skeptically characterizes consent as "moral magic": we believe that when we consent to something, the result is to modify, as if by magic, our own and others' rights and obligations. Consent transforms that which is forbidden, making it permissible so that theft, say, becomes borrowing. And an act that would have been rape is, as if by magic, just sex.[2]

Peeking into the sorcerer's cauldron, we see that sexual consent distinguishes acceptable and unacceptable sex in two senses. First, consent distinguishes between sex that is morally *right* (permissible) and sex that is morally *wrong* in the sense that it is—or should be—prohibited. Second, consent distinguishes between sex that is positively *good* and sex to which one may have moral objections—practices that are not necessarily reprehensible but that are problematic on the moral level—and which therefore is *bad*. This distinction is of central importance for this book in general and this chapter specifically, as I challenge what I take to be the conflation of these two aspects of a moral evaluation of consent: consent discourse tends to take for granted that permissible sex and good sex are the same thing, and bad and wrong sex too.

To the contrary, I argue that one sense of consent—the liberal one—may help us figure out where to draw the line between right and wrong sex, while the other, Kantian, sense is crucial to pursuing good sex. Moreover, if we want to be able to seek good sex, we must be aware that bad sex may happen on the way. We should aim to eliminate wrong sex, but it is probably impossible to prevent bad sex entirely.

Despite the constant confusion over the powers of consent, it is not hard to distinguish right sex from good sex. The following case illustrates that they are different. Casey and Pat are in a relationship.[3] Casey insists a little on having sex with Pat, but Pat does not desire sex at that moment. Casey does not blackmail or strongly pressure Pat; for example, Casey does not prevent Pat from sleeping until Pat gives in. Yet, in the face of Casey's insistence, Pat agrees and has sex with Casey to have some peace. One can argue that Pat has consented, so that this sexual intercourse is not immoral and is morally right. However, it is not morally good, insofar as it does not reflect mutual desire.

Is the Moral Philosophy of Sex Moralizing?

Before analyzing what makes sex morally good or even morally permissible, let us acknowledge that a moral evaluation of sex may seem suspicious, especially to a French mind. Isn't the study of sex from the point of view of its morality itself a form of moralism? Even more worrisome, is philosophizing about the morality of sex not a sign of puritanism, which would seek to reverse the gains of a sexual revolution that, at least in France in the 1960s, went by the pithy and powerful slogan *Il est interdit d'interdire*: it is forbidden to forbid?

The answer is no. Thinking about the morality of sex is not the same as moralizing and is definitely not puritanical. In fact, any discussion about how we should behave with one another—including discussions that no one would accuse of overwrought moralism—is a moral analysis. When we speak of sexual consent, we are immediately placing ourselves on a moral level, not in the sense that we intend to browbeat anyone but in the sense that we seek to evaluate the criteria underlying the morality of our actions. Morality can be defined as normative reflection on human actions: when we reflect on consent, we are thinking about how will and desire manifest themselves in our actions and how will and desire contribute to making these actions legitimate. Thinking about sex in terms of consent is therefore necessarily a moral analysis of sex, but moral analysis is not necessarily moralistic or paternalistic. Consider, for example, the following from French philosopher and libertarian Ruwen Ogien, who offers a moral analysis of sex without dictating sexual practices:

> Our ways of living have no moral significance as long as no harm to others comes from them (which means, among other things, that the contemplative life of the thinker or the philosopher has no moral privilege). The same is true of our conceptions of personal good. This is particularly evident in sexual life. One may have homosexual preferences, heterosexual preferences, or no sexual preferences at all; a taste for single, multiple, or no sexual relationships. We can discuss these preferences, but it would be absurd to say that one of them is more "moral" than the others. In other words, minimal ethics recommends that we adopt an attitude of neutrality regarding conceptions of personal good, especially sexual, and, more generally, that we renounce the great existential questions ("What is a good life?," "What is a successful life?," etc.).[4]

We should set aside the notion that moral reflection on sex is puritanical because every reflection on what sort of sex should be allowed proceeds from moral analysis, whether this reflection supports chastity or libertinism. When one asserts that the only criterion relevant to the quality of sexual intercourse is the amount of pleasure one derives from it, this position belongs to moral philosophy, since one is evaluating the criteria of the good. (In this case, moral philosophers would call the assertion "hedonistic.") Indeed, puritanism not only is not a necessary component of moral reflection, but it is arguably the antithesis of moral reflection. If we mean by puritanism an excessive rigorism in moral matters, then puritanism does not consist in questioning the ethics of sex. Rather, it consists precisely in surrounding sex with silence and taboo, which forbid openly thinking about and discussing sexuality. To examine philosophically what good sex is, and to distinguish sex that is "not bad" (permissible, if undesired) from positively good sex, is a profoundly antipuritanical undertaking.[5]

Moral Analysis Comes First

Why propose a moral, rather than a legal, analysis of sexual consent in the first place? To put it simply, the law proceeds from moral rules. Law, and criminal law specifically, is intended to make certain moral rules, considered particularly important for life in society, binding. Not all immoral conduct is prohibited by law; one has the right to be unpleasant with one's grandmother, even if that is not good conduct. But the conduct prohibited by criminal law is always prohibited at least in part on the grounds of its perceived immorality. Therefore, before considering what the law should permit or prohibit with respect to sex, we need to make a clear and precise assessment of what sexual activities are right and wrong, distinguishing what is acceptable—in the sense that it is not immoral—from what is positively moral and thus desirable. This distinction between morally acceptable and morally desirable sex will allow us to go further, using the concept of consent not only to identify (and punish) sexual violence but also to determine positively what morally good sex would be.

To even ask such questions—what is morally good sex, and what does consent have to do with it?—reflects cultural shifts. The centrality of consent in contemporary discussions stems from a new form of attention to sexuality: if we talk so much about consent, it is because thinking about sexuality no longer has the same function it once did. As Georges Vigarello shows in his *History of Rape,* the repression of rape was for a long time motivated by men's will to ensure that "their" women's bodies would not be used by others, and specifically to control the purity of their lineage (that is, to ensure that their children would be their own).[6] Women's desire, will, and physical integrity have only recently been sources of concern. And the modalities of sexuality and intimacy that create joy, pleasure, and happiness—these are even more recent preoccupations. The centrality of consent in contemporary discussions of sex is grounded in the hope that consent will enable us not only to fight against what is violent and immoral in certain sexual relationships, but also to emancipate sexuality from the dominations and oppressions that run through it, in order to enjoy without hindrance and in a way that makes us positively free.[7]

Three Moral Intuitions

There are good reasons, as we shall see, to be suspicious of the concept of consent, or at least of the priority that it is given. But before reflecting on criticisms of the concept on political grounds—for instance, some critics argue that consent reinforces male domination under patriarchy—let's examine consent from the inside. Setting aside the ways in which consent interacts with power in society, what, ideally, is the function of consent in the moral evaluation of sexuality? Is consent *enough* for sex to be right? And for sex to be good? In the contemporary literature on consent, three intuitions about the normative power of consent can be identified (in all these, "consent" stands for valid consent):

1. It is commonly accepted that nonconsent is a necessary condition for rape, although no legal system considers nonconsent to be a sufficient condition for rape. If sexual intercourse is consented to by all partners, then none of the partners can be considered as having raped the other. Conversely, consent is a necessary condition for sex to be permissible.

2. Most scholars of consent in moral philosophy hold that consent *makes* sex permissible. Therefore, consent is a sufficient condition for sex to be morally permissible— the consent of the partners is enough to judge that the inter- course that happened was not wrong. Given that it seems clear that good sex must at least be permissible, consent is therefore a necessary condition for sex to be morally good. Consent on its own may or may not be enough to make sex morally good, but sex without consent can never be morally good.

3. Proponents of minimal sexual ethics, such as Ogien, often argue that consent is a sufficient condition for sex to be morally good—no other conditions are needed for a sexual intercourse to be good.

The first intuition raises no issues: it is impossible to imagine morally justifiable sex that is not consented to by the partners. Although the exact definition of consent is open to debate, the idea that sex must be consensual to be permissible is not. Some people think nonconsent should be a sufficient—and not only a necessary—condition for rape, but everyone agrees that noncon- sent is at minimum a necessary condition for rape. So I will take this for granted.

The difference between the second and third intuitions is at the heart of the moral ambiguity of consent and corresponds to the following problem, which is one of the fundamental questions this book intends to answer: Does the consent of the partners *suffice* for sex to be morally good?

To start responding to this question, we need to understand how it is exactly that we think the moral magic of consent works, not only for sex but for our actions in general. In other words, how is it that consent makes something permissible? In what way or ways can consent cause actions to be justified? To respond to these questions and to set the philosophical grounds for the arguments of later chapters, the following discussion delves into details of Mill's and Kant's positions. Although I endeavor to explain them as clearly as possible, one could also skim the rest of the chapter and move on to the next without losing too much of the general argument.

The Two Philosophical Conceptions of Consent

At first sight, our intuition about the link between consent and morality is based on the following reasoning: when I consent, I express my autonomous will; if there is an expression of the autonomous will of the consenting party, then the action is good, in the sense that it is moral. But two differing conceptions of will and freedom are at stake and mixed in this reasoning. First, there is a *formal* criterion, according to which a contract or an agreement is valid if the contracting parties formally consent to it and thus express their will. Second, there is a more demanding criterion, that could be deemed *substantive,* according to which my consent to the actions I choose expresses my humanity, my dignity, and my morality.[8] It is not hard to imagine that consent will have very different powers depending on whether we see it as the expression of a decision at a given time, or whether we see it as the expression of the deep will and freedom of the subject.

What counts in the case of formal consent is respect for the *forms* of the will—for instance, a signed contract, saying "I agree." From the moment I consent in a formally acceptable way—which is to say that my consent meets criteria of validity because it is, for example, not coerced—I express my will. When I get on a bus, I tacitly communicate that I consent to a contract of transportation with the bus operator and that, therefore, I agree to pay the cost of the ticket in exchange for transportation. Other questions, such as whether I really want to be taking the bus instead of driving myself, or whether I wish to travel to the particular destination I will arrive at, are not material to the announcement (even tacit) of formal consent. Simply getting on the bus constitutes valid consent to be transported to the destinations available on the bus route, in exchange for paying the advertised fee.

But what matters according to the other, more demanding, view of consent is that the consent in question is truly a choice that engages the morality and humanity of the consenting party. For instance, when someone has to make crucial decisions regarding medical treatment, the medical community is supposed to ensure that the specific situation of the patient, and their ability to understand consequences and to express their exact desires, are taken into account such that the decision reflects the will of the patient considered in their humanity and dignity. Ultimately, these two conceptions of consent are two conceptions of the will: Do we consider that all the choices we make, even without thinking about them, manifest our will, or that will in its full sense implies deliberation about the means and ends of our actions—deliberation that might not occur in the context of every choice we make?

To Consent Is to Give Up a Right

In everyday language, to consent can mean to accept something that is offered or suggested by someone else—someone wants to borrow my bike, asks me, and I agree—or to actively choose, as in the case of negotiating a contract and agreeing to abide by its provisions. And two distinct conceptions of the normative power of consent are linked to these two meanings: one that considers that consent generates permissions based on the renunciation of a right (in the sense that one can have a moral right to one's physical integrity, for example) and one that considers that the justificatory power of consent comes from the fact that it is a manifestation of the autonomous will of the person who consents.

The common understanding in contemporary philosophical analyses of consent, in particular sexual consent, is that when one consents, one gives up a right that one previously had—the right, for example, to not be touched in an intimate way—and thus creates a permission. More precisely, consent is a formally valid agreement that "transforms an action that would otherwise wrong an agent . . . by trespassing her rights into a permissible act, consistent with her rights."[9] In this framework, sexual consent is conceived as a special case of consent, analogous to common, everyday forms of consent-based permissions whereby consenting means giving up *exclusive* right to use of one's property. When I consent to have sex with someone, I give up my right not to have that person touch me sexually and therefore I allow them to touch me in that way.

This conception of consent is a liberal one in the philosophical sense of the term, which can be linked to the claims developed by John Stuart Mill in his 1859 treatise *On Liberty*. Although contemporary liberalism is not perfectly aligned with the conceptions of Mill, his analyses are the basis of today's liberal understanding of consent—the one that is probably held by most readers of this book. It is therefore useful to understand exactly what role consent plays in the overall liberal argument. It may seem abstract at first, but a grasp of the liberal doctrine proves crucial to assessing the limits of the current understanding of sexual consent.

The liberal doctrine assumes that what human beings have in common is the search for the good life, that this search is individual (that is, what constitutes the good life varies from person to person), and that the individual must be free to pursue the good life by the means they wish. Liberals such as Mill and Jeremy Bentham are proponents of utilitarianism, which holds that it is impossible to objectively define whether choices are good or bad; all that counts in deciding whether a choice is good or bad is how much it contributes to the happiness—also called the "utility"—of the individual. Everyone must be free to choose their life as they wish. It is only because the choices of one individual living in society may have adverse consequences for another individual that one's freedom may be curtailed. Therefore, one can consent to anything as long as doing so follows from a free choice and does not harm others. The essentially individualistic perspective of this doctrine cannot be stressed enough: social life is understood solely as a series of relations between individuals, and therefore consent is essentially a phenomenon that happens between two individuals, without consideration for the social structures that may inspire individuals to make the choices they do.

Given this centrality of the individual, the key problem of political philosophy according to the liberal doctrine is to ensure that the state does not unduly impede the freedom of individuals. The capacity to have one's own will, to determine for oneself what that will is, and to cultivate one's individuality are at the foundation of human nature. "It is," Mill writes, "only the cultivation of individuality which produces, or can produce, well-developed human beings": the conception of the good is personal, and there is no objective conception of the good that society or the state can guarantee or protect. From the very first pages of *On Liberty,* Mill identifies the "tyranny of the majority" as the specific threat against which democracies must protect themselves.[10] According to Mill, the so-called will of the people on which political authority is based is in reality the will of the many and, as such, constitutes a threat to the people. It is in fact not possible to eliminate the temptation of the majority to oppress a part of the people.

The tyranny of the majority can be imposed not only by law but also by social norms. For instance, the tyranny of the majority can take the forms of paternalism and moralism that might emerge either from state action or from the functioning of society. "Paternalism" here concerns all measures whose purpose is to secure individuals from themselves, whether it be legal paternalism (e.g., compulsory wearing of protective helmets or seatbelts) or social paternalism (e.g., bosses who impose "beneficent"

limits on worker behavior, such as by refusing to pay out sala-
ries on Fridays in order to prevent workers from spending their
wages in the bar). For its part, moralism refers to measures that
are intended to proscribe certain behaviors in the name of an
alleged violation of human dignity. It is on these grounds, for
example, that homosexuality has long been both legally prohibited and socially stigmatized. According to Mill, the power of the
majority in a democracy implies in itself a risk of paternalism and
moralism that threatens the possibility for the individual to live
as they wish.

Mill's problem is then to know how to hold together, on the
one hand, the fact that the modern state is the best means of guaranteeing the natural rights of the individual so that they can
maintain their individuality, and, on the other hand, the threat
of majority tyranny inherent in any modern democratic state. To
solve this problem, Mill proposes a principle that is a criterion
for evaluating the obstacles to individual freedom, which he calls
the harm principle: an individual's freedom of action can be im-
peded by the state or society *if and only if* the exercise of their
freedom of action constitutes a risk to others. As Mill puts it,
"The only purpose for which power can be rightfully exercised
over any member of a civilized community, against his will, is to
prevent harm to others. His own good, either physical or moral,
is not a sufficient warrant. . . . The only part of the conduct of
any one, for which he is amenable to society, is that which concerns others. In the part which merely concerns himself, his independence is, of right, absolute." Put simply, only the need to
prevent an *individual* from suffering serious and concrete harm
as a result of the voluntary action of another *individual* can justify state intervention.[11]

What role does consent play in all this? For Mill, consent is
the manifestation of individual freedom and, as such, constitutes
a criterion of justice. Especially in relations between individuals,
as opposed to relations between the state and individuals,

there is a sphere of action in which society, as distinguished from the individual, has, if any, only an indirect interest; comprehending all that portion of a person's life and conduct which affects only himself, or if it also affects others, only with their free, voluntary, and undeceived consent and participation. . . . This, then, is the appropriate region of human liberty. . . . Secondly, the principle requires liberty of tastes and pursuits; of framing the plan of our life to suit our own character; of doing as we like, subject to such consequences as may follow: without impediment from our fellow creatures, so long as what we do does not harm them, even though they should think our conduct foolish, perverse, or wrong.[12]

Here Mill explains that consent is the criterion to evaluate relations between individuals outside of the strictly political sphere. Individual freedom implies, negatively, that I shall not act in such a way as to harm others (harm principle); and it implies, positively, that I may act in a way that affects others "only with their free, voluntary, and undeceived consent and participation." The concept of consent is thus central to liberalism's conception of relations between individuals: respecting the freedom of others not only means not harming them but also respecting their freedom, understood positively as self-determination, which they express through consent.

Criteria for Valid Consent

Mill offers criteria for evaluating consent: for consent to be valid, it must be free, voluntary, and undeceived. In addition, Mill requires that consenters be active participants in the activity to which they consent. This means that passive agreement is not sufficient to constitute consent. This is crucial, and we shall return to it: in most legal systems, until the recent changes I mentioned earlier, women have been seen as consenting to sex as long as they do not actively manifest opposition. This usually meant that they had to physically resist intercourse, as demonstrated through marks on the perpetrator's body. Yet, even according to the relatively unrestrictive Millian conception of consent, not saying "no," and not physically resisting, does not suffice to guarantee valid consent.

Importantly, Mill also holds that consent is the criterion for delimiting the sphere of action that should escape state intervention. To protect ourselves from the tyranny of the majority, we must ensure both that the state intervenes in public life only when there is risk of harm and that the state does not intervene in the individual's sphere of action if their action concerns only themselves or others who have consented to it. As we will see in the next chapter, this claim is critical to the argument that people have a right to privacy regarding their sexual lives.

Mill's assertion—that consent binds the state—is not entirely clear. In the passage above, his argument can be read to mean that the state should *never* intervene where individuals are isolated or have consented to interact, regardless of the content of that consent. Or the argument can be read to mean that the state should only intervene in this sphere when there is risk of harm. The first reading is more plausible because Mill tells us that he is tracing the "region of human liberty." The reiteration of the principle of nonharm ("so long as what we do does not harm them") seems to apply to those outside the association in question: when there is consent and participation, the associated individuals are conceived as a single unit, whose actions must not harm others—those outside the association. As for those within the association, the state cannot touch them because they have consented to their treatment. This reading is reinforced by the conditions Mill sets out: one can imagine that adults who are unconstrained and undeceived will consent only to what they really want in the intimacy of their conscience, and that no one should limit their actions in the name of moral considerations. On this view, consent is not only a necessary condition for precluding state intervention but also a sufficient one.

In sum, consent is genuine if it is given freely, voluntarily, and without deception; one cannot consent under other conditions. Where consent is given, it guarantees that the relationship between consenting individuals is free and therefore not be subject to intervention by the state or any other external individual, unless the activities of the consenting individuals are prohibited by the harm principle. Consent is then the criterion for the legitimacy of actions implicating multiple individuals, defeasible only by harm. No other criteria or moral considerations are relevant, for what must be protected at all costs is the capacity of individuals to lead their own lives as they wish, as long as their choices do not put nonconsenting individuals at risk. Within this framework, philosophers generally agree that consent is a formally valid agreement between informed adults, which generates permissions such that the giver of consent gives the recipient the right to do something that, without that consent, would violate the rights of the giver.

Another way to put this is that, according to the liberal framework, only individuals know what is good for them, so the best social organization consists in limiting individual freedom as little as possible—that is, in limiting it only insofar as it risks unduly limiting other people's freedom. In such a context, the only way to evaluate if an action is good is to determine whether it was consented to in a valid way. If this seems very technical, it nonetheless has important consequences, especially in the sexual realm. For instance, as Bentham already showed in 1785's "Offences against One's Self: Paederasty," the liberal framework makes it possible to affirm that no type of sexual relations—and that includes nonheterosexual, nonreproductive, and nonmarital sexual relations—should be punishable by law if they take place between consenting individuals.[13]

Consent, on this view, is a sufficient condition for sex to be permissible and a necessary, but not sufficient, condition for it to be good. By contrast, in the second conception of consent that I now turn to, consent is much more than a formal criterion. And here, consent can be a sufficient condition for sex to be good.

Consent, Autonomy, and Humanity

Although this liberal understanding of consent seems to represent the dominant view, the current emphasis on sexual consent is also grounded in the idea that consent manifests the autonomy of the will of the consenting party—something that is not necessary in the Millian conception, which does not ask what the true feelings or motivations of individuals are, only whether they have consented in a manner that is prima facie valid according to the criteria of voluntariness and nondeception. For instance, the conception of consent as manifesting autonomy is often the basis of arguments—which I do not endorse here—that sex workers may well consent in Mill's terms to the sex they have with clients but that this consent is not real consent and at best is a manifestation of deep distress because sex work necessarily infringes the human dignity of sex workers. Another, less polemical, example concerns the minimum wage: when a jurisdiction implements a minimum wage law, it says that, although a worker could agree to work for less, this agreement is void because it contravenes the humanity of the worker. The exact content of the principle of the autonomy of the will is a source of debate among legal theorists, as will be seen in the next chapter's discussion of legal disputes surrounding BDSM, but the general idea is that the function of both law and ethics is to protect the humanity or dignity of humans and therefore their autonomous will.

This conception can be linked to the moral theory developed by Immanuel Kant in his *Groundwork of the Metaphysics of Morals*. Kant is, among other things, the founder of what is called the ethics of duty, or deontology. To put it in very mundane terms, Kant is the philosopher who theorized the idea that one acts according to a sense of duty—that is, by thinking, for instance, "I do X because I have the duty to do it" rather than "I do X because that makes me happy," or "I do X because it is the right way for me to flourish." Social contract theorist Jean-Jacques Rousseau—discussed below—established a link between autonomy, freedom, and consent in the political domain, but Kant is the philosopher who demonstrates how these concepts function and are articulated in moral philosophy.

The starting question for Kant is what a moral action is—what it is to act in a good way. In his view, the morality of an action cannot be assessed by its result because what makes an action good is the good will, good in itself, which is expressed in it.[14] Kant therefore distinguishes between actions done *in conformity with* duty and those done *from* duty. Using Kant's illustration, let's say a merchant charges everyone the same price for the same goods because he believes it is in his interest to do so, lest customers, aggrieved by his favoritism, stop coming. Now let's say the merchant charges every customer the same price for the same goods because treating people equally is what the moral law demands.[15] In the first case, the merchant is acting in conformity with duty, while in the second he is acting from duty, even as in each case he takes the same action. For Kant, the moral value of an action lies not in what is done, but in the intention underlying it. Kant thus opposes the point of view of *legality*—that of conformity with the law—with the point of view of *morality,* which resides in the purity of the intention.

Results tell us nothing about morality; the fact of outwardly respecting a law, even if it is a moral law, is not enough to decide the morality of the action. What we must instead keep in mind is the principle guiding an action, which Kant calls its *maxim.* In mundane terms, we can only know if our action is moral when we look at the principle that guides us.

Kant argues that human beings, by the very fact of being rational beings, have in common a principle of the will, which is the moral law, and to which he gives the name of categorical imperative. Without going into technical details that are not important for our reasoning about consent, Kant shows that rational beings possess a universal moral law that can be stated in these terms: "Act only in accordance with that maxim through which you can at the same time will that it become a universal law."[16] Briefly, this means that an action is moral if and only if the maxim that guides the will in that action is one that could be universalized. For example, according to Kant, breaking a promise is immoral because, if everyone acted in this way, the action of making a promise would become impossible: if you don't trust that a promise will be kept, because no promises are kept, then no one can promise anything.

The Kantian analysis of action is based on the idea that rational agents have the specific characteristic of acting according to their representation of laws and not only according to laws—that is, they do not simply follow laws but also represent them—think of them—as moral laws. Now, it is the concept of humanity that allows us to establish a link between this capacity to represent one's own law and the formulation of the categorical imperative:

> Suppose there was something the *existence of which in itself* has an absolute worth, something which as *an end in itself* could be a ground of determinate laws; then in it, and in it alone, would lay the ground of a possible categorical imperative, that is, of a practical law.
>
> Now I say that the human being and in general every rational being *exists* as an end in itself, *not merely as a means* to be used by this or that will at his discretion; instead he must in all his actions, whether directed to himself or also to other rational beings, always be regarded *at the same time as an end.*[17]

The world is divided into two types of entities: things, which we use as means for our actions, and people, who have something superior in common and who cannot—or at least should not—be treated solely as means but rather must be recognized as ends in themselves. Rational beings recognize three things: that they have in common that they are rational beings; that this explains why they have in common a universal moral law; and that, as rational beings possessing a universal moral law, they are obliged to recognize and respect in themselves and in others their common humanity and dignity.

Through this notion of humanity, Kant links morality and freedom. He does so by using the notion of autonomy. Kant shows that what makes the will *good*—that is, moral—is its property of being its own law (in Greek *auto-nomos*). Unlike a will that would let itself be guided by its desires, or by external pressures, the will that acts out of duty produces the moral law and, at the same time, submits to it:

> Although in thinking the concept of duty we think of subjection to the law, yet at the same time we thereby represent a certain sublimity and *dignity* in the person who fulfills all his duties. For there is indeed no sublimity in him insofar as he is *subject* to the moral law, but there certainly is insofar as he is at the same time *lawgiving* with respect to it and only for that reason subordinated to it.[18]

When we act from duty, we submit to the moral law. But this submission, instead of being a renunciation of our autonomy, is in fact autonomous because it is the will itself that produces the moral law to which it submits.

To understand what Kant is saying here, we can see how he transposes social contract from the civil to the moral domain. With respect to social contract in the civil domain, Kant is influenced by his contemporary Rousseau, who argues that citizens are both subjects—bound to obey laws—and legislators because they are part of the sovereign and therefore decide on the laws. Therefore, in obeying the law, citizens are only obeying themselves: "Obedience to the law one has prescribed to oneself," Rousseau writes, "is freedom."[19] In a similar way, according to Kant, by setting for itself the moral law it obeys, the good will is autonomous and free. To be free is not to obey impulses or natural necessity, or to be unconstrained by law. To be free is to follow the moral law one has set for oneself.[20]

What appears here is therefore an ethics that is both objective and more demanding than Mill's—to act morally is to act according to the categorical imperative. Moral action rests on the autonomy of the will, which comes from our humanity and manifests and protects our human dignity. Every choice, every agreement, every consent that follows the moral law appears in this respect as the manifestation of our autonomy; we commit our humanity in every movement of our will and we commit ourselves as an end in every choice we make.

This conception of human agency has consequences for how we should relate to others, as manifested in the second formulation of the categorical imperative, often called the "formula of humanity":

> So act that you use humanity, whether in your own person
> or in the person of any other, always at the same time as
> an end, never merely as a means.[21]

Acting morally thus implies two different duties: a negative duty not to use others as means and a positive duty to treat them as ends—that is, to recognize them as being what Kant calls ends in themselves. In the context of a reflection on sexuality, as various feminist philosophers have shown, this negative duty can be understood as a duty not to treat others only as objects serving the satisfaction of our desire or pleasure.[22] In practice, this implies that Jo should not force Alex to have sex against their will, because in such a case Jo would treat Alex only as a means to satisfy Jo's desire and pleasure without consideration for Alex, their will, and their desire. Therefore, in this context as well, giving valid consent to have sexual intercourse with someone is a necessary condition for this intercourse to be moral.

The Sex Partner as a Person

However, the positive duty included in the formula of humanity creates additional restrictions on what a moral sexual interaction can look like. As British philosopher Onora O'Neill has shown, the positive aspect of the formula of humanity requires acting not only according to maxims that others may share, but also according to maxims whose purpose is to pursue the ends of others.[23] The formula of humanity requires having respect and love for others. One must both respect others' ends and love those others in order to help them pursue those ends. This positive duty is therefore very demanding: it requires attention to the particularities of persons, taking seriously the fact that they are not abstract autonomous beings but individuals who have their own cognitive limitations and possess only partial autonomy, affecting their ability to consent in one or another situation.

If one decides, as O'Neill does, to apply the formula of humanity to sexual consent—Kant would not have, because he had moral reservations about any sex that takes place outside of marriage—the formula highlights two important aspects of sexual ethics. First, the specificities of intimate and sexual relationships make both the positive (treat others as ends) and negative (do not treat others solely as means) duties particularly difficult to fulfill—and thus particularly likely to be unfulfilled in this setting. "Because of the implicit nature of much sexual communication and social traditions which encourage forms of sexual duplicity," deception and coercion are probable. O'Neill shows, for example, that seduction is often a form of deception that cannot pass the test of the humanity formula. In addition, "intimacy makes failures of respect and love more possible," but also intimacy "offers the best chances for treating others as the person they are."[24] Indeed, intimacy may be the best way to obtain that particular kind of understanding and knowledge of the other's circumstances and particular abilities that are prerequisites for treating them as persons. Sex is thus morally risky because of the temptation to use the other person—to deceive them and to play on the intimate knowledge that one has of them to achieve one's ends. But at the same time, sex can allow for a truly moral relationship between persons because intimacy allows for knowledge, love, and respect that make it possible to want, and to be able, to treat the other person truly as a person.

This passage through Kantian and Millian philosophy illustrates two different conceptions of consent: one in which consent is seen as a formal and formally valid agreement that generates permissions, the other in which consent is conceived as the expression of the autonomous will of human beings and thus of their dignity.[25] In the context of sexual interactions, Mill's view considers that a sexual relationship is permissible if and only if the partners have given each other permission for it to take place. Thus consent is a sufficient condition for the sex in question to be permissible and a necessary but not sufficient condition for it to be moral. This theory recognizes that individuals may hold different positions on what conditions are necessary for sex to be morally good, but only the individuals participating in sex get to decide whether those conditions have been met. In contrast, Kant's view involves a substantive conception of what sexual morality is. It sees consent as an expression of the humanity of the consenting parties and sets demanding conditions for respecting that humanity. One must pay very specific and careful attention to the other in order to know what the other really wants and what conditions need to be present for the expression of consent to be possible. If these conditions are met, then consent is a sufficient condition for sex to be not only permissible but also good.

The Normative Ambiguities of Consent

That there are two different conceptions of consent is not in itself a problem. What is a problem is that these two conceptions are mixed up in public discourse, to the point that we grant consent a justificatory power it may not have. Indeed, the commonly accepted view of sexual consent is as follows: (1) to consent is to give a formally valid agreement. This is the view of both the "no means no" position, which entails that sex is consensual if the partner has not verbally or physically expressed refusal, and the "only 'yes' means 'yes'" position, in which consent demands verbally or physically expressing positive agreement. These positions differ on the *criterion* by which validity is determined, but they agree that consent is established through *formal* validity. And (2) such consent is sufficient for the sex in question to be morally good.

Now this second part is true in the Kantian conception of consent as a manifestation of autonomy that respects humans as ends in themselves, but the first part refers to the liberal conception of consent, which says nothing about respect for humanity. One can easily imagine situations in which consent can be considered valid according to the first conception without passing the test of the second. For example, imagine that Robin meets Chris on the Tinder dating app. Robin is looking for a long-term relationship, while Chris is looking for a one-night stand. Chris does not specify that their liaison will be a one-time thing and acts in a considerate and affectionate way that is generally seen as a sign of love interest. Robin verbally and enthusiastically agrees to have sex with Chris, thinking that this is the beginning of a real relationship. Chris has not deceived Robin, and Robin has consented in a formally valid way, meeting the demanding standard of affirmative consent ("only 'yes' means 'yes'"). However, it can easily be argued that even if Chris has not purely used Robin as a means, Chris, by not being interested in what Robin might really want, does not show the respect and love for Robin necessary to treat someone as a person. Put in general terms, the liberal conception of consent cannot be thought to have the normative power of the Kantian conception. Nor can consent on the liberal model be sufficient in determining that sex is good.

This interpretation may seem unnecessarily technical, but it is actually deeply important. Even before examining the criticisms that can be made of consent from a legal or feminist point of view, it is essential to clarify what can reasonably be expected of this concept. The confusion between a liberal and a Kantian understanding of consent has serious consequences. It means that contrary to our immediate intuitions, the normative and justifying power of consent on the moral level is not what we think it is. Our intuitions come from a faulty superposition between, on the one hand, a formal conception that is easily implemented but carries only moderate normative power, and, on the other hand, a substantive conception that is hard to implement but has deep normative power.

One conclusion we can draw is that consent's moral magic may be considerably less powerful than we tend to think. We are trying to use the methods of liberal, Millian consent to secure the aims of substantive, Kantian consent. This is an ethical project that simply doesn't work. The methods of liberal consent have nothing to do with recognizing dignity and respecting humanity, only with establishing the fact of formal agreement. We are faced with a choice: If we want to stick to a formal definition of consent, possibly sanctioned by law, then consent alone cannot suffice to lay the foundations of good sexuality. And if we want a conception of consent that lays the foundation for morally good sexuality, then that conception is likely to be too demanding to be sanctioned by law. So where do we go from here?

3

"HIT ME BABY ONE MORE TIME"

THE MORAL MAGIC OF CONSENT rests on confusion between two different conceptions of consent, so let us keep them apart and see what happens if we allow each to hold sway separately. What are the concrete consequences, for people's sex lives, of a liberal and of a Kantian conception of sexual consent? Perhaps surprisingly, the most fruitful arena in which to test each approach to consent may be BDSM.

In a way, the philosophical and legal debates surrounding consent in BDSM are a magnified version of debates surrounding sexual consent generally. BDSM practices illustrate how the liberal view of consent can legitimize and normalize sex that was once prohibited. Yet the case of BDSM also demonstrates the limits of liberal consent. In that regard, BDSM shows how a Kantian analysis of human dignity can be useful in pinpointing moral issues that stem from society's antagonism toward particular sexual practices.

What Is BDSM?

For those new to these questions, some definitions may be helpful. The acronym BDSM stands for bondage and discipline, domination and submission, and sadism and masochism. BDSM has become the umbrella term to describe what was for a long time called sadomasochism, or S&M, and other sorts of pain play and power play. Sadism is generally understood as taking pleasure in the pain of another. In sexual contexts, sadism can involve taking pleasure in witnessing, causing, or creating conditions in which another person experiences pain. Masochism involves taking pleasure in one's own experience of physical or emotional pain, humiliation, degradation, or submission. Bondage and discipline do not have such precise definitions. Participants in these activities conceive of them in a range of ways—as role-playing, as fantasy, as requiring master-slave contracts that extend beyond the bedroom, and so on. The practices covered by BDSM are therefore extremely diverse and can seem almost limitless. BDSM has its own vocabulary: the participants, called *players* or *kinksters,* carry out *scenes.* There is usually a submissive party called a *sub* and a dominant called a *dom.* BDSM has specific social contexts: people meet in *dungeons* or leather bars or in specialized online communities like Fetlife.[1]

Practitioners tend not to describe BDSM as a set of practices but rather as a community, identity, or even a form of therapy.[2] Participants constitute a subculture—a group that distinguishes itself through certain traits, beliefs, and behaviors that constitute symbolic resistance to norms of mainstream culture. In the case of BDSM, these are sexual norms, whether heterosexuality or conventional sex—"vanilla," in the argot of BDSM. Following the typical evolution of subcultures highlighted by the sociologist Dick Hebdige, BDSM has gradually become accessible to popular culture. The codes and practices of BDSM first gained a footing in independent cinema—where they retained an element of protest—and later took the spotlight in popular culture in the broadest sense.[3] The success of the *Fifty Shades* trilogy is the most tangible sign of this "mainstreaming." Practitioners themselves have been strongly critical of these developments, arguing that depictions in mass-market entertainment defuse BDSM's capacity to contest the social order.[4]

The Use of the Contract in Masochism

BDSM subculture has for some time been considered an interesting source of philosophical reflection on sexual consent.[5] In particular, a fascinating aspect of BDSM practices is the use of contracts. BDSM practitioners use the contractual form for erotic reasons but also as a tool of justification within a liberal framework. The reasoning is as follows: if the use of contracts makes it possible to guarantee the consent of the involved parties, and if the consent of the parties manifests their freedom, then sadomasochistic practices governed by contract are manifestations of individual freedom. Importantly, criminalization of these practices would then be contrary to individual freedom.

This sense of the purpose of BDSM contracts reflects an evolution, as historically BDSM contracts had nothing to do with consent. The contract as the vector par excellence of masochism was developed by the nineteenth-century Austrian writer Leopold von Sacher-Masoch, whose name provides the root of the word "masochism." Sacher-Masoch, in his novels and in his life, made contracts with the women he wanted to serve as a "slave."[6] In his best-known work, 1870's *Venus in Furs*, Sacher-Masoch includes the following contract between himself and one Wanda von Dunajew:

> My Slave,
> The conditions under which I accept you as my slave and tolerate you at my side are as follows:
>> You shall renounce your identity completely.
>> You shall submit totally to my will.
>> In my hands you are a blind instrument that carries out all my orders without discussion. If ever you should forget that you are my slave and do not obey me implicitly in all matters, I shall have the right to punish and correct you as I please, without your daring to complain.

Anything pleasant and enjoyable that I shall grant you will be a favor on my part which you must acknowledge with gratitude. I shall always behave faultlessly toward you but shall have no obligations to do so.

You shall be neither a son nor a brother nor a friend; you shall be no more than my slave groveling in the dust.

Your body and your soul too shall belong to me, and even if this causes you great suffering, you shall submit your feelings and sentiments to my authority.

I shall be allowed to exercise the greatest cruelty, and if I should mutilate you, you shall bear it without complaint. You shall work for me like a slave and although I may wallow in luxury whilst leaving you in privation and treading you underfoot, you shall kiss the foot that tramples you without a murmur. I shall have the right to dismiss you at any time, but you shall not be allowed to leave me against my will, and if you should escape, you hereby recognize that I have the power and the right to torture you to death by the most horrible methods imaginable.

You have nothing save me; for you I am everything, your life, your future, your happiness, your unhappiness, your torment and your joy.

You shall carry out everything I ask of you, whether it is good or evil, and if I should demand that you commit a crime, you shall turn criminal to obey my will.

Your honor belongs to me, as does your blood, your mind and your ability to work.

Should you ever find my domination unendurable and should your chains ever become too heavy, you will be obliged to kill yourself, for I will never set you free.

"I undertake, on my word of honor, to be the slave of Mrs. Wanda von Dunajew, in the exact way that she demands, and to submit myself without resistance to everything she will impose on me."

Dr. Leopold, Knight of Sacher-Masoch.[7]

The "masochian" origin of the use of the contract makes clear that consent was not at issue. The contract form was used for two main reasons. First, and most obviously, the contract between Wanda and Sacher-Masoch produces sexual excitement. Sacher-Masoch is aroused not only by his submission but by the idea of his submission. The contract is erotic literature in which each new description of abuse and punishment is a source of desire and pleasure. The second function of the contract lies in the fact that it is drawn up, or at least wished by, the masochist himself: the woman-whore, if she tortures, if she dominates, does so at the request and for the pleasure of the one she tortures. There is no sadism here, strictly speaking, because violence and humiliation serve the pleasure of the submissive participant. Thus the second function of the contract is to announce the demands of the submissive masochist. As such, the contract is an expression of the submissive's will, to which the woman-torturer consents but only in the passive sense. The woman accepts the terms, but she has no role in establishing them. Meanwhile the submissive does not consent to experience violence and humiliation; he asks for it and imposes it on himself. The request of the submissive participant, embodied in the contract he has written, expresses his autonomy—his will to be dominated.

Consent and Contract in BDSM Practices

Contemporary BDSM culture has inherited the masochistic use of the contract but has profoundly modified it, making it an expression of consent. The rationale for the use of contracts comes now from a liberal perspective in the sense established in the previous chapter: the contract is seen as formalizing consent and thereby establishing that all participants are enacting their free will. Consent is thus the criterion that demarcates BDSM from sexual violence.

In particular, contracts are essential to the realization of the BDSM community's mantra of "safe, sane, and consensual," sometimes referred to by the initials SSC.[8] On the strength of these three fundamental pillars rests a space in which sexual practices considered deviant by society can take place freely and without risk to participants—that is, under better conditions than many everyday sexual practices. To ensure that the goal of safe, sane, and consensual BDSM play is achieved, participants in a sadomasochistic scene will typically establish a contract beforehand.[9] These contracts take countless forms, but certain common features can be identified.[10] The contracts, which may involve two or more people, adopt legal language establishing the rights and duties of all parties and, in so doing, establish boundaries of what may and may not happen during the scene. For instance, the contract will typically specify limits beyond which the submissive party refuses to allow the scene to go.[11] Contracts also may specify safe words: if uttered during the scene, safe words signify that the submissive either wants to end the scene or wants to halt a particular practice.[12] Safe words are popular because the usual ways of asserting one's desire for something to stop—for example, saying "no, no stop"—can be part of the scene being played out, so participants need some way to distinguish a false refusal from a true one. Therefore safe words often have no relation to what is happening: a participant might shout some unrelated, innocuous language—"cherry" or "cupboard" or whatever you can imagine—and the activity underway must immediately cease. Finally, if the contract is of a long-term nature, governing more than one scene, it usually sets out conditions under which it can be terminated as well as procedures for doing so. By all of these means, BDSM contracts ensure safety, sanity, and, above all, consent.

Crucially, BDSM contracts are not tacit commitments: they are negotiated, drafted, and signed by both parties. The requirement for negotiation is strict and subject to rigorously enforced social norms. As Jill Weinberg shows, the negotiation can be a lengthy process, and often—particularly where beginners are involved—is supervised by experienced practitioners who are not parties to the contract. A given couple or larger group will commonly undertake several rounds of negotiation as well.[13] All of these norms ensure that all of the parties, dominant and submissive, consent to the contract in the sense that they actively choose it. Consent is therefore at the origin of the contract.

The list of permitted and prohibited practices and the establishment of safe words are intended to guarantee that consent is ongoing throughout the sexual scene and throughout the relationship of domination and submission as a whole. This special concern for *durable* consent reflects a recognition by all parties of the compromised position that the submissive is embracing. The state of the submissive during the scene is often compared to one of intoxication or semiconsciousness, in which it is difficult to ensure the validity of consent. The submissive may also be too compromised to employ safe words. For this reason, it is crucial that the boundaries of what the submissive consents to are established in advance, outside the situation of domination. The preemptive establishment of limits overturns the usual rule of "no means no," replacing it with the positive rule of "yes means yes": the dominant can take only those actions that the submissive, in an uncompromised state, has positively recognized as acceptable.

The BDSM community has continually developed new models of consent, reflecting a profound commitment to informed, enthusiastic participation. For instance, some BDSM practitioners have moved away from the framework of safe, sane, and consensual, judging that the primacy of safety and sanity is too limiting: BDSM practitioners may be aroused by situations that are *not* safe. This has led to a new model called risk-aware consensual kink, or RACK, in which consent is conceived as necessary communication around risk. Yet another approach—known as caring, communication, consent, and caution (4Cs)—insists on mutual care among the partners as well as constant communication of consent.[14] Followers of the 4Cs distinguish among three levels of consent: *surface consent,* the verbal agreement to participate in a scene; *scene consent,* referring to the pre-scene negotiation of limits and safe words; and *deep consent,* which is the true, willing, desiring agreement of the parties and often implies that the participants will review the scene after the fact and honestly evaluate their consenting status.

The distinctions of the 4Cs point to a profound truth: consent is a temporal condition, subject to variation over time. Consent intervenes at different moments and has different forms depending on what is going on in these moments. In addition, these distinctions recognize that consent given before or during a scene does not necessarily imply consent afterward. One may agree to certain activities beforehand and in the moment, yet later conclude that these were not really what one wanted. This dissonance may not imply that the other partners did something wrong—they did what they were given permission to do—yet after-the-fact nonconsensual feelings are real and ought to mean something to all participants. Sociological studies of BDSM practitioners confirm that many take these distinctions seriously, and in ways that are quite telling. While law and mainstream discourse prioritize surface consent—did the parties clearly state willingness to participate ahead of time?—BDSM practitioners often skip surface consent, suggesting that in their view it is not the most important variety of consent. More significant are indicators of deep consent, which may be nonverbal, and the establishment of consent after the fact, through post-scene debriefings. Surface consent may be necessary to legal conceptions of permissible sex, but the communities most invested in an ethos of consent do not see it as sufficient to guarantee the free-willed action of the parties: BDSM practitioners know that legal and moral consent are two quite different things, and that the latter is what really counts for good sex.

Contracts without Legal Value

BDSM contracts, unlike the Sacher-Masoch contract, are drawn up in the form of a legal document and seek to comport with legal formalism. However, in both civil and common law jurisdictions, these contracts have no legal value. Yet, from the perspective of BDSM participants, the legal formalism of these unenforceable contracts is critical. This only further emphasizes the BDSM community's acknowledgment of a profound disconnect between law and morality, with elaborate rituals of consent designed to establish that the demands of the latter are satisfied.

In French law, the sadomasochistic contract has no contractual legal value because it contains provisions contrary to public order. French law recognizes the preeminence of public law over private contract in stating that "one may not by private agreement derogate from laws that concern public order and good morals."[15] In other words, two people may agree to an act that is forbidden by law, but their agreement won't be legally recognized. In practice this means that contracting parties cannot consent to what the law considers a crime; their consent cannot eliminate the offense. The crime of battery is independent of the consent of the victim, and under French law the sexual practices described in BDSM contracts generally fall under this category. The sadomasochistic contract therefore has no contractual value and as such cannot truly constitute an obligation. The only possible legal use of such a contract would be for mitigation: a person convicted of a criminal offense in the context of BDSM play could argue for lenience by showing, by means of the contract, that the battery they inflicted was consented to by the "victim" and thereby hope to secure a lighter penalty.[16] As for the common law context, the primary basis for the legal invalidity of BDSM contracts is the rule against contracts for sex.[17] In the few US court cases that cover BDSM, the consent of the "victims" has not been considered.[18]

Importantly, BDSM participants know that their contracts are not enforceable—that, from the standpoint of the law, their contracts are not actually contracts. After all, one of the foundations of the contract is that its breach can lead to prosecution—that is, the contract is protected by the institution of justice.[19] However, since no BDSM contract is ever used as a basis for lawsuits, and since the contracting parties never seem to enter a contract with the idea that their contract could be legally enforceable, this contract is not a contract, despite the legal formalism that characterizes it. It is not called upon to have a contractual legal function.

Why go to all this trouble? Why do BDSM practitioners—who have few illusions about the legal value of their contracts—persist in using legal language to express consent that courts cannot recognize? Because the function of these contracts is not strictly legal. If these contracts have no legal value, they nevertheless have the function of manifesting in the most formalized way possible the consent of the parties. These contracts may not matter in court, but they matter to the participants in their ambition to achieve a Millian vision of consent: BDSM contracts guarantee the absence of physical and psychological damage, and thus show that the harm principle cannot justify state intervention. More importantly, even legally invalid contracts demonstrate that consent is understood as a necessary and sufficient condition for an interindividual relationship to be just and permissible.

The Liberal Defense of BDSM

The use of contract in sadomasochism can be explained as a liberal claim and thus helps to illustrate the centrality of consent within liberalism.

As we have seen, liberalism as inherited from Mill insists on the need to limit the intervention of the state in the lives of individuals in the name of the primacy of the individual over the collective. In this framework, the state's sole function is to guarantee the security and property of individuals. Determining the legitimate field of action of the state is necessary so that state interventions serve only to protect, and never to endanger, the freedom of the individual. Thus the harm principle, which holds that the state can only, and indeed must, intervene whenever the free action of an individual poses a risk to the security and freedom of another individual. In all other cases, the individual must be free to act as they wish and to have the relationships of their choosing.

The function of the contract is to establish the physical and moral safety of the participants, thus ensuring that no harm will come to them and that, therefore, the state has no business involving itself in their relationship. In this respect, the use of contract serves to legitimize BDSM within the liberal framework.[20] This is an important gesture of self-defense on the part of participants, whose sexual practices have long appeared, and to some extent still appear, deviant, pathological, even legally condemnable.[21] Moreover, the supposed deviance of BDSM practices historically has been used to persecute gays and, to a lesser extent, lesbians. Indeed, one of the main arguments for prosecution and legal harassment of US gays and lesbians in the 1970s was the association, in public discourse, between gays and lesbians generally and the supposedly dangerous S&M practices of the "leather" subculture.[22] BDSM practices were and still are criticized on two fronts. First, supporters of strict sexual moralism find them to be against nature. Second, some feminists have criticized BDSM practices for perpetuating patriarchy. Particularly in the 1970s and 1980s, some feminists argued that BDSM was a smokescreen for violence and sexual exploitation, a topic I discuss in detail in Chapter 4.[23]

Against both critiques, the use of contract is seen a guarantee of consent. More specifically, the conformity of BDSM to liberal requirements is at the heart of the claim that practitioners cannot justly be prosecuted.[24] Given that, especially in common law countries, liberalism is conventionally considered the best theory of justice and best guarantor of freedom, the use of contracts allows BDSM to claim a moral character. This is why BDSM contracts are so rich in formalism: it serves to highlight the paternalism and sexual moralism at work in prohibitions against BDSM. The language may not render the contract valid, but it shows that the parties respect contractual norms. Given that they do respect contractual norms, and given that the contract guarantees both the consent of the parties and the harmlessness of the practices covered, then only the moral condemnation of the practice can explain its prohibition, and this condemnation, in its moralism, is contrary to the very principles of liberalism.

The *reductio ad absurdum* of a liberal ban on BDSM has been central to its philosophical and legal defense. For instance, many defenders of BDSM have based their arguments on the idea that a right to privacy is central to the guarantee of individual freedom. This is the basis for an interpretation of BDSM as falling within the principles enunciated by the US Supreme Court in the 2003 decision *Lawrence v. Texas*. There, the Court held that the right to privacy applies to consensual intimate sexual practices, so long as they are not dangerous.[25] If they are dangerous, then the imperative of protecting the health of individuals would constitute a compelling state interest and justify state intervention. The Court found that homosexual sex was not dangerous and so could not provoke state intervention. Some BDSM advocates argue that, likewise, sadomasochistic practices are not dangerous— in the sense that they do not lead to serious injury, require medical attention, or leave permanent marks—and so should fall under the same privacy protection.

The Sports Objection

The first objection to this defense of BDSM is to refute its harmlessness. Indeed, the individuals who engage in BDSM, whether bondage or sadomasochism, are almost necessarily hurt physically.

Therefore, the harm principle would require state intervention. The common response to this objection is based on a comparison of sex and sports.[26] Jill Weinberg opens her book *Consensual Violence* with a comparison of strangulation as practiced in mixed martial arts (MMA) and in a sadomasochistic setting, arguing that the gesture is exactly similar and similarly risky in both cases.[27] Yet strangulation is legal in MMA and illegal when it happens during sex. Thus the argument that sadomasochism should be forbidden because it is violent is inconsistent and probably covers for sexual paternalism. Sports practices illustrate that there is no basis for banning a practice simply because it may involve violence that hurts participants.

The comparison between sadomasochism and sports highlights a complex problem: Is it possible to consent to evil? In some cases, it seems the answer is an obvious yes. It is reasonable to assume that any American football player has embarked on his career consenting to the very high risks to his health.[28] He also consents to obey his coach's orders, even if those orders lead to injury. However, there is still some doubt as to whether consent to sadomasochistic practices is possible, or at least whether it is ever valid.

If there is a difference between the two practices in terms of both consent and harm, it is, according to pre-2005 French and European Union case law, to be found in the infringement of human dignity. Below I discuss this law and its implications for ideas of consent, as well as changes to the law and what we can learn from these new approaches.

Jurisprudence: The Importance of Human Dignity

French and EU law, influenced by the Kantian model presented in the previous chapter, establish dignity as a fundamental right protected by the state.[29] This concept of human dignity accounts for limitations French and EU law impose on the validity of consent, in particular sexual consent. But it is important to note that the law does not correspond to the subtleties of the Kantian argument. The law uses the idea of human dignity mostly as a way of putting human rights into practice.[30]

In France, the most discussed example of nonrecognition of consent in the name of preventing infringement of human dignity is the decision of the Conseil d'État of October 27, 1995, Commune de Morsang-sur-Orge, concerning "dwarf-tossing."[31] In this case, an entertainer of short stature practiced the activity for economic purposes, until the mayor of Morsang-sur-Orge prohibited it. The entertainer then petitioned for annulment of the ban. The Conseil d'État ruled that "the 'dwarf-tossing' attraction, which consists of having spectators throw a dwarf, leads to the use of a person with a physical handicap," so that, "by its very purpose, such an attraction violates the dignity of the human person."[32]

This is a hard case because it abstracts human dignity from consent. Had the entertainer denounced the practice to which he was subject, the ban on the basis of human dignity would be unproblematic. But, given that the entertainer did not complain, the effect of the Conseil d'État's decision was to legalize a measure that discriminates against little people in the name of protecting their dignity.[33] By asserting that the entertainer's interest in freedom of trade could not justify a practice that disturbed public order by infringing on human dignity, the Conseil d'État established a hierarchy in which individual freedoms manifest by consent must give way to the imperative of protecting human dignity. The Human Rights Committee of the United Nations affirmed the decision, holding that the French state did not infringe on the entertainer's rights.[34]

It is also in the name of human dignity that the European Court of Human Rights issued its first verdict on sadomasochistic practices. In December 1995 the ECHR heard a case concerning violent sadomasochistic encounters involving dozens of gay men in the United Kingdom. British police had seized video recordings of the encounters, which were used to convict some of the men with assault and battery. The convictions were appealed and upheld, albeit the men's sentences were reduced, as a judge decided that they "did not appreciate that their actions in inflicting injuries were criminal."[35]

The European Court was then asked to rule on whether the United Kingdom had complied with Article 8 of the European Convention for the Protection of Human Rights and Fundamental Freedoms, which requires that, "in a democratic society" the right to privacy is protected from unnecessary state interference.[36] The court acknowledged that the men's "activities were consensual and were conducted in private for no apparent purpose other than the achievement of sexual gratification" and that, further, the usual limitations found in BDSM contracts were implemented and respected.[37] Still, the court rejected the appellants' argument that, because all parties consented—definitively and emphatically—they had engaged in sexual expression, not violence. The court held that the consent of the "victims" did not preclude state intervention to prevent infliction of harm:

> The State was entitled to punish acts of violence, such as those for which the applicants were convicted, that could not be considered of a trifling or transient nature, irrespective of the consent of the victim. In fact, in the present case, some of these acts could well be compared to "genital torture" and a Contracting State could not be said to have an obligation to tolerate acts of torture because they are committed in the context of a consenting sexual relationship. The State was, moreover, entitled to prohibit activities because of their potential danger. . . . Acts of torture—such as those in the present case—may be also banned on the ground that they undermine the respect which human beings should confer upon each

other. . . . The Court considers that one of the roles which
the State is unquestionably entitled to undertake is to seek
to regulate, through the operation of the criminal law,
activities which involve the infliction of physical harm.
This is so whether the activities in question occur in the
course of sexual conduct or otherwise.[38]

In this case, *Laskey and Others v. the United Kingdom,* BDSM
practices are proscribed in the name of preserving both the health
of individuals and the moral order embodied by the notion of
human dignity. This decision has two effects. First, it gives the
harm principle underlying Article 8 an extensive definition according to which harmfulness is assessed not on the basis of
actual harm experienced but rather on the basis of the risks
incurred. Second, the ruling establishes that not only this expan-
sive harm principle but also the principle of respect for human
dignity overrides the consent of the parties.

The Jurisprudential Defense of Sexual Autonomy

In 2002 the ECHR reversed the position it had established in
Laskey, stating in *Pretty v. the United Kingdom:*

The ability to conduct one's life in a manner of one's own
choosing may also include the opportunity to pursue
activities perceived to be of a physically or morally harmful
or dangerous nature for the individual concerned.[39]

This ruling has had direct consequences on jurisprudence
concerning BDSM, as illustrated by the court's judgment of
February 17, 2005, in *K. A. and A. D. v. Belgium.* In this case, the
sadomasochistic practices were more violent than those at issue
in *Laskey:* the two petitioners appealed to the court after having
been convicted in Belgium for having practiced acts of extreme
violence on a woman to whom one of them was married.[40] Here

the court accepted that "criminal law cannot, in principle, intervene in the area of consensual sexual practices, which are a
matter of individual free will." Violations of human dignity and
the seriousness of the injuries the woman suffered could not
overcome this consent principle, or, at any rate, did not in this
case. But the court nonetheless ruled against the appellants, on
the grounds that the victim did not consent. "If a person can
claim the right to engage in sexual practices as freely as possible,
a limit that must be applied is that of respect for the will of the
'victim' of these practices, whose own right to free choice as to
the modalities of exercising his or her sexuality must also be
guaranteed," the court held. "This implies that the practices take
place in conditions that allow such respect." For several reasons,
the court ruled, this "was not the case."[41] Recordings showed
that the woman repeatedly uttered the word "mercy," previously established as a safe word, yet the practices continued.
The two men also consumed large quantities of alcohol, which
BDSM standards forbid because of the loss of control resulting
from heavy drinking.

Still, the reversal of jurisprudence is clear. Where previously
consent was not sufficient to legitimize sexual practices, the court
later decided that it is sufficient. The court did not directly pro-
nounce itself in favor of decriminalizing BDSM, but it opened
the door to a reversal of the hierarchy between consent and
human dignity. Sure enough, that position provoked virulent criticism from defenders of the priority of human dignity.

BDSM, Consent, and Human Dignity

This dispute, between liberal legal theorists and legal theorists
for whom the defense of human dignity trumps liberal freedom,
is crucial for us because it illustrates the ways in which Kantian and liberal approaches to sexual consent stand in tension.
And, more importantly, the dispute sheds light on structural

issues at play in sexual consent, which the liberal approach cannot tackle.

French legal theorist Muriel Fabre-Magnan opposed the court's new jurisprudence as "a real reversal of the philosophy of human rights."[42] Although I am not convinced that the court's endorsement of what she calls a legal "right to sadism" is as problematic as she thinks, her argument is useful in unveiling crucial deficits of liberal sexual consent. According to Fabre-Magnan, the core issue at stake in the decision is the extent to which state intervention in private life is justified in a democratic society. The court could have simply rejected the appeal on the grounds of the victim's lack of consent, but instead the court did much more: it affirmed, in the name of personal autonomy, that criminal law cannot in principle intervene in the area of consensual sexual practices. In other words, the court affirmed that freedom—demonstrated by means of valid consent—takes precedence over the need to protect the physical integrity of the person, seen as a manifestation of her dignity.

For Fabre-Magnan and many others, this is a bridge too far. She points out that this ruling contravenes other legal doctrines, such as those undergirding labor law, based in the conviction that consent is not a trump card. Fabre-Magnan argues that if the law is intended to protect individuals, it must account for the fact that individuals are not always aware of the risks involved in acts to which they consent, or that their consent may be compromised by forms of social domination. In other words, one weakness of liberal consent is that it considers all individuals to be free and equal, whereas in truth individuals live in society and therefore are placed in different social strata so that they are in fact not equal: some have more power than others, greater or lesser ability to express their desires, and so on. Thus it is normal to write and enforce laws that account for the asymmetrical positions of bosses and their employees, protecting the latter from the power of the former. Likewise, we might consider that race, gender, and social class are likely to have tangible effects on what sexual partners can say about their desire and their pleasure.

According to Fabre-Magnan, these limits of consent, alongside the extreme violence of the acts at issue in *K. A. and A. D. v. Belgium*, justify reliance on the concept of human dignity: because the acts are torture—or, at least, inhumane and degrading—they must be prohibited, regardless of participants' consent. In this view, the violation of human dignity does not concern only the person who experiences it. The law shapes society, giving others in society an interest in the rights that law recognizes and the effects of this recognition. If a hypothetical right to sadism has deleterious social consequences, then the wider public is justified in denying this right.

Fabre-Magnan, whether or not we agree with her whole argument, mounts at least two effective challenges to the liberal conception of sexual consent. First, the absolute value that liberals want to attach to consent is shown to be incompatible with the function of criminal law. Criminal law is justified by the recognition that the protection of individuals is one of the fundamental functions of the state; to allow individuals to consent to criminal violation would vitiate the state's purpose. This is why the criminal law cannot, for example, recognize the consent of those who want to be killed and eaten, as in the case of the so-called German cannibal, who was convicted of murder after killing and eating a person with their consent in 2001.[43] Unlike civil law, criminal law does not have the function of arbitrating between individuals but of guaranteeing the rights and freedom of all. Thus, in the criminal trial, what is judged is the harm done not solely to an individual but to society as a whole. This means that the effect of the crime on human dignity is important *even if* the "victim" consents to their treatment.

Second, *K. A. and A. D. v. Belgium* demonstrates how difficult it is to establish consent. There are three main obstacles.

First, the fact that sex usually happens in private spaces, involving no one but the partners, makes it difficult to know exactly what happened. In this instance, the judicial authority was in the highly unusual position of possessing a recording of the scene but still struggled to determine that the woman did not fully consent, ultimately determining that this was in fact the case.

The second obstacle to establishing consent is more serious than the first and has to do with the social situations of individuals: How can we establish consent when there is a severe power differential between the individuals, such as when the partners are on different sides of a dyad of social domination? Consider that, in *K. A. and A. D.*, the woman involved was the stay-at-home wife of a wealthy husband. Did she have the genuine option to not consent, which is a crucial condition of valid consent? Undoubtedly, she might enthusiastically wish to engage in BDSM with her husband and his friend, but she also might not and yet proceed because the consequences of rejection are potentially great—and from the outside, it could be hard to tell the difference. Faced with this scenario, the liberal representation of consent is revealed to be highly simplistic and inadequate: it presumes that consent is exchanged among equals, who are perfectly free to consent or not and are unencumbered by long-term considerations, a situation that does not look much like real life. This blindness to the difference between consenting to sex with a stranger and sex with a partner sharing one's bed, marriage, children, and bank account is glaring.

As I discuss later in detail, this presumed equality of consenting parties is all the more problematic when we appreciate that sexual consent is implicitly understood to concern only women: men are seen as constantly wanting and propositioning sex, so it is the responsibility of their potential partners—most often women—to give a green or a red light to men's ardors. In such a situation, men and women are not equal, if only because of the social structure of patriarchy. So how can we be sure that women consent and do not simply give in? One could readily imagine that, in the same way that a worker might consent to inhumane working conditions in hopes of obtaining some advantage offered under capitalism—for instance, a future reward from his boss or a better opportunity at another business—a woman might consent to inhumane sexual practices in order to achieve rewards or escape hardships within the patriarchal system.

A third and even higher obstacle to establishing consent lies in liberalism's assumption that humans are rational agents who face no epistemic or emotional complications. As Fabre-Magnan puts it, liberalism "refers to a very ethereal vision of the human being, considered as omniscient and above all transparent to himself, that is to say, of course, without a subconscious."[44] The philosopher Michela Marzano raises a similar concern: liberal consent implies a rational, voluntary, and nonvulnerable subject, who is conscious at every moment of their will and of what underlies it.[45] But we know from extensive studies of human psychology, from the social sciences, and probably from our own experience that this liberal human is not at all the norm. To the contrary, most people are far from transparent to themselves and are not always sure of what they want. Indeed, for reasons I explore in the last chapter, we probably are least sure of what we want where sex is concerned. If the subject cannot be sure of what they want, how can we be sure they really consented to sex?

And so we come full circle. BDSM advocates have worked harder than anyone to draw the blood of Kantian, moral consent from the stone of liberal consent, by using elaborate, legalistic procedures to affirm repeatedly the true willingness and desire of participants. In *K. A. and A. D. v. Belgium,* the European high court essentially blessed this program, affirming that one can consent to BDSM, albeit that in the case in question the woman involved did not. Yet in doing so, the court roused critics who cogently argue that the law's liberalism dramatically oversimplifies the human condition. The law may (sometimes) insist otherwise, but individuals are not always—in fact, rarely are—perfectly equal and free. Social hierarchies influence what individuals can want and can express. In the case of sexual consent specifically, the impact of gender oppression on the distribution of sexual duties—who must initiate and who must consent—and on the possibilities for women to withhold consent gives ground to think that a strictly liberal approach to consent is insufficient to ensure good sex.

4

SEX IS POLITICAL

THE PRECEDING STUDY OF BDSM points to several conclusions: the concept of consent is central to a liberal theory of sexuality; the legal doctrine of consent is structured around an opposition between liberalism and human dignity; and power relations and gender inequalities permeate intimate relationships in a way that complicates the act and meaning of consent. BDSM shows that consent is crucial for those who want to explore sexual desires and pleasures, including the risks they may entail. But the story of consent in the context of BDSM also suggests that the liberal framework—by apprehending sex purely as a relationship between individuals, without attention to the influence of the social structure on the positions and possibilities of these individuals—is insufficient. This is also true beyond the case of BDSM. Liberal consent is insufficient because social position influences what one can want or refuse: neither are we totally free, nor are the sources of arousal entirely personal and within our control. They, too, are products of the world around us, and of earlier life experiences that are part of who we are, whether we chose them or not.[1]

What role might consent play in a new, egalitarian sexual ethic? Two are possible: the concept of consent could, negatively, allow us to fight effectively against sexual violence by enabling us to distinguish not only between sexual violence and BDSM but also between sex and rape. Positively, consent might enable new modalities of love and sexual relationships that are more just and more pleasurable. In this way, we could hope to protect our integrity and what autonomy we already possess and at the same time create the conditions of possibility for a fuller, deeper sexual autonomy than is currently possible.

This chapter argues that neither of these two goals—discerning sex from rape and achieving genuine sexual autonomy—can be pursued through liberalism's individualist register. Feminists have long known this, hence the motto "the personal is political." What this means, for our purposes, is that the power relations playing out through sex cannot be abstracted from those of society as a whole. It is impossible to understand what we do and what we want sexually if we fail to recognize that patriarchy prescribes certain attitudes, desires, and practices.

To foster that recognition, this chapter offers an intellectual history of the idea that sex is political. This history casts doubt on the possibility of knowing exactly what we desire and in turn leads to the conclusion that consent cannot manifest an already-there will of the subject. We are left to reckon with a difficult suspicion: that our sexual individuality is not in fact our own but rather a product of power relations.

A Sexual Revolution

The absence of a self-evident distinction between sex and rape is of a piece with many of the factors that make for unsatisfactory intimate relationships. If this is hard to grasp, consider the global conversation about intimacy initiated by the Harvey Weinstein case. To be sure, the #MeToo discourse concerns sexual violence—by men against women, against other men, and against children.[2] But there is also more to it: a general critique of sex and love. Indeed, whether we talk about rape culture, gray zones, toxic masculinity, or the absence of the clitoris from school textbooks, one observation is inescapable: intimate relationships—

and not only heterosexual ones—are shaped by patriarchy, a sociopolitical system that organizes the domination of women by men.

One of the fundamental contributions of feminist theory and the feminist movement has been to show that sex is political and that these politics are, among other things, (hetero)patriarchal. Today, this observation may seem rather obvious; since the sexual revolution of the 1970s, since Michel Foucault's writings on the history of sexuality, and since #MeToo, the permeation of sex by power relations has been discussed at length. But what exactly does this mean, and how did the embeddedness of sex in power relations come to be a given? Much is at stake in this intellectual evolution.

Contemporary debates about consent, including incommensurable positions taken in these debates, are products of the so-called sexual revolution. This revolution was structured by the idea that society wrongly repressed sexuality and that it was necessary—for the good of all people, but especially women and noncis and nonstraight people—to liberate what was deemed shameful and was hidden. Against a social order in which licit sexuality was conceived as heterosexual and reproductive, the objective was to free oneself to recognize the joys of nonreproductive, nonheterosexual, and nonmarital sex. But this critique of sexual interdiction could err in the direction of fundamentalism, hence that French slogan we encountered: it was *interdit d'interdire,* forbidden to forbid. Liberation at any cost led to radical and contested positions, especially concerning children's sexuality.[3] The feminist movement that developed alongside this sexual revolution was both a result and a critique of it: feminists underlined the sexist dimensions of sexual liberation as it was practiced. Sexuality, feminists argued, was seen through a male prism that made women invisible, and liberation was not accessible to women in the same way it was to men.[4]

Psychoanalysis and the Repression of the Sexual

From the beginning, then, the meaning of the sexual revolution was unsettled, but it was undoubtedly political. And a key source of this political reading of sex was psychoanalysis.

To grasp how psychoanalysis inaugurated an understanding of sex and power as intertwined, we first must understand something about the role of sex in the theories of its Austrian founder, Sigmund Freud. One of Freud's central theses is that sexuality plays an essential role in the psychic development and in the psychic life of individuals. Freud and his followers argue that neuroses—psychological disorders—result from the repression of sexual impulses in the unconscious. In this way, Freud brings to light the determining impact of desire and sexuality in human subjectivity.

Freud has a capacious concept of the sexual, which includes not just sexual intercourse but all of the acts, fantasies, and thoughts since childhood that are related to pleasure. Yet sexual life does not come easily, nor is it purely joyful: for Freud, sexuality is often the cause of suffering, owing to the repression of the sexual in the unconscious. Freud uses a spatial metaphor to illustrate consciousness and the unconscious: we can imagine consciousness as a living room in which the people (or psychic movements) milling about represent perceptions. But before anything can enter the living room, it passes through an antechamber—the unconscious. Between the antechamber and the living room stands a guard. Like a nightclub bouncer, he inspects those who wish to enter the living room that is consciousness, admitting some and rejecting others. Whatever is refused is, in the terms of psychoanalysis, repressed—pushed back into the antechamber of the unconscious. However, the separation between the living room and the antechamber is not perfectly hermetic; the unconscious recalls itself to consciousness like unwelcome guests making noise outside. These are the repressed impulses, they are often sexual in nature, and they are a source of suffering.

This metaphor of the guard shows that there are, within our psychic apparatuses, effects of control and repression. In his later writings, Freud indicates that this repression, this control of the sexual impulses, is substantially a product of society. Life in society requires a restriction of the impulses, so that cultural impositions influence the repression of the sexual at the individual level. It is because the whole society restricts the sexual impulses that the individual reproduces in himself the restriction of sexual impulses and consequently suffers neuroses. Freud builds a political theory on the basis of sexual repression. In *Totem and Taboo* (1913) and then in *Moses and Monotheism* (1939), he presents the emergence of democracy through the myth of a powerful father who alone has the right to sex with the women of the tribe. His sons, suffering from the sexual restriction their father imposes, revolt and kill their father in the name of a more equal distribution of pleasure. But while the democracy born of this process does feature a more equal distribution of pleasure, it also necessitates new restrictions. In order to prevent struggle among the brothers, they all must foreswear sex with—and even avoid socially—potential partners within the family they share. Freud sees in this narrative the origin of incest taboos, although the boundaries of his incest restriction go beyond the immediate family, encompassing a larger social unit more akin to a tribe. In any case, the precise details of the boundaries matter less than Freud's insight that sexual repression is imposed on the individual from the outside, so as to maintain social peace.

There is much more to be said about Freudian social theory, but this quick overview points to what is essential for our purposes: Freud's ideas open the door to an understanding of sexuality in terms of social restriction and relations of power. These restrictions are constitutive of the social order, but they may be felt as, and in fact are, oppressive. This leads to the hypothesis that sexuality can, and perhaps must, be *liberated* (from repression). This hypothesis was the seed of much of the activism and thought underlying the sexual revolution. But Freud's ideas, as insightful as they are and as influential as they have been, were only a beginning. They, and the activism they inspired, came under intense criticism from those who argued that overcoming repression, once and for all, means doing the impossible: separating sex from power.

The Unbreakable Link between Power and Sex

Michel Foucault's *History of Sexuality*, the first volume of which was published in 1976, takes Freud's theories of repression as one of its starting points.[5] Foucault's theory of sexuality is important for us for two main reasons. First, he demonstrates that sexuality is a construct that is intrinsically political; sexuality cannot be understood if we consider it a product of nature that ends with individual desires and practices. Second, Foucault shows that we cannot disentangle the ways in which we think of ourselves as subjects from the ways in which sexuality shapes us. Put differently, the particular ways in which each of us thinks about the world and ourselves—our tastes, wishes, emotions, moral judgments, political convictions, and so on—are influenced by a sexuality that exists outside of and prior to ourselves. This last idea is in itself interesting, but it is all the more fundamental for an analysis of consent that casts doubt on the idea that there is a subject that precedes sex and that knows what they want from sex. To the contrary, Foucault's writings suggest that the subject who consents is also shaped by their consent and by their sexual experiences, each of which is shaped by relations of power. Given this, it may be impossible to consent or withhold consent in the sense proposed by liberalism.

Rejecting the Repressive Hypothesis

Foucault refutes Freud's claim that sex has been the object of continuous oppression, secrecy, and prohibition during the modern era, especially during and after the nineteenth century. But, from the start, it is important to understand that Foucault is not suggesting that people do not in fact face social control in the arena of sex. Rather, he has a distinctive view of what this means and how it works, a view at odds with Freud's and that of successors like the psychoanalyst Wilhelm Reich and the philosopher Herbert Marcuse, whose readings of Freud were the intellectual bases of the sexual revolution.

Foucault contests their claim that bourgeois life made sex taboo and secret and therefore silenced our desires and our pleasures—pleasures and desires that can be revealed through psychoanalysis. Foucault calls this the "repressive hypothesis": individuals have been forced by society to limit their pleasures, reducing sex to its reproductive function, which is the same as eliminating pleasure.[6] Thus Foucault writes, summarizing the argument of Freud and his followers, "Modern puritanism imposed its triple edict of taboo, nonexistence, and silence."[7] We have been forced not just to abstain from pleasure but also to keep quiet about it because language has performative force— the power to transform the state of the world. According to this hypothesis, sex has disappeared because of the silence surrounding it and is only waiting to be liberated, brought to light, and expressed.

However, Foucault points out that reality is more complex. Most obviously, society has hardly been quiet on the matter of sex. "Since the classical age," Foucault writes, "there has been a constant optimization and an increasing valorization of the discourse on sex."[8] Hardly forbidden, sex talk happens all time, through an ever-increasing production of discourses. But these discourses—for example, scientific discourses or Christian discourses of confession—do not see sex as positive. Instead they analyze pleasure and desire in either neutral or negative terms, while discourses exalting pleasure or desire are, indeed, reduced to silence. We have been talking more and more about sex, but not in order to have better sex. Rather, we talk about sex in order to know and control ourselves by controlling our sexuality.

Sexuality, Power, Knowledge, and Truth

Foucault demonstrates how simplistic the repressive hypothesis is and, by extension, shows that representing sexuality as something natural but repressed by puritanism is itself wrong. The power relations running through the discourses of sex are too intricate to characterize in this way.

Recognizing this, in the *History of Sexuality* Foucault develops a new analysis of power not as a unidirectional force—emanating from one person or group that has power and exerts it against others that don't—but as a field of forces.[9] Domination is unidirectional, but power is not. Power is relational, a web of interactions in which everyone both exerts power and is an object of the power of others. To see this concretely, consider gender roles in what is typically considered a traditional nuclear family. The father exerts power over all members, but this does not mean that the mother is powerless; she is in a position of power vis-à-vis her children and perhaps others in society, such as domestic workers. Meanwhile the children, though they have no explicit authority over their parents, have the capacity to extract certain concessions and may exert a degree of power over each other, their friends, nonhuman animals, and even human adults in some contexts. And a father who exerts tyrannical power at home is nonetheless under the thumb of his boss at work—unless perhaps he is a member of a union that uses its own power to resist domination. No one, then, is just the target of power. In the case of sexuality, "pleasure and power do not cancel or turn back against one another; they seek out, overlap, and reinforce one another.

They are linked together by complex mechanisms and devices of excitation and incitement."[10]

In order to understand exactly how this power functions, Foucault creates a concept that he calls *dispositif*, which has been translated as device, machinery, or apparatus. Scholars usually stick with dispositif, though, describing what Foucault called "a thoroughly heterogeneous ensemble consisting of discourses, institutions, architectural forms, regulatory decisions, laws, administrative measures, scientific statements, philosophical, moral and philanthropic propositions—in short, the said as much as the unsaid."[11] This mixture of forces and structures is the infrastructure of power, creating and transmitting it.

The *History of Sexuality* is devoted to the analysis of the dispositif of sexuality, which rests on a certain relation to truth: one seeks the truth of sex and, according to this truth, one seeks to shape what sex should be. This search for the truth of sex manifests in the explosion of discourses on sex. The minds of the modern age have not sought to take more pleasure or even to understand how pleasures should be governed; these minds have not thought about pleasure at all but instead have sought to know the truth of sex and, by doing so, to influence it. To use Foucault's words, instead of proposing an *ars erotica* that learns from the sensations of one's body, our civilization practices a *scientia sexualis,* a form of power resting on knowledge.[12] Whereas "in the erotic art, truth is drawn from pleasure itself, understood as a practice and accumulated as experience," the *scientia sexualis* seeks to learn the truth of sex, that is, the truth of desire and pleasure, through the confession of desires and pleasures.[13] The avowal of one's faults—in considerable degree, one's sexual sins—through Christian confession is a paradigmatic case of this science of sexuality that develops in the modern era.[14] Confession, alongside a multiplicity of other institutions, moral and religious frameworks, and social rules (including laws), organizes a certain way of relating to what we call sex. This multiplicity gives sex its meaning: it imprints in our bodies a certain way to behave, to seduce, to desire; it teaches us to see certain desires as natural and others as shameful.

Foucault's history, then, is not of sexual behavior but of sex as an object of knowledge. How, in the tradition that Foucault studies, did sexual behavior become the focus of a science of sexuality whose discourses of truth are linked to mechanisms of power? To answer this, he examines what he calls the procedures of truth production. The very term "procedure" illustrates entanglement between knowledge and power: the confessor, the physician, and the psychiatrist acquire knowledge about sex and, at the same time, power over the sex of the confessing person by the simple fact of their confession.[15] In turn, the knowledge that these arbiters of truth gain becomes the stuff of politics.

Sex as an Object of Politics

Through the analysis of this discourse on sexuality, Foucault highlights three ways in which sexuality and power are linked. First, sex gradually becomes the central preoccupation of politics, so that it becomes a political object. Policy becomes increasingly concerned with what sex people have, how often, with whom, and for which purposes. Indeed, political power sees sexuality as the best way to control life.[16] Governments want people to have children, but not too many; they want the family to be understood as the nuclear family, so that people live in small units; they want to increase the population's life expectancy in order to expand the workforce; and so on. In this way, beyond the dispositif of sexuality which applies to individuals as such, emerges what Foucault calls *biopower:* the way in which the political power tries to govern individuals, understood both as members of the society and as elements of the general population. The dispositif of sexuality is personal, intervening in the lives of persons interacting one-on-one with authorities in the areas of religion, science, and medicine. Biopower is impersonal, enacted by modern states setting policies that apply to all social members: "an explosion of numerous and diverse techniques for achieving the subjugations of bodies and the control of populations," with the goal of ensuring the economic and military health of the whole social body.[17]

Second—and this is one of Foucault's most important ideas for our analysis of sexual consent—*scientia sexualis* determines the subject in two ways: it is both controlled and made subject by the discourse on sexuality. Through confession—to a priest or to a psychoanalyst—the subject must recognize themself as a desiring subject, and the kind of subject that they are is specified by the joint evolution of medicine, psychiatry, and justice. A good example of what admittedly is an abstract process is the emergence of the figure of the homosexual. Before the nineteenth century, the category of the homosexual did not exist as such. Some people had sex with people of the same sex, and they could be prosecuted on the basis of these acts, but these acts were not determinative of their identity. In other words, society deemed it was wrong to practice sodomy, but practicing sodomy was not a sign that one was a certain type of person, much less a person who could, or needed to be, cured of wrong desires. It is only amid certain developments in medicine and psychology that people's sexual practices come to be perceived as saying something about what kind of subject they are—in other words, about their subjectivity. As Foucault says, "The psychological, psychiatric, medical category of homosexuality was constituted from the moment it was characterized . . . less by a type of sexual relations than by a certain quality of sexual sensitivity."[18] What makes a homosexual is not the practice of sodomy, which has no meaning in itself. The homosexual starts existing as a category, and therefore as a subject, once a link is posited between the practice of sodomy and the supposed essence of the individual. The homosexual is no longer seen as an individual having a certain type of sexual practices; rather, these practices are a sign of what he is, which is determined by his sexuality. The dispositif of sexuality, then, unveils how the modern subject is constituted: it is by one's sexuality, constituted primarily by one's desires, that the individual is specified.[19] Our desires and our sexual practices say who we are.

We are now very close to appreciating what Foucault's argument that sex is political means for discourses of consent. The last step is to understand how the process of "subjectivation" described above is at the same time a process of *subjection*. Foucault is arguing that you desire in a certain way because of the way you are shaped by the world you live in, and that way of desiring is what makes you the person you are. Foucault explicitly distinguishes between two meanings of the word *subject*: "subject to someone else by control and dependence, and tied to his own identity by a conscience or self-knowledge. Both meanings suggest a form of power which subjugates and makes subject to."[20] Sex constitutes the individual as a subject in these two senses: first, the confession, the medicalization, the control of sexual practices subjugate the individual to the dispositif of sexuality; second, the individual who confesses their sexual practices—because they think that those practices display something of their own truth—is attached to their sexual identity, which they take to constitute themself. You do not have to realize this. You may take your particular desires to be expressions of your own, personal, individual truth. Or, conversely, you may see therapists and put yourself through this disciplining practice of scrutinizing your darkest thoughts and reporting them to someone else because you think that what you will find in this process will tell you *who you are*. In either case, what you understand as your essence and therefore as a place of *nonsubjection* to power—that is, what you understand to be your self—is in fact a product of the dispositif of sex and of other such forces. Judith Butler sums up the matter in *The Psychic Life of Power:*

> We are used to thinking of power as what presses the subject from the outside, as what subordinates, sets underneath, and relegates to a lower order. . . . But if, following Foucault, we understand power as *forming* the subject as well, as providing the very condition of its existence and the trajectory of its desire, then power is not simply what we oppose, but also, in a strong sense, what we depend on for our existence and what we harbor and preserve in the beings that we are. . . . Subjection consists precisely in this fundamental dependency on a discourse we never chose but that, paradoxically, initiates and sustains our agency. "Subjection" signifies the process of becoming subordinated by power as well as the process of becoming a subject.[21]

Each of us is a subject in two senses: we are subjugated by power and we are created by it. By constituting themself as a subject conscious of their own being and their own truth, the subject is in reality the product of a power that is exercised over them.

The scope of this conclusion is vast. First, it implies that everything, including the subject, is historically determined. That is to say, there is nothing that is not dependent on the dispositifs of power in place. This poses a deep problem concerning the very possibility of knowledge, suggesting that there is nothing to know objectively; there is no knowledge besides the knowledge situated in and varying by social context. Second, Foucault's argument raises concerns about the possibility of knowing what we want: if the subject is shaped by the dispositif of sexuality in such a way that their sexuality becomes their identity, and if this dispositif is the product of political power, then there is no such thing as a stable subject who knows what they want. Power shapes the subject's sexual desires, which shape their practices, which shape who they are, which shapes their desires, and so on. There is no escape from being the subject that power has created. There is no outside-of-power from which we could think about the power that is exercised over us and fight against it.

Through this intricate derivation—from the dispositif of sexuality, to the assignment of identities according to sex acts, to sex itself, and finally to desire—Foucault succeeds in showing that the supposedly natural is in fact socially and historically constructed and, above all, that the causal character that we commonly attribute to sex is wrong. Sex is not the cause of what we are; it does not tell us any truth about ourselves. It is an *effect,* an effect of the power that makes us but does not tell us the truth about itself. Sex does not result from desire that may be repressed and unearthed via psychoanalysis. On the contrary, desire results from sex through the process of the dispositif of sexuality, which insists on correspondence between desire and the identity of the subject. We may well experience certain pleasures through our bodies, but desire is something different—the product of a certain way in which a subject is made. The man's desire for the woman, and the woman's desire for the man, are not natural, inherent, or prior. They are created by the constitution of the heterosexual subject—a subject whose existence comes with particular desires. Likewise the man's desire for the man and the woman's desire for the woman are not natural but created by the constitution of the homosexual subject. There is no nature to repress, nothing independent of the structures of power that could be surfaced and liberated.

The reader of Foucault is left with a feeling of unease: If the dispositif of power that we call the dispositif of sexuality acts on our constitution as subject, constructs the sexuality that we believe to be a given, and determines the very nature of our desire, what can we do? If this power is so concerned with our bodies, what is left to us that is not determined by it? Is there any freedom to be exerted in the arena of sexuality? Foucault himself felt this unease and so issued a call to "counter the grips of power with the claims of bodies, pleasures, and knowledges, in their multiplicity and their possibility of resistance. The rallying point for the counterattack against the deployment of sexuality," he wrote, "ought not to be sex-desire, but bodies and pleasures."[22] We ought to think deeply about this rejoinder, about our own anguished questions about sexual autonomy, if we want to decide what good sex might be.

It is no exaggeration to say that Foucault's ideas have shaped subsequent discourse on sexuality in Western academia and societies. Foucault's conception of sex has thoroughly challenged religious discourses and secular "sexology" that imagine a natural sexuality, highlighting the political character of these discourses. Every student of sexuality since Foucault has reckoned with his ideas, or at least with discourses of sexuality that are shaped by his ideas.[23]

But Foucault's legacy is very complex. We can see from the above survey how his ideas might be used for multiple purposes. One might use Foucault to recognize the ways in which the relations of power that weave society—the relations of gender in particular—are replayed in sexuality and consequently make sexuality a politically nonneutral ground and therefore one in which an egalitarian state might take interest. But one might also use Foucault to raise suspicion against any state intervention where desires and pleasures are concerned. One can easily imagine a critique of sexual consent as just another dispositif of sexuality, analogous in certain ways to confession. Some of the critiques of campus consent rules can take this form when they argue that the focus on consent creates a "bureaucracy" of its own.[24] One can also imagine—all the more so because Foucault himself defended this position—how these ideas could be used against discourses and policies aimed at protecting children from sexual encounters.[25]

Indeed, Foucault has been marshaled for and against almost all visions of sexual consent, from the most libertarian positions—necessitating absence of state control and thus a central place for consent—to the most radical feminist positions in which women's consent to heterosexual sex is conceived as not even possible. My own argument is inspired by Foucault's approach, but, as I discuss next, also departs from it.

The Intimate Is Political

Foucault makes a convincing case that there is something political going on in sex. But his argumentation is rather abstract. When he talks about the power relations intrinsic to sex, there is a surprising omission: he barely mentions the core manifestation of those relations, which is the social domination of women by men. The feminist politicization of intimacy—whereby consent cannot be understood as involving strictly the two or more people engaged in a specific sex act—is therefore the third crucial step in the evolution toward a political analysis of sex, after Freud and Foucault.

We can, with Freud, say that culture represses sexual desires and thus leads to a repression of sexual impulses. With Foucault, we can say that sexuality is at the heart of devices of knowledge-power and is thus crossed by power relations. With the feminists who arose during the sexual revolution, we can say something further: through sexuality, a certain form of social domination is played out—that of men over women. Some feminists have called this heteropatriarchy, and it constitutes the last phase of the intellectual history reconstructed here.[26]

Various feminist practices, in particular the discussion groups that go under the heading of "consciousness raising," have increased awareness of the oppressive mechanisms of patriarchy.[27]

In consciousness-raising groups, women take the floor to talk about their mundane daily experiences. (Typically, consciousness-raising groups have only women members.) When women share intimate aspects of their lives, they often come to see that their experiences are not unique; rather than the product of a particular individual history, experience becomes a manifestation of a social dynamics, in particular the oppressive dynamics of male domination. This practice emphasizes that the intimate sphere is, in reality, the context in which "each woman, in her own particular, even chosen, way reproduces in her most private relations a structure of dominance and submission that characterizes the entire public order."[28] In other words, the personal—the intimate—is political. Legal scholar Catharine MacKinnon sees four dimensions of this political character of the personal:

> First, women as a group are dominated by men as a group, and therefore as individuals. Second, women are subordinated in society, not by personal nature or by biology. Third, the gender division, which includes the sex division of labor which keeps women in high-heeled low-status jobs, pervades and determines even women's personal feelings in relationships. Fourth, since a woman's problems are not hers individually but those of women as a whole, they cannot be addressed except as a whole.[29]

Consciousness raising illuminates the functioning of male domination in all its complexity. And it highlights that intimacy, and in particular sexuality, is political and must therefore be the object of political struggles. A central focus of that struggle has been rape.

A New Understanding of Rape

Discussion groups have produced their share of concrete knowledge about women's lives. In particular, as Maria Bevacqua and

Nicola Gavey show, these conversations have radically changed the way rape is represented.[30] Rape was previously commonly conceived as an exceptional crime, committed by deviant individuals, in a public context—the stranger raping a woman in a parking lot. But when women began to come together and talk about their sexual experiences, it became clear that sexual violence in general, and rape in particular, was committed primarily by their husbands, boyfriends, exes, fathers, brothers, and uncles. It also became clear that sexual violence was far from being out of the ordinary. Thus, both in their activism and their theoretical work, feminists in the 1970s developed the idea that rape was not a crime emanating from individual psychology but a manifestation of patriarchy. As such, rape was inherently linked to the domination of women by men. Rather suddenly, rape became a political issue.

If rape is no longer the work of sick and isolated beings, but instead a routine manifestation of male domination in the context of intimate relations with women, then how can we distinguish rape from sex? This distinction was apparently obvious before: sex was what one did with one's husband; rape was what was imposed by a violent stranger. But with large numbers of women testifying to rape within marriage, distinguishing rape from sex was suddenly complicated, raising new questions. Is rape necessarily physically violent, after all? Is sex in fact rape if obtained by husbands who make their wives live in terror? If a woman is completely dependent on her husband financially, does that potentially constitute threat or coercion in the context of sex?

All of these questions, and others besides, can be reduced to another, which in itself distills the radical feminism of the 1970s: If rape is a manifestation of male domination that is structural, and if it is not the exceptional act of sick or evil men, does that mean that a significant portion of what is considered sex is actually rape? In essence, feminists were unsettling the rape/sex binary and suggesting that perhaps we should think of intimacy occurring along a continuum from the most desired sex to the most violent rape. In this important intellectual move, we see feminists embracing Foucault's analysis but also taking it in a new direction. That analysis holds that what we call sex is rarely, maybe never, fully chosen by any of the parties involved. Now feminists were naming the power relation that made sexual agency arguably impossible: heteropatriarchy. Rapists were not sick men; they were men carrying out their social roles in a political context that assigned them a dominant position and women a submissive one. Indeed, rape—or, as it was previously known, sex—was one of the means by which heteropatriarchy reproduced itself.

The "Sex Wars"

At the end of the 1970s and the beginning of the 1980s, this feminist politicization of intimacy—and in particular the question of a rape-sex continuum—gave rise to what became known as the "sex wars."[31] To put the matter succinctly, the awareness that sexuality is crossed by relations of power inspired two major, conflicting positions among feminists and in particular lesbian feminists. As bell hooks put it, some held "the utopian notion that feminism would be the theory and lesbianism the practice."[32] One political camp, including Andrea Dworkin and Adrienne Rich, defended the idea of a continuum between rape and sex in heterosexual relations, which made it difficult to imagine heterosexual relations liberated from male domination. These feminists, who were heavily influenced by the movement for women's liberation, rejected pornography as form of misogynistic dehumanization of women.[33] They also were highly suspicious of the idea that sex could be an emancipatory practice and so opposed prostitution. For this group if emancipation from male domination was possible, it would come through lesbianism. The other camp, comprising radical lesbians, gays, and queers, was associated more with gay liberation than with women's lib and constituted what was then called the "leather community." For this group, emancipation from male domination was indeed possible, and its vehicle would be BDSM.[34] At this point BDSM practices were a defining feature of US gay culture, inseparable from the aesthetics of the leather subculture, and were claimed as an identity marker in the context of the fight for equal rights for homosexuals.[35] Against a radical feminism criticizing sadomasochism as reproducing hegemonic and oppressive sexual norms harmful to women, other lesbian activists defended BDSM as a space of freedom and reappropriation of pleasure outside the frameworks of so-called normal sexuality.[36] These lesbian activists had many allies among gay men, perhaps above all Foucault himself.

Foucault found in BDSM a response to his worry about the impossibility of resistance to the dispositif of sexuality. Recall his somewhat enigmatic exhortation: "Counter the grips of power with the claims of bodies, pleasures, and knowledges, in their multiplicity and their possibility of resistance. The rallying point for the counterattack against the deployment of sexuality ought not to be sex-desire, but bodies and pleasures." What Foucault is suggesting is that bodies and pleasures can be sites of resistance because they are not determined by power in the way that sexuality is. Bodies are only secondarily constructs of power, in the sense that biopower is concerned with the health of the population; essentially and initially, bodies are a biological given.[37] The body that is given has certainly been eroticized, turned into a field of desires that are themselves creations of power. Yet, though the body is touched by the dispositif of sexuality, it is not itself a fiction invented by power, and so it is possible to invent an aside-from-power through the exploration and invention of the body's pleasures. In a 1984 interview, Foucault notes that the "S&M subculture" undertakes this "kind of creation, a creative enterprise, which has as one of its main features what I call the desexualization of pleasure"—that is, pleasure freed from the power of the dispositif of sexuality. He adds, "The idea that bodily pleasure should always come from sexual pleasure as the root of *all* our possible pleasure—I think *that's* something quite wrong."[38]

It is not by accident that Foucault relates BDSM's "desexualization of pleasure" to "pleasures . . . in their multiplicity." Pleasure in the singular is the constructed and imposed character of desire and sex according to the dispositif of sexuality. It is the pleasures, in their multiplicity, that can be desexualized. The dispositif of sexuality reduces pleasure to what is experienced in monogamous, heterosexual, reproductive intercourse. Other tactics, like fist-fucking and the wider range of activities associated with BDSM, exemplify potential sources of pleasure that escape the dispositif of sexuality. They are the pleasures of the body and not those of sex.

Lesbian defenders of BDSM developed similar views, which they brought to debates on sexuality in women's emancipation. Some of these debates became extremely heated, notably at the famous Barnard Conference on Sexuality in 1982, where antipornography activists faced off with BDSM backers, and conference participants levied highly personal accusations. Controversies like these were widely represented as evidence of a division in the feminist movement. On one side were so-called prosex activists, who believed that women's sexual fulfillment was possible, that it could be achieved even through heterosexual relations, and that achieving this fulfillment should be one of the objectives of feminism. On the other side were so-called antisex activists, for whom heterosexual sex could not be emancipatory because it was so similar to rape.

As hard-nosed as the debate could be, the notion of sex wars, suggesting two belligerents duking it out, is deeply misguided. For one thing, the "antisex" label obviously aims to discredit certain activists, suggesting that they are spinsters incapable of knowing the joys of sex. More broadly, the simplistic pro- and antisex duality denies the sophistication of the positions involved and perpetuates the stereotype of the catfight whereby women have some natural affinity for mutual hostility. But above all, as Lorna Bracewell argues, the notion of sex wars emphasizes only disagreement, while overlooking the essential area of agreement between the camps: sexuality is political, "compulsory heterosexuality" is the theater of patriarchy, and it is vital to find alternative practices.[39] One might even say that the popularity of the "sex wars" epithet—which was bandied about in the heavy, and profoundly sexist, media coverage of feminist debates in the 1980s—reflects patriarchy protecting itself against feminist critiques of every stripe.

Is BDSM Really Emancipatory?

Another deficit of the "sex wars" framing is that it implies that some party could be, or was, victorious and the other defeated. Unsurprisingly, from the standpoint of the wider culture—invested as it is in "normal" heterosexual sex—the prosex camp, sometimes referred to as "sex-positive," won. That the argument is settled may seem obviously true just because heterosexual sex is hardly extinct; many women, including feminist women, want sex with men; and it has become common to consider sexual experimentation empowering and kink a cool and edgy practice.[40]

Rather than participate in this trivialization of a serious debate, though, we would do better to learn something from it. In particular, we might learn something about consent from one of the core areas of "sex wars" contestation: whether BDSM constitutes a form of emancipation or whether it is a replay, under the pretext of emancipatory parody, of sexist and patriarchal norms. Let us give credit to those who see genuine potential in BDSM. But let us also recognize that *kink*—a generic term for nonstandard sexual practices—is common outside the

BDSM scene and may be coincident with sexual violence. For instance, a 2019 survey commissioned by the BBC showed that 38 percent of adult British women under age forty had experienced unwanted slapping, choking, spitting, or gagging during sex.[41] Nonconsensual strangulation practices, often minimized by the terms "choking" or "erotic asphyxiation," are especially problematic because they are so dangerous.[42] When abusers, usually men, are called out for engaging in these practices without consent, they may well claim the mantle of BDSM to defend themselves against accusations of sexual violence, just as many feminists feared they would. For example, when former New York attorney general Eric Schneiderman resigned amid allegations that he sexually abused women, he also justified his conduct by referencing the liberal moral and political framework of BDSM. "In the privacy of intimate relationships, I have engaged in role-playing and other consensual sexual activity," he said. "I have not assaulted anyone. I have never engaged in nonconsensual sex, which is a line I would not cross." Schneiderman later admitted to abuse ranging from "slapping [women] to applying pressure with his hands onto women's necks without consent."[43]

From the standpoint of my analysis, the crucial question that BDSM raises is whether and to what extent these practices, which give a particularly central place to consent in its liberal sense, are permeated by gender inequalities. "Antisex" feminists of the 1970s and 1980s—and, as we saw in the last chapter, Muriel Fabre-Magnan and others more recently—have argued that BDSM can and does serve to eroticize existing power relations based on the domination of women by men. On this view, BDSM is just one of the forms taken by patriarchy, one of the many means by which it imprints itself on our sex lives. The contrary view, held by gay and lesbian defenders of BDSM, is that BDSM's parody of power relations is sincere, not pretextual. It can therefore actually reverse relations of power, liberating participants sexually. Let us consider this debate more closely and see what we find.

The Art of Reversal and the Parody of Power Relations

One argument against BDSM's alleged complicity in social domination begins with the contractual practice itself. While social structure and oppressive social hierarchies are always already there for the subject, the contract positions the BDSM participants as being in an initial state of equality and freedom. The BDSM relationship is necessarily one of domination and submission, but in order to consensually establish this relationship, the partners must first negotiate from positions of equality. The contracting individuals are conceived in this respect as independent, rational, and not vulnerable. They freely choose to commit themselves to one another in order to obtain sexual pleasure. The hierarchical power relationship between the partners is a fiction created by the contract: the power relationship exists during the scene, but it is fictitious in the sense that the participants know themselves to be equal and equally creators of their relationship. The contract introduces a clear separation between the sexual scene, where power relationships are invented for purposes of pleasure, and the outside world, where power relationships are brute facts of social life.

The negotiation embodied in the contract is also central to the conception of BDSM as a liberating practice. Negotiation necessitates a discussion of consent and its limits that is often absent from conventional sex, an absence that can result in nonconsensual sexual practices. To quote legal scholar Janet Halley, all sexual intercourse is confronted with the "problematic of wantedness": desire is driven by the paradox that one may want not to know what one wants, which creates a risk of unwanted sex.[44] The "elaborate consent rituals" of BDSM reduce the risk that sex will take an unwanted turn.[45]

Another argument in favor of BDSM as a genuine practice of resistance lies in the way power relations are played out in the sub-dom relationship. If indeed BDSM is shot through with power relations, they look little like those of the world outside. They are, in an important way, not real. Anne McClintock writes, "To argue that in consensual S/M the 'dominant' has power, and the slave has not, is to read theater for reality. The economy of S/M is an economy of conversion: slave to master, adult to baby, pain to pleasure, man to woman, and back again. . . . Contrary to popular stigma, S/M theatrically flouts the edict that manhood is synonymous with mastery, and submission a feminine fate."[46]

The organization of BDSM in clubs, the recourse to contract, the formalization of the scenes—all of these work to support the theatrical dimension of the eroticized power relation. The economy of conversion creates the possibility of a cathartic, freeing relation to the hierarchies played out during the scene. And by replaying, magnifying, and parodying these hierarchies, participants highlight power relations in society, opening them to contestation. The relation of BDSM to society's power relations is thus analogous to the relation of drag with the stereotypes of gender: magnifying and parodying social norms positions them as objects that can be critiqued and shows off the constructed character of what is supposedly natural.

The reversal that arrives in the BDSM performance is reinforced by the contract, which also manifests the transferable character of power. The contract reverses the usual hierarchies because, as we have seen in Sacher-Masoch's work, it is the submissive who establishes the rules necessary for their own pleasure. This is confirmed by the sociologist Damien Lagauzère, who finds that BDSM is essentially masochistic and "masocentric": in the overwhelming majority of cases, the masochist organizes the staging, which transforms reality in correspondence with his fantasy.[47] The "victim" chooses the persecutor, educates them, and trains them in their fantasy; the sub thus actively constructs the context of their passivity. As such, the victim *makes* the persecutor, insofar as the persecutor carries out what their victim asks.[48]

BDSM does not, therefore, seem to constitute a practice of reproducing social hierarchies but rather an emancipatory practice of revising and parodying those hierarchies. In this framework, BDSM submission should be distinguished from other types of submission. BDSM submission is the result of erotic role-playing governed by a contract between independent and consenting individuals. Submission is neither more nor less valued than its counterpart, domination, and both share the same goal: sexual pleasure, considered purely physical and as such apolitical.

Submission Contracts and Reinforcement of Gender Hierarchies

Yet what is perhaps true of BDSM in theory does not seem to be as clear-cut in practice. Although it is difficult to obtain reliable figures concerning sexuality in general and BDSM in particular, what evidence we do have suggests that, contrary to the image of reversing power relations, BDSM often reflects society's gender hierarchies. For a recent study of the psychological health of BDSM practitioners, researchers interviewed 902 BDSM practitioners and 434 control-group participants and asked about, among other things, which roles they inhabited in scenes. The researchers found that 33.4 percent of men were submissives, while 48.3 percent dominants. (The rest switched between roles depending on the scene.) Among women, 75.6 percent were submissive and only 8 percent were dominant.[49] According to this study, therefore, men are predominantly in a dominant position and women are overwhelmingly in a submissive position during BDSM practices. These figures, which are in line with the information that appears in the scientific literature on BDSM, are worrying: if BDSM is mostly heterosexual, if women are overwhelmingly submissive and men overwhelmingly dominant, then is BDSM really reversing the power relations we experience in society at large?

Again, lack of data makes it hard to know for sure what is going on here, but it is fair to speculate that the vast majority of BDSM scenes involve one or more dominant men and one or more submissive women. In cases when these roles are reversed, submissive men often obtain the services of a professional domi-natrix.[50] This distinction is important, and all the more so in light of participants' contractual obligations. As we saw previously, contracts can cover two types of circumstances: they can set out the rules for a specific scene, or they can set out the rules for a domination-submission relationship that persists over time and constitutes a way of life. In the first case, the contract lasts only as long as the scene; in the second, the contract lasts as long as the dominant desires or until the submissive terminates the contract according to its provisions. The fact that very few women are in positions of domination—and that those who are in such positions are often professionals, who therefore use scene-specific contracts—suggests that long-term BDSM relationships are predominantly between a dominant man and a submissive woman.

This type of contract—a long-term one, between a dominant man and a submissive woman—poses particular difficulty with regard to the consent of the submissive and the type of exchange at stake. It gives reason to fear, alongside the radical "antisex" feminists, that heterosexual BDSM masks male domination.

An example of this contract can be found in the famous novel *Fifty Shades of Grey*. In this text, which is more of a romance than it is BDSM literature, the heroine falls in love with a rich and handsome businessman who happens to be keen on long-term domination-submission relationships. He proposes that she become "his" submissive and sign a contract. Fully repro-duced in the novel, the contract is very similar to the long-term BDSM contracts commonly found online and in specialized literature. The contract adopts legal vocabulary and form, establishes the obligations of both parties, establishes safe words, and indicates the limits to which the submissive has agreed. The three pillars of safe, sane, and consensual are respected, notably through detailed attention to questions of hygiene understood in a very broad sense (clauses 2, 3, 6, 14.1, 14.4). The contract further provides that no lasting traces will be left on the body of the submissive and that the practices planned will never be so painful or otherwise hazardous as to necessitate medical care. Conditions of dissolution are included, and the contract sets a time limit (three months) and notes the possible need for renegotiation (clause 14).

At the same time, a number of provisions imply that the signatories are not equals. In the first place, the contract is formulated in terms that make the submissive an object. Clause 15.2: "accepts the Submissive as his own." Clause 15.13: "she is now the property of the Dominant." Moreover, the submissive is an object for the maintenance of which the dominant will pay, as emphasized in clause 14. Notably, she is not his employee: the contract suggests ownership rather than employment because the dominant is responsible for maintenance, not compensation.

This is not the contract of Sacher-Masoch, which secures the autonomy of the submissive in their pursuit of pleasure through pain. This contract specifies the abandonment of any form of freedom for its duration. During these three months, the submissive no longer belongs to herself, insofar as she "shall serve the Dominant in any way the Dominant sees fit and shall endeavor to please the Dominant at all times to the best of her ability." The only limits to the obedience the dominant commands are the sexual limits established by the contract; otherwise, the submissive must do the dominant's every bidding. The contract does impose some obligations on the dominant, the nonfulfillment of which would lead to immediate breach of the contract (clauses 15.1–15.12). Then, too, the contract enjoins the dominant to ensure "the wellbeing and the proper training, guidance, and discipline of the Submissive" (clause 7). In sum, then, this agreement could be described as a benevolent contract of slavery.[51] Although benevolent, it nonetheless deprives the submissive of most of her agency.

In its apparent benevolence, in its the concern to ensure not only the consent but also the safety of the submissive, and in several other respects, this contract is resolutely paternalistic. The submissive is not allowed to question the dominant's actions toward her, or even to ask for an explanation. Clause 15.18: "shall accept without question any and all disciplinary action." Clause 15.20: "without hesitation or argument." Clause 15.21: "without hesitation, inquiry, or complaint." The dominant controls the submissive's conduct at all times and in all places because he decides how much she sleeps, what she eats, what physical exercise she gets, and so on. The contract manifests not only a desire for control on the part of the dominant but also the conviction that the dominant knows what is best for the submissive and should, therefore, substitute his judgment and his decisions for her own. Such a substitution is contrary to the very foundation of Mill's liberalism, which holds that the purpose of limiting the power of the state over individuals is to guarantee those individuals the freedom to make choices for themselves.

The contract in *Fifty Shades of Grey* does not subvert existing social hierarchies; it reinforces them. The contract's appendix has the function of ensuring that the submissive corresponds to stereotypes of femininity: that she is slim, athletic, and healthy; that she shaves her legs; that she is discreet; and above all that she is modest. Conversely, the contract manifests the masculinity of the dominant, who not only controls the submissive and knows what is good for her, but also pays for all the expenses involved in their relationship.

Fifty Shades of Grey is fiction, but similar contracts are implemented in real life and include provisions restricting the female submissive's food intake, forcing her to exercise, and requiring her to handle household chores and childrearing. Such contracts may reinforce the male dominant's position by allowing him to permit the submissive "treats" that would otherwise be proscribed.[52] Such a contract seems merely to reproduce the gendered hierarchy that already exists in society; without the label of BDSM, the distribution of roles in such contracts looks like run-of-the-mill sexist distribution. In these cases, BDSM is not social critique but rather an "edgy" screen behind which male domination in its most traditional form hides itself.

In addition to reinforcing gender inequalities behind the veil of BDSM, such contracts, through their conformity with installed social hierarchies, raise suspicion about the validity of the consent they embody. Can a woman in need of financial support truly consent to such a contract—is she not coerced by her circumstances? What if the contract in question is proposed by her husband? Does refusal not come with potentially serious consequences? Fabre-Magnan indirectly expresses these concerns when she asks whether the European Court of Human Rights, by enshrining consent in its jurisprudence, goes too far in insulating the home from state interference, particularly when it comes to the protection of battered women.[53] The absence of complaint by battered women—which is common—could appear as an expression of consent, even as feminists have shown that these women are often fearful of being punished by abusive spouses and are too poor to escape. As noted, it is difficult to ascertain whether the wife in the case of *K. A. and A. D. v. Belgium*, by virtue of her marriage, was capable of expressing full consent. In cases where consent cannot be established with certainty, the distinction between BDSM submission and submission tout court is no longer clear.

Even where women's consent to BDSM submission is valid, this does not guarantee that they will escape violation in the context of a scene. Contracts notwithstanding, many women report having

been raped during BDSM practices.[54] Jay Wiseman, author of
SM 101, considered the definitive introduction to BDSM practices, has himself reported on this problem. In a blog post entitled "Are We Men a Bunch of Lying Pricks?" he describes his
disbelief upon discovering that male dominants regularly break
the boundaries of their negotiated contracts and that female
submissives, including some of his partners, tolerate their participation in what can only be described as nonconsensual sex.[55]
What is striking about this realization, besides the author's immense disappointment, is his astonishment at the fact that the
women don't just "run away." It seems obvious to Wiseman
that, in light of nonconsensual activities, women should give up
the practice of BDSM. Yet they do not. Wiseman does not consider the possibility that it is precisely because they are women
that they endure and tolerate nonconsensual sex, conceived as
the price to pay for being able, at times, to live out their sexual
desires and pleasures as they see fit. Perhaps it is precisely because,
as women, they are accustomed to having their choices or wishes
disregarded that they continue such practices despite the risk of
rape. Wiseman is unable to break from the liberal assumption
underlying the use of contract and the valuing of consent—that
individual identity and social affiliation need not be taken into
account. It is impossible for this leader of the BDSM community
to appreciate that a woman may not consent to her submission
in the same way a man does—that women's social subordination
makes it easier for them to consent to sexual subordination.

This overview of the politicization of sex and intimacy, informed
by the theory and practice of BDSM, is fundamental to understanding what is at stake in contemporary thinking about sexual
consent. For one thing, it highlights the reason why this debate
is recent: various intellectual changes had to happen before we
could begin to think of sexual consent the way we now do. Sex

had to appear as the center of our subjectivity; psychoanalysis provided for this. Then there needed to arise a critique of the imperative of liberation itself, which Foucault offered. Only after power relations within sexuality had been theorized could they be interpreted as vectors of injustice so that a legal and political vocabulary, that of consent, could be applied to sexuality. This application of consent to sexuality is not by any means universal: it is an object of disagreement. But only recently have we even been able to discuss it. It is thanks to feminist activism and theory that the two major contemporary questions about sexual consent appear: How can we understand and establish the difference between sex and rape? And how can we conceive of harmonious and maximally depoliticized intimate relationships, freed from the mechanisms of social domination?

These two questions manifest the ambivalent place of the sexual revolution in women's lives. The advances for women represented by the liberalization of contraception, the (precarious) legalization of abortion, and the end of virtually compulsory heterosexual marriage are undeniable. The sexual revolution also fostered the development of a new form of feminist activism, with new priorities, among them the politicization of intimacy. That having been said, and as Catharine MacKinnon notes, the sexual revolution was above all a source of liberation for men, not for women. She shows, among other things, that the sex conceived as requiring liberation corresponds with what constitutes sex from men's point of view: penile penetration. Both the claim that repressed urges must be let free and the related pathologization of low female desire for men ("frigidity") serve men's interest in having sexual access to the greatest possible number of women.[56] More broadly, various received ideas that factor in women's subordination remain robust. Among these: women should not have "too many" sexual relations, while men are encouraged to be "players"; female pleasure is of a psychological nature and thus not something men could learn to give; and women's principal sexual desire is for submission. In addition, we have witnessed the emergence of a new form of heterosexual couple in which men are no longer bound by the traditional imperatives to provide for the family and at the same time do not feel bound to a more egalitarian sharing of family duties. All of this adds up to the observation at the heart of the #MeToo movement: for women, sexual liberation has not happened.[57]

The intellectual, psychological, and rhetorical investment in consent, then, reflects the failed promise of sexual liberation. If consent has been central for the passage from authoritarianism to democracy, perhaps it can also enable the passage from a repressive and heteronormative sexuality to egalitarian intimate and erotic relationships. As I discuss next, such an egalitarian promise can only be realized if we learn to oppose the ways in which the vocabulary of consent can reinforce gender inequality.

5

IS CONSENT A WOMAN'S PROBLEM?

CAN A REAL FEMINIST use the concept of consent? Although we are accustomed to the idea that feminists are the ones pushing for the adoption of affirmative consent policies or consent-based laws against rape, many feminist scholars are in fact wary of consent. They worry that consent may be used to give an appearance of legitimacy to situations that are actually unequal and unfair. Women have, after all, consented to marriage for centuries, and yet marriage has mostly been bad for them. And it sometimes looks like criminal law against sex offenses is built in such a way that no matter what a woman does, she will always be seen as consenting. More generally, women are often accused of accepting their roles in patriarchal society and thereby silently consenting to it. Consent, then, appears to be very much a double-edged sword, potentially valuable in protecting women from violation but also capable of justifying injustice.

We saw as much in the previous chapter. When we abandon a strictly individual approach and instead adopt a structural one—when we consider that power relations structuring society as a whole affect what happens when individuals have sex with each other—we see that sex is political. In such a context, activities that appear innocuous and consensual may be revealed as seriously harmful, and according to certain radical critiques are necessarily so.

In this chapter, I turn to another troubling and revealing feature of consent: sexual consent is almost always presented as exclusively a woman's concern. In every campaign against sexual violence, every poster on a dormitory wall, and in most philosophical analysis, it is taken for granted that only women must consent to sex. Thus a classic philosophical text on the subject begins, "Although this book ranges more widely, its central organizing question is this: when does a woman give valid consent to sexual relations?"[1] It is presumed that men always want sex and are always in the position of proposing it, while women receive and vet proposals, accepting some and rejecting others.

We can certainly imagine exceptions to this scenario, wherein women propose sex, and the men to whom they propose are uninterested. Yet the presumption remains, and it does reflect the broad sociological truth of how heterosexual sex actually works. So why does it matter that consent is seen as concerning only women? And if there is a problem here, couldn't we solve it by just revising our posters and our slogans—by just saying that men's consent also counts? On the contrary, I believe the intuitive connection drawn between consent and womanhood cannot be waved away. It is something we can learn from and that we ought to learn from if we want to use consent to build better sex lives.

Against the optimistic view that consent is unequivocally emancipatory for women, in this chapter I discuss four feminist arguments supporting the claim that the concept of consent can harm women. This chapter is slightly different from others as I am mostly explaining other scholars' views (except when I criticize the sexism of the supposed French art of love). But, trust me, understanding these views is crucial. Collectively, these arguments clarify the tension within the concept of consent: why we simultaneously need it in order to attain sexual autonomy *and* why we should be constantly suspicious of the ways in which our intuitive liberal view of consent disguises the inequalities of a patriarchal world.

There is no way to salvage consent if we do not fully apprehend this tension. On the one hand, consent is the best tool we think we have for claiming the sexual agency that patriarchy has denied to women. Therefore consent is of primary importance for achieving feminist goals. On the other hand, consent is the product of an intellectual universe, constructed over time, that does not conceive of women as men's equals. That means that under the guise of guaranteeing equality, consent can enable, and even legitimize, relationships of power and domination that harm women and perpetuate patriarchal structures. If we want, as I do, to salvage consent, we need to carefully evaluate the arguments of its feminist critics. In their ideas, we may find a road to sex that doesn't reinforce patriarchal norms.

Consent, Feminism, and Liberalism

First, I want to show that the very liberalism that makes consent so appealing to feminists is also what makes it potentially dangerous. In its liberal understanding, consent is both a path toward women's autonomy and a mechanism to render patriarchy invisible.

We have seen that consent is a central concept in the liberal tradition. It is also at the heart of contemporary theories of social justice based in what is called the "high liberalism" developed in the second half of the twentieth century by the US philosopher John Rawls.[2] In important respects, this version of liberalism both shares in and differs from the "classical" liberalism of Mill. A key difference is that Mill was concerned only with the relationship between individuals and governments. There is no place for society in this liberalism; there are only individuals associating, and governments can legitimately intervene in these associations only if they involve harm. Rawls's liberalism, by contrast, is a social theory. It seeks to establish how a society should be organized in order to be just and therefore what possible type of relationship between the state and society is just. However, this twentieth-century liberalism maintains the central hypothesis of traditional liberalism, according to which each individual decides for themselves what the good life is. Rawls is interested in how the democratic state might use its capacities to structure society, so that individuals have the space necessary for building the moral life of their choosing. Rawls's methodological individualism places him in the liberal tradition, and it leads him, like other authors in that tradition, to assume that the world is divided between a public sphere, in which individuals live with and influence each other, and a private sphere, in which the individual chooses the meaning they want to give to their life.

For Rawls, the importance of preserving and protecting personal autonomy assures consent a central role in guaranteeing justice. Consent is valid—that is, it is deemed to express a choice that is free enough to justify the consequences it produces—if the conditions under which the choice is made are satisfactory. For example, consent cannot be valid if the person who gave it did so under threat. Consent is the basis of what Rawls calls "pure procedural justice": if the procedure through which an individual makes a decision is just, then the individual is free enough to be held responsible for the consequence of their decision. Consent, when it manifests the autonomy of the individual—that is, when it is exercised in a sufficiently free manner—guarantees that the outcome of the consented-to act is just.

Given that liberalism in the context of social justice retains the firm association between consent and self-determination, it is not surprising that feminists of the social-justice era are often invested in consent. Feminism and liberalism share an emphasis on autonomy, both personal and political. As philosopher Anne Phillips notes, the freedom to decide for oneself is both an aspiration of and a concern for feminists.[3] Feminists aim to break with centuries of dependence and submission during which women have been compelled to accept husbands chosen by their fathers, to follow religious injunctions about appropriate forms of sexuality and motherhood, to obey paternalistic legislation claiming to protect them from their own fragility, and to conform to the expectation that a good woman will sacrifice her needs and ambitions for the benefit of those she loves. Feminists have thus repeatedly made self-determination the condition for women's liberation. The fact that women have historically been deprived of rights that men had—the right to vote but also the right to drive a car, testify in court, have a bank account, and so on—in the name of a supposed natural incapacity to make decisions for themselves has reinforced the structuring of feminism around the claim of autonomy. Although this autonomy can take diverse forms, it remains at the heart of feminist claims.[4]

Yet some feminists have also observed that contemporary theories of justice err in their treatment of gender-based social inequalities. The first major feminist revision of liberal theories of justice is Susan Moller Okin's 1989 book *Justice, Gender, and the Family*.[5] Okin contrasts the egalitarian ideals of the United States with the permanence of gender inequalities in US society, at the heart of which is the unequal distribution of unpaid work within the family. Noting how family structure—neglected in liberal theory—affects the moral development of children, she writes:

> What is a child of either sex to learn about fairness in the average household with two full-time working parents, where the mother does, at the very least, twice as much family work as the father? What is a child to learn about the value of nurturing and domestic work in a home with a traditional division of labor in which the father either subtly or not so subtly uses the fact that he

is the wage earner to "pull rank" on or to abuse his wife? What is a child to learn about responsibility for others in a family in which, after many years of arranging her life around the needs of her husband and children, a woman is faced with having to provide for herself and her children but is totally ill-equipped for the task by the life she agreed to lead, has led, and expected to go on leading?[6]

This excerpt is striking because it highlights the contradiction between women's consent—what women have "agreed to"— and women's freedom under conditions of structural inferiority. Okin does not say that gender injustices make this hypothetical woman's consent invalid, but she shows that consenting does not guarantee a free life. This woman consented to an arrangement that, in the long run, placed her in a position of subordination and dependence on her husband and family. The behavior of her and her husband's provide a powerful model for their children, thus perpetuating the structural inequality that she herself experienced.

That this woman can give her consent and still be in a situation that is unjust for her is not, in principle, contrary to Rawls's theory. Pure procedural justice only works when the conditions under which a choice is made are satisfactory. Yet, given Rawls's assumption that the family is a just institution, the choices made in the family sphere satisfy the conditions for valid consent. Since this woman's situation clearly appears to be unjust, and yet this situation conforms to Rawlsian criteria of justice, his theory of justice fails in this case to address injustice. If, as Okin claims, cases like these are typical, then the Rawlsian theory of justice needs to be amended in a feminist sense—that is, to ensure that the specific situation of women is taken into account.[7]

Rawls's view of the family as a just institution is of a piece with a broader problem of liberalism. As we saw, liberalism's concern for the individual and their rights calls for a separation between public and private spheres. But, as feminists have shown, this separation is inherently harmful for women. The feminist critique of liberalism initially took the form of a critical rereading of classical texts in the light of feminist issues.[8] These critical readings showed that the ineffectiveness of liberal theories on gender inequalities derives from the public-private distinction, which grounds these theories and results in the exclusion on principle of the family as an object of philosophical and political analysis.

Most liberals take for granted that the public sphere is constructed, while the private sphere of the individual and the family is a matter of nature. Historically it was understood that men can develop in both spheres, but women are confined to the private sphere. This distinction originates centuries ago in a dispute between John Locke and Sir Robert Filmer, a political theorist who defends monarchy on the grounds that the power of the king over his subjects is analogous to the power of the father over his family. Locke disagrees: the power of the father is natural and therefore unlike that of the king, for political power is constructed. That male authority in the household is ordained by nature is obvious from men's greater strength and because "we see that generally the laws of mankind and customs of nations have ordered it so." The subjection of wives to husbands is not political: "It can be only a conjugal power, not political, the power that every husband hath to order the things of private concernment in his family . . . and to have his will take place before that of his wife in all things of their common concernment."[9] Since the power relations we witness within the family are only natural, political theorists following Locke have typically not been interested in it: there are no questions of obligation and legitimacy to reckon with, and likewise there can be neither justice nor injustice. Thus the distinction between the private and public spheres has been at the root of the exclusion of the family from reflections about justice and of the special status of women from political thought.

Consent and Citizenship

The distinction between the public and private spheres is particularly important in understanding why, despite its apparent usefulness to feminism, consent has provoked suspicion among feminist theorists. The historical exclusion of women from the public sphere, in classical theories of social contract, meant that women were deprived of liberalism's cherished individuality. Strictly speaking, as nonindividuals, women could not enter into contracts, whether everyday contracts or the social contract. Women were therefore excluded from the very possibility of citizenship and deprived of legal personality. Hence various laws that may now seem bizarre: until the second half of the twentieth century, a woman could not open a bank account without her husband's authorization, property ownership and inheritance laws treated women as adjuncts of their male relatives, women were often barred from participating in legal proceedings without special permission, and so on. This is to say nothing of the voting rights that slowly came online for women in the twentieth century.

The individual, conversely, is recognized as free and equal to other individuals in society and is deemed to have participated, even virtually, in the social contract by which the social order is created. Women are excluded from these two conditions of individuality: they do not participate in the social contract; they are recognized neither as naturally free nor as equal to other individuals—their submission to the authority of men is taken for granted. Recognizing this, some feminist theorists have argued that the notion of the individual is historically constructed to apply only to men and to exclude women.

Of course, one could easily read this exclusion as a mistake of the past that, thanks to the corrective of feminism, belongs to the past. However, some feminist theorists think these philosophical foundations continue to influence the place of women in society. According to Carole Pateman, the eventual opening of citizenship to women does not change the fact that the political theory on which citizenship is based considered it impossible and unnatural for women to be citizens.[10] Social developments in the nineteenth and twentieth centuries certainly enabled women to acquire formal legal equality with men and thus to be recognized as citizens and as individuals. Yet the inequality between men and women is woven into liberal theory. For instance, one of the central qualities of the citizen is his independence—independence that implicitly is made possible by the fact that this citizen has a wife who takes care of feeding, clothing, and caring for him and for raising his children. Even today the freedom of individuals in the public sphere is made possible by a private sphere in which male domination reigns.

Importantly, consent is essential to women's historical exclusion from citizenship. On the one hand, women could not consent like men because they were not individuals; on the other hand, women's consent made, and continues to make, the distinction between the public and private spheres *possible*.[11] According to classical contract theorists, consent belongs to the public sphere, to political agreement. Consent is the work of men who have agreed to the social contract and who revive this original consent in each of the contracts to which they consent. Because of their exclusion from this original contract, women seem therefore to be deprived of the capacity to consent. Yet consent is at the heart of the marriage contract, and it is the marriage contract that creates the family and therefore the private sphere. Thus even when women were everywhere seen as formally unequal to men, their consent mattered. But far from securing them equality, consent rooted their inferiority. Consent to marriage served to locate the spouses' relationship outside the public sphere: until the end of the twentieth century and the recognition of domestic violence and marital rape, the spouses' consent to marry made their relationship a private matter, of concern only to its members—the law had very little say in what went on. We are thus faced with a paradox: on the one hand, the separation of the spheres deprives women of the capacity to consent; on the other hand, this separation rests on women's consent to marry.

Marriage and Consent

Pateman identifies and explores the implications of this paradox in her 1988 book *The Sexual Contract,* one of the most radical feminist critiques of consent and of the contractual form in general. Her analysis raises critical questions: What sense does it make to talk about consent in a world where nature is supposed to be the source of authority? How, in such a world, can women consent? In particular, she takes on these questions in the context of the marriage contract and women's consent to it.

Pateman notes two distinct problems inherent to the marriage contract: first, the way in which this contract organizes gender relations and, second, what this contract says about the legal personality of the woman. The marriage contract looks like a normal contract—an agreement between equals—yet it establishes the individual subordination of the woman by the man. As Pateman shows, the marriage contract evolved with this purpose in mind, hence, for instance, the doctrine of coverture in force until the end of the nineteenth century.[12] According to this doctrine, the wife was her husband's possession and slave: she was "civilly dead," melting into her husband's personality in the sense that any interaction she might have with state and other institutions was carried out through him. The married woman had no rights of her own and could not have possessions, sign legal documents or contracts, keep a salary, or receive an education without her husband's permission. Pateman argues that, despite its gradual demise, the coverture doctrine has left a lasting impression on the conception of marital relations. "Some decisive reforms in the legal standing of wives are so recent," she writes, "that most of us still bear marks of subjection, notably that we are known by our husbands' names."[13] Adopting one's husband's name can seem like a meaningless detail, but what does it say if not that, through marriage, a woman ceases to be her father's possession and becomes her husband's?

According to Pateman, the traditional marriage contract belongs to a category of contracts that create relationships of subordination. (The labor contract is another example.) Drawing on Claude Lévi-Strauss, who asserts in *The Elementary Structures of Kinship* that women in "primitive" societies are "the most precious category of goods" and that marriage is "the archetype of exchange," Pateman interprets the marriage contract as a double exchange.[14] First, although the contract implicates the spouses, the woman is in fact the *object* of an exchange between her father and future husband: the woman passes from one master to the other. The second exchange is indeed between the spouses: the wife trades obedience to her husband for his protection.[15] The key moment of the marriage ceremony stages this "exchange of consents," whereby both parties agree that she will be subordinated to and secured by him.

The marriage contract is alienating for women because it allows men to appropriate women's bodies sexually. This can be hard to recognize when the law imposes what, on its face at least, is reciprocal conjugal duty. For instance, this has been the case of French law since 1810. However, the construction of heterosexual sexuality makes clear the duty is, at best, reciprocal on paper. Where sex is constituted as women yielding to men's desire, the conjugal duty is in fact a right of the man to have sexual relations with his wife without any obligation to take her will into account. Thus, for instance, the famous 1888 Australian ruling *R v. Clarence*, which guaranteed the right of the husband to demand sex from his wife, even though in this case the husband knew he had contracted gonorrhea from a prostitute. In essence, through the marriage contract, the woman consents to any sex her husband wants, so long as the marriage remains in place. Only very recently has this state of affairs changed significantly, through the legal recognition of the possibility of marital rape.[16]

The man's possession of his wife's body is not limited to her sexuality: she is also his possession in an economic sense, a body that works for him. Thus, the marriage contract establishes not only a relationship of sexual subordination but also a labor relationship, similar to that of the labor contract. Capitalism and patriarchy are inextricably linked in the very institution of marriage: the husband is also a boss. Through marriage, the husband appropriates his wife's body as a sexual body and as a labor force.[17]

If the marriage contract is indeed an appropriation of the woman by the husband, it is difficult to understand "why . . . a free and equal female individual [would] enter a contract that *always* places her in subjection and subordination to a male individual."[18] As long as marital rape was not recognized as a possibility, consenting to marriage meant that a woman would permanently relinquish the right to consent or not to consent to sexual relations with her husband. Why would a woman consent to this? There is a tension between, on the one hand, the appearance of consent in the marriage contract and, on the other, the reality of marriage, which deprives the woman of the capacity to consent to either sex or work.

According to Pateman, this tension is resolved only when we understand that women's consent in marriage is not what we normally mean by consent: the woman does not consent to the marriage contract in the same way that an individual consents to an ordinary contract, because the marriage agreement is not taken between equals. The marriage contract is just the woman's formal, public acknowledgment of her supposedly natural submission to the man and in that sense is itself an act of submission.

This consent is not real consent because the parties are not equals, which in concrete terms means that the woman does not have the option of refusing consent. For one thing, the woman has no say in the exchange between her father and her future husband. Moreover, Pateman shows that linguistic conditions are such that women's nonconsent cannot be heard. She cites Rousseau's prescription that women *"must always say 'no,' even when they desire to say 'yes.'* . . . Apparent refusal of consent can *never,* in a woman, be taken at face value."[19] If a woman's every "no" can or must be understood as a "yes," then the "yes" that the woman utters at the time of her consent to marriage has no value in indicating actual agreement. To have such a value, the woman would have to be able to say no in a way that would be understood as refusal. The imperatives of modesty have corrupted the meaning of women's language, so that they cannot refuse and therefore also cannot accept fully—so that no means yes and therefore authentic consent is not possible.

These issues of exchange and language supplement the further coercive factor of social stigma. To the extent that unmarried women are viewed as suspect or dishonorable, the choice of whether to marry is not really a choice at all. It is important to realize that these impingements on women's capacity to consent to marriage are not identical; they are distinct, and they add up, making for immense pressure on women to accept marriage regardless of their true preference.

Pateman does not adopt the liberal perspective of starting from the individual and their choices. Rather, hers is a critical perspective that understands society as deeply structured by the domination of men over women. This complicates what is often a reductive sense of consent. The question is no longer whether the woman has consented to marry or whether she has consented to submit to the partner who is, by contract, her master, but instead the extent to which the patriarchal organization of society affects not only her ability to choose but also the kinds of choices she can make. We are compelled to recognize that, under conditions of male domination, women's subordination is disguised as the natural or consensual order.[20]

It might be objected that women today are freer than Pateman's analysis assumes. It would be more accurate, however, to say that some women feel freer to test these limits, while many others do not and still others believe that men's appropriative rights are indeed endowed by nature rather than by patriarchy. Consider the so-called Deneuve op-ed. In 2017 *Le Monde*, the French newspaper of record, published a letter signed by a hundred women including the actress Catherine Deneuve, claiming that men have a right to sexually harass women. This right is implicitly a product of men's conquering nature, and women are left to, at most, gently repel these assaults. Women should "not feel forever traumatized by being rubbed in the subway," the signatories claim. Such activities are just what we should expect given men's naturally inexhaustible desire.

Sexual Consent and the So-Called French Art of Love

There has been in France, in the last fifteen years or so, resistance to supposed American puritanism based in a liberal, contractual, view of intimacy. Critics argue that this vision is contrary to a typically French romantic art of love. Anyone who has watched the TV series *Emily in Paris* has a (slightly deformed) idea of what this may look like to a young American woman: a great deal of flirting, constant sexual jokes, people having lots of sex with lots of different partners. But also *a lot* of sexual harassment, in addition to assault and rape.

This may be the French art of love through American eyes, but it is not entirely wrong. Still, French partisans would draw a somewhat different picture. Various scholars trace this art to the inheritance of eighteenth- and early nineteenth-century French and English literature—think for instance of Samuel Richardson's *Pamela* or, later, the model of love that prevails in many of Jane Austen's novels. The literary scholar Claude Habib, an apologist for this supposed French art of love, links its vision of consent to the writings of Rousseau in particular, which distinguish between a public sphere where freedom must reign and a private, intimate sphere structured by the bonds of dependence and subordination that we have identified in liberalism.[21] On this view, the freedom of citizens is possible and desirable only because it is limited to the public sphere, while the private sphere is organized partly by love, considered antithetical to freedom. In Habib's reading of Rousseau, "The reflection on love . . . is indissociable from a reflection on the nature of women—on their propensity to bend for love, on their natural subordination." Habib asserts that "there is no sense in imagining love as an exchange between equals," which she adds, "is the eternal misunderstanding of homosexuality, and its simplicity."[22] In this framework, consent is the sole business of modest, restrained women:

> Rousseau discovered that the expression of feminine agreement is minimal and concessive: "It suffices that she does not resist much." This discovery does not amount to making shyness compulsory. This does not prevent a woman from joyfully joining her lover and throwing herself into his arms, looking him in the eyes. It is just that, in this case, she is doing more than her position requires. . . . In the female position, saying "yes" conveys emphasis, compared to the natural mode of consent, which consists in letting things happen.[23]

As described here, the notion of consent embedded in the French way of intimate relations presumes a certain idea of women's nature and of their place: women are objects of love and desire but are not citizens. They are not equals but rather prey to

be seduced. In this context, consent can only be that of women—
l'homme propose, la femme dispose, as the saying goes—and
nothing kills the mood like the equality of the sexes:

> This is where Rousseau has something to teach us,
> because, unlike the sexual liberation activists of the
> 1970s, he does not reason in terms of prohibitions—
> whether it is a question of fighting them or, thirty years
> later, of reestablishing them. His question is not: How
> to limit desire? The question is to understand how de-
> sire is limited by nature. . . . If women acted as men
> with regard to the things of the body, the desire would
> make itself unlimited; the situation which would result
> from it would not be a liberation, but an anguish of ex-
> haustion: such is the diagnosis of Rousseau. No doubt
> Rousseau would have reproved, had he known it, the
> lifestyle of the gays of our time.[24]

Homophobia seems irremediably entangled with this vision of
love, for it presumes a complementarity of the partners that is
only possible when they are of different sexes. Men are understood to be active, chasing women as a hunter does good game,
while women must behave with the modesty (and submission)
that befits their sex. Women can have sexual desire—actually,
Rousseau is worried they may have too much—but this desire
should be reined in to the point of being undetectable. Heterosexual love is understood as complementarity (in a somewhat
analogous way to religious complementarianism but with a twist
of sexiness on top), and homosexuality as an offense to the supposedly natural condition of heterosexual sexual commerce, in
which consent can only be a feminine attitude. Indeed, under the
guise of interpreting Rousseau, Habib is advancing a militant
claim: against the sexual revolution of the "soixante-huitards"
(the sexual liberation activists of the late 1960s and 1970s), and

against a contemporary feminism suspected of seeking to reestablish the prohibitions this same sexual revolution contested, there is another model of sex and love, unequal but supposedly happy. This is every bit the model of the Deneuve op-ed—of the woman who, because she is a woman, lets a sufficiently bold man have what he wants.

Fundamentally, defenders of "French-style gallantry" envision positive consent—consent that has to actually speak for itself—as incompatible with love.[25] Consent is not absent from the French way of love, but it must be grounded less in women's autonomy than in their submission to dominant men. As such, this version of consent reinforces Pateman's argument: we need to pay attention to the ways in which, under supposedly neutral if not egalitarian conditions, consent can ground and promote patriarchy.

"To Yield Is Not to Consent": The Anthropological Critique

Not only can consent add an egalitarian veneer to highly unequal gender relations, but it can also become a vehicle for blaming women for ostensible complicity with patriarchy. Thus one of the major scholarly debates of the 1980s, kicked off by the famous French anthropologist Maurice Godelier, who claimed that women's subordination to men is at least as much a result of women's consent as of men's violence. This was met with a thorough rebuke from a feminist anthropologist, Nicole-Claude Mathieu, who argued that Godelier confuses yielding for consent and thereby demonstrates how certain concepts of consent can impair women's autonomy.

This dispute highlights one of the key challenges to our understanding of the social dynamics of gender—understanding that colors how to think about consent and its multiple possible meanings. Anthropologists and others readily observe that societies are organized according to dynamics of social domination—men over women, for example, or capitalists over workers. But how are we to make sense of the form and persistence of domination?—a question that naturally encourages us to seek as well the *origin* of domination. One might readily affirm that domination originates in violence and the threat of it, yet this is not the only explanatory framework we might look to. It is not, for instance, Godelier's. Rather, his argument is of a piece with Étienne La Boétie's in the 1577 essay *Discourse on Voluntary Servitude,* which argues that the advent and endurance of social domination lies in the behavior of the dominated. Applied to the question of patriarchy, this consists in saying that male domination springs not only, if indeed at all, from men's violence but also and perhaps primarily or exclusively from women's consent to be dominated. Godelier does not take the most extreme position— that violence has nothing to do with domination—but he comes close:

> Any power of domination is composed of two indissolubly mixed elements which make its strength: violence and consent. Our analysis necessarily leads us to affirm that of the two components of power, *the most important force is not the violence of the dominants but the consent of the dominated to their domination.* To put and maintain "in power"—that is to say, above and at the center of society—a part of society, men in relation to women, an order, a caste or a class in relation to other orders, castes, or classes, repression is less effective than adhesion, physical and psychological violence less effective than the conviction of thought that brings the adhesion of the will, the acceptance, if not the "cooperation" of the dominated.[26]

It might seem as though Godelier is arguing that not only men but also women are invested in patriarchy, a position also acknowledged by many feminists. "Adherence" and "conviction of thought" are both consistent with a description of social reality, not just with a normative claim about women's submissive "nature." But Godelier goes quite a bit further, asserting that women consent to their domination because domination "appears to them *as a service* rendered to them by the dominants" and that this consent of the dominated plays a bigger role in the permanence of domination than does the violence of the dominants.[27] In other words, Godelier claims that women are at least as responsible for the permanence of patriarchy as men are.

Mathieu's refutation constitutes one of the most important feminist critiques of consent. Her first step is to show that Godelier's theory wrongly assumes symmetry of consciousness between oppressor and oppressed. In reality, the material and psychological oppression of women is such that this symmetry does not exist.[28] Drawing on anthropological studies from across the globe, Mathieu first shows that women's material conditions have psychological consequences. The demands on women are fundamentally unlike those on men: women are supposed to be physically available—for sex, household chores, educating children—to a degree and with a continuousness that men ordinarily are not. "How could she *on top of that* think clearly . . . about her situation?" Mathieu asks.[29] Moreover, women are structurally malnourished, which diminishes the physical and mental capacities necessary to resist. The burden of caring for children imposes further limits. Male domination thus constrains women physically and mentally, consuming time, energy, and mental space needed to think carefully about conditions of domination. The experience of domination may give these women the feeling that they have no option apart from giving in. Are we really prepared to equate giving in with consent? Mathieu says no; she suggests that these constraints seriously undermine the claim that women consent to the domination exercised over them.

Male domination further constrains women by defining them relationally: women's value is seen as deriving from their husband's, their brother's, or their children's. Learned inferiority is imprinted on women's consciousness, so that they may feel comfortable when participating in rituals of male dominance. Contrary to Godelier's view that this participation bespeaks the consent of the dominated, it in fact shows the extent of the physical and mental limitations placed upon women. Of women's tendency to join in activities that manifest and reinforce patriarchy, Mathieu writes:

> It does not seem difficult to understand that: 1) if they did not do so, they would suffer ostracism, if not physical repression in some societies; 2) given that their own submission in their youth was their means of survival, in the sense of escaping death in case of revolt, and more generally in the sense of living anyway ("one must live"), that is, adapting to the given social conditions in order to make a life for themselves as human beings and to be more or less at peace—old women can imagine no other method than to teach young people what they believe to be "their" method of personal adaptation and which is presented to them, moreover, as constituting their value or courage *as women*.[30]

The idea—often defended today—that older women's participation in rituals of male domination manifests their consent to this domination ignores both the real dangers to which they would otherwise be exposed and the psychic consequences of domination. Due to these dangers and consequences, submission appears to women as the best possible adaptation to the circumstances they face and as an adaptation valued by social norms.

Mathieu adds another layer to her refutation by showing that men have control over values and knowledge in society and that the contents of these values and this knowledge reflect domination.[31] She rejects the position, held by some feminists, that the masculine dimension of values necessitates their refusal—Pateman, for example, argues that feminism necessitates the renunciation of the contractual form. But at the same time, Mathieu highlights how masculine values shape the consciousness of the dominant and the dominated alike, if in different ways. She shows that social organization according to men's values is a *consequence* of male domination, not a cause. It is *because* prevailing values are those of men—and it is because male domination enables men to shape the oppressed consciousnesses of women to the point that they conceive of themselves as inferior—that women are mystified and perpetuate male domination. Male domination does not originate in a set of ideas justifying male superiority—ideas shared by men and women equally. The starting point of male superiority is male domination, not the other way around. Domination limits women's consciousness to the point that they come to share men's ideas about their own inferiority.

After showing how the material conditions of male domination constrain women's consciousness, Mathieu refutes Godelier's claim that violence is not the primary source of male domination. Direct violence and psychological abuse are never-ending, Mathieu argues, such that women have "neither the right nor the time nor the strength" to even think of resisting male domination.[32] Violence and abuse buttress patriarchal "training": "First the girl is, for example, prevented from running, first she is made to serve her father, her brothers . . . then she will observe: men can run, must be served. An observation. A forced observation is not a consensus."[33] Girls may wonder at the terms of their training, and if they do, they face a corrective social response in the form of violence and threats of it. In other words, violence and coercion are applied long before women imbibe ideas legitimizing domination, so that when women accept—even promote—the ideology of male domination, we cannot call this consent. Indeed, we cannot even call acceptance of patriarchy a belief; it is a psychological reaction to the threat of greater suffering. On this view Godelier's thesis springs from his position as dominant: it is the dominant man, not the submitted woman, who has mental representations that justify male domination, lest the man be forced to acknowledge the moral wrong of his privilege. Women have no need to justify men's violence—they need only fear it.

If consciousness of patriarchy's workings is constrained by psychological violence—psychological violence that rests on the constant threat of physical violence—then it is clearly absurd to judge women as consenting to patriarchy:

> The oppressive relationships based on the exploitation of labor and the body result in a real *anesthesia of the consciousness inherent* to the concrete, material, and intellectual limitations imposed on the oppressed, which means that one cannot speak of consent. And in case the patient wakes up during the anesthesia (resistance), the violence that is then applied to her does not only consist of beatings, death, or insults: the *main violence* of the oppressive situation is that *there are no* possibilities of escape for women in the majority of societies.[34]

It is not only consent that we cannot presume. We also cannot presume symmetry between men's and women's choices. Dominant and dominated consciousnesses differ essentially because the material conditions of domination produce the limitations experienced by the dominated consciousness. The two parties may announce the same ideas, but the underlying reasons for doing so are dramatically different.

Mathieu's argument has three significant consequences. The first is that consent does indeed lie at the origin of domination, but the consent in question is that of *men*. Among men, the representations of self and world that legitimize domination are constantly present to mind, and it is these that justify the use of violence to establish domination. Men, not women, consent to women's domination. Second, it is illegitimate to equate women's consent with men's. Women's obedience to men cannot be thought of as expressing consent, if by consent we mean the expression of an autonomous will. As the title of Mathieu's article points out, "to yield is not to consent."

The third consequence is that the dominated cannot consent to domination because such consent would presuppose that the dominated are aware of the relation of domination in which they find themselves.[35] To consent, one needs to be at least minimally aware of what one is consenting to. To say that the dominated consent to domination presupposes that they are conscious of consenting not only to whatever is occurring in the moment but also to an action that participates in and perpetuates the social domination that applies to them. Concretely, this means that a woman who, say, spares her husband all domestic work cannot for this reason be said to consent to male domination. She consents to male domination if and only if she is aware that she does all of the domestic work because she is dominated and, further, if and only if she shares with her husband the conviction that she is his inferior and must therefore serve him. Yet such an epistemic circumstance rarely obtains; dominated people seldom fully recognize their oppression. And when they do, they are unlikely to endorse it:

> The denial by the oppressed of their own oppression is not surprising if one knows (but to know it, one has to be on this side of the fence) that it is quite *unbearable* and traumatic to recognize *oneself* as oppressed. Why is this so? Because in the very movement [of thought] where the person sees their oppression, they constitute themselves as a new subject (subject of oppression) and as a judge of the other subject: this other self that they

believed themselves to be before. . . . It is at the moment, and only at the moment, when not only the *idea*
of domination will no longer be repressed, but when the
person will have admitted *that they are, themselves,
part of* the relation of domination that they may be able
to say to themselves: "But how could I have consented
to that?" because then *they* understand themselves as
actors of a struggle to come. . . . It is thus only from the
point of view of awareness (individual and collective)
that the word "consent"—assuming it is adequate—could
be used.[36]

When we adopt the point of view of the dominated, it appears very difficult to conceive of consent to domination that
is recognized as such. Consent presupposes a full ability to
understand what is going on. However, such an awareness is
so costly for the oppressed that they tend to avoid it. When
the dominated become aware of their domination, they
typically do not consent to domination but instead resist this
domination.[37]

From Mathieu's arguments, we can conclude that women do
not so much consent to male domination as they *assent* to it. Assent is not like consent, in that it does not manifest an autonomous individual will. We cannot speak of consent where genuine
choice is not possible, and it is not possible where the parties involved are in conditions of inequality. For this reason, the
problem of women's consent can only be posed in societies where
women are at least formally equal to men—that is, in societies
that at least officially recognize the equality of men and women
before the law. This minimal condition is necessary for the act
of consent to be recognized as such, insofar as women are recognized as having an autonomous will in the same way as men.
Yet even formal equality is not enough to assure true choice. The
psychological dimension of domination is such that, even in for-

mally equal societies, women's oppression can end up looking like consent.

When we abandon liberalism's strict focus on the individual and instead account for the relation between consent and the power relations that structure society—in particular patriarchy—it becomes clear that consent does not guarantee social justice. Rather, consent can and does make domination look as if women choose it of their own free will. At the absolute least, we should have an ambivalent stance toward consent, recognizing that it is at once both a possible tool of emancipation and an instrument of women's oppression. Whatever its potential, consent also is at the heart of women's exclusion from the public sphere and of their confinement to a private sphere where their work and bodies are appropriated by men.

Sexual Consent as Men's Law

Consent's contributions to inequality are especially dramatic in the context of the law of sex. Under the guise of protecting women from men's violence, law reinforces men's access to women's bodies.

This, at least, is the position that Catharine MacKinnon, the leading philosopher and legal theorist of the "antisex" movement, has defended for decades.[38] Her argument is different from Pateman's. Pateman contends that the vocabulary of consent is used incorrectly—that we assess women as consenting even when the conditions of consent are not met. But in this view, consent can live up to its potential: under patriarchal circumstances, genuine consent is rare but conceivable. MacKinnon's position, however, is that women's oppression does not merely sever the apparently obvious link between consent and autonomy; rather, women can consent to nothing but their submission.[39] Consent is not a criterion of justice or even justification that may be misapplied, as in Pateman's case. From

MacKinnon's perspective, consent is at best a *description* of the situation faced by women: the effect of male domination is that women's consent is not and cannot be a manifestation of their freedom. Women's consent under patriarchy is a sign of their subjugation.

MacKinnon is asking us to recognize that, if women's submissiveness is so common as to be the statistically normal attitude, then neither their submissiveness nor their consent is attributable to them. Consent, then, no longer has moral implications, in the sense that it does not say anything about people's autonomy or freedom. It is purely a legal category: we cannot sensibly ask whether a woman consents, only whether the conditions for legally valid consent are met in a context where the law is established by men to rule over women's lives.[40] Women's consent, in other words, is not an expression of their will but a self-reinforcing ritual of submission to male power, embodied in and enforced by a legal system made by men to serve their interests.

Women's Consent, Men's Laws

MacKinnon argues that male dominance and the sexual objectification it induces challenge the usual conceptualization of consent—women are mostly considered sexual *objects* by men, wheras only *subjects* can consent. First, MacKinnon criticizes the way in which the Freudian assumption of sexual repression, and its counterpart, the sexual revolution's assumption that sex should be de-repressed, has been put to work in the interests of men. Recall Freud's view that all humans possess sexual desires that have been hidden, quieted, and confined to heterosexual marriage as a result of political and hygienic repression of the sexual nature of individuals. It follows that, if this hypothesis is true, we ought to free ourselves from this repression and give rein to our natural impulses which, by the very fact of their naturalness, are good for us.

According to MacKinnon, such a position is consistent with male desires, since it implies that women wish, even unknowingly, to have as much sex with men as men do with women. Such a position implies that a woman's refusal of sex cannot be sincere: she must be repressing her own natural sexual desires. "No" does not mean "no," it means "I am repressed and need to be liberated." As MacKinnon puts it, "One function of the Freudian theory of repression (a function furthered rather than qualified by neo-Freudian adaptations) is ideologically to support the freeing of male aggression while delegitimizing women's refusal to respond."[41] Thus the sexual revolution gave men further justification for pursuing their objects of desire, for now men could position women's refusal as prudery or frigidity to be overcome. Women here are burdened by false consciousness: they believe they do not want sex, but this is only social repression talking. In fact, by announcing what they do not want, women entreat desiring men to have sex with them. It is Rousseau all over again.

The repressive hypothesis at the heart of the sexual revolution undermines women's capacity to consent because it implies that women want sex even when they refuse it. If refusal can be interpreted as consent, then there is no room for real consent, and the boundary between (consensual) sex and assault disappears.[42] While women's consent is presumed by the call to de-repress sex, MacKinnon argues that its function is not so much to respect women but rather to hide the violence of sex. In particular, in pornography, the appearance of consent is a necessity, so as to shroud its violence:

> The appearance of choice or consent, with their attribution to inherent nature, is crucial in concealing the reality of force. Love of violation, variously termed female masochism and consent, comes to define female sexuality, legitimizing this political system by concealing the force on which it is based.[43]

In MacKinnon's view, consent has the same function as the myth of female masochism.[44] The point of both myths is to make people believe that the violence suffered by women is not really violence but rather is what they enjoy (masochism) or choose (consent). MacKinnon's comparison reinforces the idea that all submission is of a piece: not only is sexual submission essentially the same thing as social submission, but masochism, understood as the psychological desire for submission, partakes of the same logic. Whether we are talking about consent to sex or domesticity, or whether we are talking about a supposed womanly desire to be violated, the goal is to portray women as in accordance with the desires of men, the better to ensure that women conform to this representation.

Why Legal Consent Is Worse than Useless

By showing how consent, in pornography and other circumstances, camouflages men's violence against women, MacKinnon opens the door to a critique of the legal concept of consent. "'Consent' is supposed the crucial line between rape and intercourse," she writes, "but the legal standard for it is so passive, so acquiescent, that a woman can be dead and have consented under it."[45] This is a provocation, but it is not that outlandish: when MacKinnon wrote these words in 1989, US law equated nonconsent only with an expression of refusal, so that the failure to refuse—which of course is a dead woman's only option—was considered consent.[46]

This is not just an argument against the no-means-no model of consent; it also highlights the otherwise-unexamined ideology embedded in consent as a legal concept. MacKinnon argues that the problem with the traditional legal perspective is that it assumes equality among individuals. In reality, individuals live in a society in which they are not equal and in which, in particular, men have power over women. Social inequality has an impact on the way individuals make choices, on the choices they think they can or cannot make. If this social inequality is not considered, then "the interaction between A and B may break no law, even if B says that A raped or otherwise violated her." In this framework, which MacKinnon wrote about in 2016, "consent emerges as an intrinsically unequal concept, whether in real life, philosophically, historically, or in legal practice, as well as a legally impractical tool through which to pursue sex equality in a sex-unequal context."[47]

MacKinnon shows that, even as the legal definition of sexual consent presumes an equality that does not prevail, it is structured by stereotypical representations of conquering masculinity and passive femininity. Traditional legal theory pretends that this definition of consent as a woman's passive assent is neutral, when in fact it is based on gender difference, which is itself structured by male domination. The legal definition of consent is structured by the dominance-submission pattern that leads to conceiving of men as active and women as passive.[48] In the male-female relationship described by the legal concept of consent, the *voluntary* dimension of assent disappears.[49] As MacKinnon shows, the law is not interested in what motivates assent, in what could make assent voluntary. In a context where men have structural power over women, the fact that a woman assents to an action carried out on her body—remember, she is the passive recipient—reveals "the core logic of consent," which is that of "assimilating accommodation to inequality to freedom for women in sex." That is, accommodation of inequality is configured as freedom. "More narrowly," consent configures "accommodation to inequality" as "non-criminal sexual intercourse under the consent standard."[50]

Fundamentally, consent as a legal tool is not concerned with women's active, voluntary participation in sex. Law presumes that sexual intercourse is initiated by men and acquiesced to by women. As such, not only does legal consent fail to fulfill its function of demarcating sexual intercourse from rape, but it also conveys a representation of sexuality structured by male domination.

The Psychic Dimension of Power

MacKinnon agrees with Mathieu that male domination is more than a material phenomenon. True, women are economically dependent on men and, in many societies historically and today, legally dependent as well. But above all it is the psychological dimension of male domination that explains why women's consent does not convey authentic freedom. Male domination can be subject to a Marxist analysis of material relations, but this is insufficient. What makes male domination so intractable is that it ensnares women in a psychological alienation that renders resistance almost impossible.

Here again, MacKinnon is not critiquing consent as a good that is denied women by virtue of their oppression. Rather she is rejecting the very idea that consent manifests the freedom and equality of individuals. The choices made by individuals are not products of the freedom they all share equally but of social structure, in particular the structure of male domination. Under male domination, the equality and natural freedom on which the individualist perspective of liberalism is based are illusions springing from the epistemological consequences of male domination. First, because men's power allows them to pass off their desires and values as neutral and objective—and because women's submission cannot be other than voluntary, according to the normative rules of liberalism set by men—women can be blamed for their submission without betraying demands of neutrality and universality. Second, because men's power is based on an epistemic norm of taking the regularities of the actual world as indications of the nature of things, women's submission can be interpreted as a sign of women's submissive nature and thus allows for the reinforcement of sexual difference in the name of a specifically male taste for freedom.[51]

It is therefore impossible to think of women's agency in terms of individual choices that women, independently of each other and of the social structure, would make and through which they would express their freedom. Women's choices are always made in the context of men's structural domination, and this structural domination is such that women are not free in their actions or in their thoughts. MacKinnon points out the fallacy of thinking about women's agency separately from male domination through another provocative comparison, this time between women's sexuality and Black American culture: "Interpreting female sexuality as an expression of women's agency and autonomy is always denigrating and bizarre and reductive, as if sexism does not exist, just as it would be to interpret black culture as if racism did not exist."[52]

In sum, to think of women's choices outside the confines of male domination is to indulge in a fantasy maintained by this very same male domination—a fantasy according to which unchanging human nature always and forever inscribes gender-differentiated patterns of sexual desire and submission, which owe nothing to male domination.

This assessment of women's sexual autonomy must worry us deeply. Is there no way to be sexually free—even to want to be sexually free? Is the ground on which we race toward the goals of equality and autonomy in fact a treadmill, going nowhere? These worries are not easy to shake off, especially once we have been convinced by Foucault that our subjectivity and our desires are shaped by the power relations we live with and in. I confess that I do not have a solution that will enable us to escape these worries once and for all. But I also am less convinced of consent's worthlessness—indeed, its harmfulness—than are some critics, like MacKinnon. With that in mind, I will use the last two chapters to argue that consent can and should be part of the feminist toolbox. Consent can indeed be bad for women; it has long been so. But understood in all its complications and subject to probing reflection, consent need be neither useless nor harmful. It can very well ease the road to equality, in the bedroom and elsewhere.

6

RAPE IS NOT SEX MINUS CONSENT

OUR LIBERAL INTUITIONS ABOUT THE emancipatory power of consent have been shattered. Now it is time to build something new.

We know that, on the one hand, consent can be a useful tool to free our sex lives from moralizing—that consent can be a means of expressing sexual autonomy. The moralistic regulation of sexuality—the historical criminalization of sex outside of marriage, for example, or bans on homosexuality—has been destructive of liberty and personal wellbeing, demonstrating the need for an ethical framework that allows individuals to decide what they want to do with their sex lives. On the other hand, the reality is that male domination profoundly shapes our sexualities, whether or not we are straight, to the point that women's consent can appear an empty shell that serves to conceal or even legitimize an unjust social and sexual order. This gives reason to think we should abandon consent and find a new vocabulary to promote sexual equality and autonomy. Thus, we face a profound tension. If we want to keep using consent to achieve autonomy, we need to make sure it does not also enable patriarchy.

In this chapter, I argue that, contrary to widespread intuition, consent is not the ultimate tool to fight sexual violence. Consent may help us identify part of the harm done to victims of sexual violence, but it tends also to hide the real wrongness of sexual violence. That is, the consent framework personalizes what is in fact a social and political problem: it renders sexual violence a problem of communication between individuals, whereas the true foundation of sexual violence is a patriarchal ideology that justifies men's use of women for their pleasure. Liberalism invites us to blame individuals—perpetrators, but also victims—instead of reforming the structure. In other words, there can be no substantive personal autonomy in a world riddled with gender injustices.

The next step toward an emancipatory sexual politics and ethical framework for sex is to understand more precisely how social norms generate these injustices, such that men and women are not the equals presumed by the liberal model of consent. Male domination structures our sexualities, including, albeit to a lesser extent, nonheterosexual sexualities. Furthermore, because of the place it is given in the social world, sexuality is a site of particular vulnerability for women, nonheterosexual men, nonbinary people, and children. This vulnerability is reinforced by hierarchies of race and class, as well as by epistemic injustice. I will detail this issue below, but, briefly, there is a strong tendency to distrust women and people of color and to refuse to try to understand their experiences or integrate them into a broader picture of social inequality.

One of the central themes of this chapter is that, to date, efforts to respond to these inequalities and injustices through articulations of consent have been misguided. In particular, I refute the claim that consent, including affirmative consent, is sufficient to distinguish rape from permissible sex. The notion that sex without consent necessarily is rape is at odds with common sexual practices that bring pleasure to people of all genders and sexual orientations. Furthermore, drawing the line at consent can reinforce patriarchy in multiple ways. Doing so constitutes a further investment in the liberal model on which patriarchy thrives by disregarding the structural inequalities that dilute the capacity of consent to express women's genuine will. Distinguishing rape on the basis of consent alone also burdens women with the unrealistic expectation of directing the sexual behavior of men whom they understandably perceive as physically threatening. Given the inequalities enforced by patriarchy, it is unreasonable both that women should "just say no" and that they should have to say yes. Then too, given that women do experience sexual pleasure under patriarchy—in spite of the way that it corrupts women's ability to consent, even affirmatively—we must accept that the problems of both protecting women and achieving good sex are too complicated to solve by means of consent alone.

This critique will drive us toward the two fundamental questions that we must eventually answer: How do we get men to stop raping, violating, and forcing others to have sex? And how do we ensure that gender norms do not prevent people, especially women, from realizing their chosen sexuality?

Gender Norms and Injustices

Gender norms are the source of recurrent injustices, particularly in the area of sexuality, and these injustices place men and women in structurally different positions regarding sex. Let's be clear from the start of this discussion that, as elsewhere in the book, the categories "men" and "women" are not meant to represent every single man or woman, but rather the average behavior within social groups. In particular, there is no doubt that not all men fit the representation of hegemonic masculinity here. Notably, men of color and gay men experience what sociologist R. W. Connell calls "marginalized masculinity" and "subordinate masculinity." Often, they suffer from hegemonic masculinity more than they draw benefits from it.[1]

As I argued previously in *We Are Not Born Submissive,* the norms of femininity are norms of submission. Women are educated, in varying degrees, to submit to men because society values their submission more than their freedom. In concrete terms, women are expected to take care of those around them, to be generous, altruistic, kind—in short, to put the needs and desires of others, and in particular of men, before their own. Now, it is easy to imagine what problems this may generate in the sexual domain: if women generally give priority to the desires of others, especially those they love, then we can expect the same behavior in the bedroom.

The norms surrounding women's sexuality also make it difficult for women to express and even conceive of their desire; as MacKinnon says, "All women live in sexual objectification like fish in water."[2] Women are educated to conceive of themselves as objects of desire for men—not as active pursuers of sexual fulfillment but as prey to be hunted. Our social practices leave it up to the man to "make the first move" and to the woman to take him up on his offer. While men achieve social status by actively expressing sexual desire and claiming sexual pleasure, women who behave similarly risk being condemned in the name of virtue and modesty. The contrast between "easy" or "slut" and "player" testifies to these prejudices, according to which a woman should always resist first—that she should be conquered rather than decide autonomously what she wants. It is no wonder that, as social psychologist Nicola Gavey points out, women commonly do not seek sex for its own sake but for the secondary benefits they can derive from it. In particular, by "giving" sex to men, women might obtain something they desire: a long-term monogamous relationship. This norm is strikingly illustrated by the pressure on French women to resume sexual relations very soon after childbirth. Resuming a (penetrative) sex life is presented as necessary to ensure that the partner will not be tempted to be unfaithful or to leave the new mother.[3]

Social norms of masculinity are also very much a factor in fostering gender injustice. The first source of injustice and patriar-

chal violence is the idea that men always want sex and are unable
to control their urges. For example, this idea structures discourses
legitimizing prostitution on the grounds that doing so would
protect women—meaning "respectable women," who do not sell
sexual favors—from sexual aggression by allowing men to satisfy their desire by other means. No scientific study supports these
notions that men experience constant sexual desire or that what
desire they do experience cannot be controlled.[4]

A second source of injustice, linked to the first, is the idea that
men have a right to have sex and a right to sexual access to
women. This discourse of a "right to sex" manifests in all its
horror through the activities of those calling themselves *incels* (involuntary celibates). These men, who hold in common the view
that they have been unjustly rejected by women, gather in online
forums to complain, humiliate women whose disinterest they
cannot stand, and fantasize about punishing men whose beauty
or social status they envy. Incels might be laughable if their rhetoric were not at the heart of several misogynistically motivated
crimes, including the 2014 attack in Isla Vista, California, that killed
six and injured fourteen; a 2018 Toronto van attack that killed ten
and injured sixteen; and a March 2021 shooting at Atlanta-area
spas that killed eight people and injured another. The language
of involuntary celibacy is new, but the violence associated with
it is not. All of these killings were preceded by an ideologically
similar mass murder at the École Polytechnique in Montréal in
1989. These are acts of terrorism against women generally, perpetrated by men who feel entitled to avenge themselves for the
refusal of their supposed right to use the bodies of the women
they desire.[5]

That men can think they have such a right—to women's
bodies, attention, and even love—is at the heart of numerous
contemporary philosophical and feminist reflections on sexuality. The philosopher Kate Manne shows that structures of
male domination give men a sense of entitlement, particularly

in their relationship with women. This feeling provides the ideo-
logical basis for men's recourse to violence: it is because they are
deprived of that to which they are entitled—and which constitutes a fundamental part of their masculinity—that it seems
possible, and even legitimate, to resort to violence. This violence
is routinely pathologized and made to seem incidental, hence
rhetoric like "blowing a fuse" or "losing it," which classes men
as personally in the wrong for momentary errors. In fact, at the
level of society as a whole, violence against women is not momentary but constant—and it is not a mistake. Misogynist violence serves the purpose of establishing and reestablishing a
world order considered normal and desirable, in which women
stay in their place.[6]

Of course, violence is not the only manifestation of male sexual
entitlement. Men undertake a range of entitled behaviors, from
pressuring women to have sex to ignoring consent, which seems
either self-evident—because their partner necessarily consents—
or irrelevant because sex is their due. If men believe that women
owe them sex, it is highly unlikely that they will recognize and
accept a "no." Instead, men who feel entitled to sex will likely
ignore signs of refusal and insist until the woman yields. Some
will eventually resort to force. Behavior like this obviates consent: there can be no real consent or refusal if the pursuer of
sex is socialized to hear a "yes" in every response. And, here
too, we see why consent cannot be the individual responsibility
of the woman, for it must also be respected by her (potential)
partner. Patriarchy makes it less likely that such respect will be
forthcoming.

Let's take a concrete example. A man and a woman meet, enjoy
themselves at a party, and are about to spend the night together.
The man is sure that the woman wants it, he kisses her, undresses
her. She is not sure that she is in the mood for sex, but she does
not dare say no to him. After all, she tells herself, she should not
have left the party with him. She worries she will be seen as a

"tease," that she will be accused of having seduced him without accepting the "logical consequence"—penetration. (The representation of the tease is clearly an adjunct of this idea of a right to sex.) If, in the moment, the man asked her, "Do you want to go further?" she would probably hesitate, perhaps mumble something in embarrassment; that could convey to her partner that they are not in the same state of mind. But gathering the courage to stop him and to explain that, actually, she would prefer to leave, seems impossible to her.

Why? Not least because women are generally taught to be kind, personable, smiling, caring, even at expense to themselves—to say yes. Conversely, men are taught to be assertive, to express and defend their will, to think of their sexual desire as a need. How else to explain the findings of a recent study, which asked 150 men how they would respond to a woman's refusal of sexual advances and found that 30 percent would knowingly engage in rape if it were guaranteed that they would not be prosecuted.[7] But men do not have to rape women in order to make clear their entitlement. They need only take rejection badly. How many women have ignored propositions—including from street harassers—only to suffer men screaming and swearing at them for their indifference? Experiences like these lead women to fear refusing men, lest their anger explode into violence.

The gender norms enabling male entitlement, threat, and violence collectively train women to do what men want, regardless of what women want. And these norms function alongside others that instruct women that their role is to serve, care for, and attend to men. The effect of norms of femininity is to say yes, while norms of masculinity give good reason to fear the consequences of saying no.

Again, this brief foray into gender norms is not intended to argue that all men are misogynistic and violent or that all women are submissive and alienated. But while there is a diversity of experience, we nonetheless live in societies structured by male domination of women. As a result, society pushes men and women to behave in certain ways that perpetuate gender inequalities and that, in the sexual context as in others, give rise to gender injustices. These social norms and the injustices they cause are central to the problems posed by consent. On the one hand, legitimizing sex through consent has emancipatory potential in relation to these gender norms: the idea that sex must be consensual for all parties involved goes against the idea that women owe sex to men, that they say no but think yes, that they are frigid if they do not want to have sex. On the other hand, these gender norms raise suspicion of the supposed "moral magic" of consent, which would suffice to make any consensual relationship legitimate. Indeed, as we saw in the case of the French art of love, the vocabulary of consent is essential to an unjust vision of seduction relationships, in which the woman must make herself virtuous and passive prey to be chased and carried away by an eager man. In such a situation, women's consent is not a sign of autonomy but of the behavior expected of her in a hushed battle of the sexes in which the man is called to triumph over the woman's defenses.

Epistemic Injustices

One of the fundamental problems standing in the way of an uncritical adoption of the vocabulary of consent is that of epistemic injustice. To put it bluntly, women are too often deprived of the opportunity to be heard and listened to. The British philosopher Miranda Fricker coined the term "epistemic injustice" to reflect this state of affairs, in which prejudice ensures that certain people's claims and knowledge are routinely ignored or distrusted.[8] This is a new field of epistemology, the branch of philosophy devoted to the study of the way knowledge is produced. Its purpose is to shed light on injustices in the production and reception of knowledge and to respond to the following questions: Who gets to produce knowledge? Who has a voice, and who does not? Who gets to be understood and believed? Which knowledge productions are considered legitimate or important, and which are not?[9]

These questions are fundamental to understanding the effects of various forms of social domination not only on the production and dissemination of knowledge but also on the social positions that individuals occupy: the capacity to be listened to and believed is not shared equally by all, which influences social hierarchies. An example of epistemic injustice is to be found in the claim that the #MeToo movement has finally provided women, gay men, and victims of incest a forum in which to speak out. According to this view, the disclosure of famous cases of sexual violence gave otherwise-silent women license to finally share their experiences. But the reality is quite different. Certainly, the #MeToo movement has contributed to a new awareness of violence committed by men against women, men, and children. But this awareness does not arise only or even mainly from new testimonies; it comes from a new *reception* of this speech. The story of #MeToo is not one of victims no longer forced to keep secret their violations; it is one of people suddenly being willing to listen to those victims.

To the extent that victims have in fact been silent, it is because, historically, there has been little point in speaking. Their words were not listened to, their complaints were not taken seriously, police doubted the truth of their statements, courts refused to accept their testimony as evidence. Stigmatizing discourse, like the idea that a rape victim is forever damaged, has served to discount the knowledge of victims. Why speak out when you have every reason to expect that no one will listen—and that, if anyone does, the consequences will be deleterious to oneself? When victims are racialized, poor, trans, disabled, or sex workers—and potentially all of these—they tend to have an even harder time being heard. It is not unimportant that well-known and powerful women have spoken out, thereby catalyzing a change in the conditions of reception of these people's voices. But while victims can now find a somewhat more sympathetic audience in the general public, there is little evidence that the statements and knowledge of women and other marginalized people are treated differently in an interindividual context—meaning, for instance, during sex.

Philosopher Kristie Dotson distinguishes three types of epistemic injustices that should be addressed: testimonial and hermeneutical injustice, already identified by Fricker, and contributory injustice, which Dotson herself theorizes. *Testimonial* injustice is the injustice of giving less credibility to a speaker because of one's prejudices against them. Another way of putting it is that testimonial injustice implicates the ability to be seen as a credible source of knowledge and experience. For example, the legal scholar Patricia Williams, a Black woman, recounts an incident at Stanford University in which students met her account of experiencing racist treatment with suspicion. Here, the students were acting on their racist bias, according to which Black women are "liars" and "paranoid."[10]

Hermeneutical injustice is a bit more abstract, in large part because it arises in the breach. This injustice stems from the fact that structures of social domination prevent the experiences of certain individuals from being known because the broader society cannot recognize these experiences. This type of injustice has been highlighted extensively by the work of women of color who have shown how racism and sexism prevent them from having the language and tools necessary to understand their own experience of the world.[11] As the social theorist Patricia Hill Collins writes, "Oppressed groups are frequently placed in the situation of being listened to only if we frame our ideas in the language that is familiar to and comfortable for a dominant group." Collins's own analyses defy hermeneutical injustice by drawing almost exclusively from the words and theories of Black women, rather than relying on the tools of white feminism, Black men, and mainstream Marxism.[12]

Finally, *contributory* injustice is the injustice that occurs when privileged people refuse to use or even seek hermeneutical resources apart from those that silence oppressed people and prevent them from contributing to the creation of knowledge. This is, for example, the injustice pointed out by many feminist people of color when white feminists do not make the effort to read, learn about, and discuss the work of people of color. In so doing, white feminists erase the ideas and knowledge of people of color and perpetuate a body of theory that does not allow for an account of experiences different from their own. This third form of epistemic injustice is related to the phenomenon that philosopher José Medina refers to as "active ignorance"—that is, the efforts a person in a position of social power may make to avoid learning about possibly unpleasant truths. Medina distinguishes not needing to know something from needing not to know it: sometimes socially privileged people neglect to learn because they are lazy, and sometimes they actively try to hide and ignore—in the double sense of not knowing and pretending not to see—significant dimensions of social life.[13]

Epistemic injustice may seem strictly fodder for an academic argument, but it is not: this framework explains not only why women's consent and refusal may not be heard but also how men can actively choose to not hear women's refusal and women's desires generally. Indeed, these various forms of epistemic injustice have far-reaching consequences for oppressed people as a whole and manifest in particularly severe ways in the sexual realm. The occasions for epistemic injustice are too numerous to list, but we have already come across a few, which may suffice to demonstrate the real-life importance of this problem. For instance, we have already noted the large gap between incidence and reporting of sexual violence, which reflects in part a failure of what philosophers of language call "uptake": testimonies concerning sexual violence may be announced but are not necessarily received, in the sense that the message does not get through to the people addressed. If women refuse to report their own violation, it is in large part because they know that there is a high risk they will not be believed, whether by a judicial institution or by parents, friends, mentors, or other trusted individuals. This risk is that much greater for poor women and women of color, to say nothing of sex workers who still very often appear as unrapeable on the basis of how they make their living.

Epistemic injustice is clearly a major challenge in responding to the problem of sexual violence. Beyond this, the framework also helps us grasp why heterosexual women report significantly lower likelihood of achieving orgasm during sex than do men—gay or straight—and lesbians.[14] The fact is that large numbers of heterosexual men do not care about women's pleasure or desire, and a major reason why they do not care is that they don't seek to know whether their partners are fulfilled or to understand what they might do to ensure that fulfillment. Sex as a social practice is known and understood from the perspective of those in power, which is to say white heterosexual men. This results in hermeneutical inequities: for example, there is a strong tendency to represent the normal sexual act as penetration and particularly as vaginal penetration. All sex that is not heterosexual or penetrative appears as a deviation from the norm.[15] Yet when women are asked about their pleasure, only a third report achieving orgasms through vaginal penetration alone.[16] A third of women also report experiencing pain during their most recent sexual encounter with a man.[17] What is commonly considered "foreplay" (meaning, not penetrative intercourse) is actually most likely to bring women orgasms.

There must be mechanisms of epistemic laziness and active ignorance on the part of men regarding women's pleasure, otherwise we would not see such imbalances. And men's lack of interest in women's desire and pleasure in turn affects heterosexual women's ability to express their desire and the terms of their pleasure: anyone who knows that their partner is not listening to them will tend to stop expressing themselves. Indeed, the failure to be received may lead a person to cease recognizing even their own desire and pleasure. Furthermore, as men are not socialized to pay attention to women's pleasure, but are socialized to think that the quality of their sexual performance is an important indicator of their manhood, women regularly find themselves simulating sexual pleasure that they are not experiencing, thus feeding the vicious circle of male ignorance.

A further source of epistemic injustice is pornography, which influences both women's capacity to voice their pleasure and men's interest in paying attention to women's pleasure. Following Catharine MacKinnon's claim that pornography silences women, the effect of pornography on the reception of women's speech has become the focus of important philosophical work.[18] According to Rae Langton, pornography, by repeatedly depicting women saying no when they mean yes, has the consequence that women's real-life refusals are not taken seriously by men.[19] I do not agree with Langton that watching pornography is bad in itself, and it is not the case, as she asserts, that only "porn addicts" watch or that these viewers are incapable of enjoying happy sex lives with real partners. However, the question of how pornography, especially mainstream porn, affects women's ability to be listened to and taken seriously, both in their sexual lives and elsewhere, is the subject of important philosophical debates that are far more interesting than the caricatures of the sex wars suggest.[20] And empirical research raises worries: recent quantitative work on the films available at the most-visited online platforms and on their consumption suggests that mainstream pornography is associated with real-life sexual violence.[21] There are good reasons to think that, at the very least, watching pornographic actresses' repeated refusals lead to violent sex is not exactly making it easy for women to refuse sex in everyday life. Certainly such depictions eroticize sexual violence.

The preceding examples do not exhaust the range of gender-based epistemic injustices that make for women's sexual disempowerment, but they offer a start. We can see clearly that gender injustices in sexuality take, among other forms, the form of injustice concerning the production and reception of knowledge about sexuality, with adverse effects on sexual practices. There are ample grounds to worry that social norms make it difficult for women to be heard and easy for men to ignore, actively or not, what the women they have sex with want.

Adaptive Preferences

Another worry springs from mainstream porn consumption: if so many people—in particular, so many women—watch mainstream porn, and therefore arguably like it, this may mean that their sexual desires correspond to some extent with what they see on video. It is commonplace to see this correspondence as reflecting the supposed harmful effect of watching porn, but another explanation is simpler and more worrisome: maybe patriarchy is powerful enough to provoke in men and women alike a taste for gendered sexual violence. In other words, the situation is not so much that porn inspires sexual violence but that patriarchy shapes our fantasies, to which porn simply caters.

This brings us to a further problem that must be confronted if the vocabulary of consent is to address gender inequities: adaptive preferences. Individuals' preferences can adapt to the oppression they experience, which creates a challenge for a consent-based model of good sex. One of the reasons that consent is conceived as a way to ensure sexual justice is that it is seen as expressing the individual's preferences and is therefore understood as manifesting autonomy. However, philosophers and social scientists have shown that, in contexts of oppression, individuals adapt not only their choices but also their preferences in light of the narrow range of options available to them. The philosopher and economist Amartya Sen writes:

> In situations of long-standing deprivation, the victims do not go on grieving and lamenting all the time, and very often make great efforts to take pleasure in small mercies and to cut down personal desires to modest—"realistic"—proportions. Indeed, in situations of adversity which the victims cannot individually change, *prudential reasoning* would suggest that the victims should concentrate their desires on those limited things that they *can* possibly achieve, rather than fruitlessly pining for what is unattainable. The extent of a person's deprivation, then, may not at all show up in the metric of desire-fulfilment, even though he or she may be quite unable to be adequately nourished, decently clothed, minimally educated, and properly sheltered.[22]

Sen shows that preference adaptation is a rational act: the people he describes, who are very often women, make "great efforts" to adapt to a situation they know they have no power to change. This is not self-deception; on the contrary, adaptation is, at least to some extent, conscious, otherwise it would not involve effort. And preference adaptation is rational—a matter of prudential reasoning. There is likely an implicit reference here to Aristotle, according to whom prudence is the virtue that allows one to choose a criterion or a rule of action when one has knowledge of the contingent circumstances in which one finds oneself.[23] Prudence is then a manifestation of reflection and reasoned apprehension of the situation. In a situation of acute deprivation from which one cannot escape, prudence calls for the adaptation of preferences. And by speaking of prudential "reasoning," Sen asserts that this adaptation is rational not only from the point of view of the persons who carry it out but also objectively.

Likewise, if women know that they cannot expect anything besides patriarchal sex, they may well stop desiring anything but patriarchal sex. This point is decisive because it allows us to understand how certain situations or sexual practices can be both chosen by women and harmful to them. For instance, feminist media outlets often raise concern about feminists who like to be sexually dominated. How to approach this apparent conundrum? The philosopher Serene Khader lays out two possible understandings of practices like these:

> People with adaptive preferences are both people who actively choose and whose deeply held conceptions of the good deserve respect and people who participate in their situation of deprivation and whose behaviors that perpetuate that situation need to be challenged.[24]

The problem that arises is what Khader calls the "agency dilemma": the difficulty of recognizing and analyzing the vulnerability of oppressed people while at the same time recognizing and respecting their capacity to act.[25] We need to understand how oppression both hinders autonomy *and* shapes agency, so that oppressed people can seemingly both choose their situation *and* be disempowered. Being treated as a sexual object can be disempowering for women *and*, at the same time, be desired by women.

The idea of the agency dilemma helps us think about this sort of situation without simply asserting that women should not have such desires and that those who do are responsible for their own victimization and those of women generally. Once we are aware, thanks to Foucault, that the sexual desires we have are not idiosyncratic—that they are not only ours but also are products of power relations—it becomes clear that everyone, to at least some degree, adapts their sexual preferences to social norms. The goal, then, is not to go back to a pre-oppression, presocial time where we would find our real desires but to try to solve the agency dilemma to which women, specifically, are subjected under patriarchy.

It is not hard to imagine how the problem might arise in relation to sexual consent: one is enjoined both to respect the sexual choices women make—to recognize these as their choices—and understand how these choices are produced by male domination and harm women. Women are raised to care for others and to want what others want. It is thus very likely that their sexual desires are at least in part a product of this upbringing and their gendered socialization and therefore contribute to the injustices they experience. Yet it is crucial to respect their choices precisely because choices manifest their autonomy. If we don't respect women's choices, we risk doubling the injustice done to them by gender norms. But we also need to see how these norms are obstacles to autonomy insofar as they make it hard for women to know and seek what they want and also insofar as they make it likely that women will not be heard or taken seriously. More generally, epistemic injustices and adaptive preferences invite us to be wary of the idea that consent offers an immediately readable expression of each person's freedom: if preferences adapt to oppression, if there are injustices that create biases not only in the reception of these preferences but also in their expression, then we cannot automatically equate consent with full autonomy.

Consent, Autonomy, and Free Will

So how are we supposed to take everyone's autonomy seriously without reinforcing oppressive social norms? The first step is no doubt to give up on a liberal ideal of autonomy, in which individuals are, by definition, fully autonomous. Instead we might seek to increase the nonideal, limited autonomy that we actually have.

The question of sexual consent is analogous to the classic philosophical problem of free will, which places two claims in opposition: first, that individuals can choose their actions—and are therefore morally responsible for them; second, that our actions are determined by social laws and laws of nature. On the one hand, the social norms just mentioned are such that it seems impossible to fully consent to anything in the area of sexuality: if patriarchy shapes our desires and pleasures—inducing men to understand sex as performance and violence and compelling women toward obedience, availability, and submission—then none of us really choose what we desire or how to express it. On the other hand, we intuitively recognize that there are sexual relationships that we have chosen, that we have wanted, that we have enjoyed, and that this makes them absolutely different from sexual relationships that we have not wanted. This tension is crucial for feminists for two reasons. First, because, again, recognizing the choice that women say they make is important in order not to replay the injustice of not taking their word seriously. And second, because recognizing that we are not absolutely compelled to behave in the way that gender norms prescribe is essential if we are to believe that men have an individual responsibility for the sexual violence they commit.

Many philosophers interested in consent are focused on this tension. Their approach to solutions involves distinguishing between what can be called an ideal theory of consent—which considers the exact conditions under which sexual consent justifies a sexual act—and a nonideal theory of consent, which considers the mechanisms of domination at play in sexuality in order to assess the conditions under which consent can be valid.[26] As philosopher Quill Kukla shows, no one seriously believes that there can be no consent without full autonomy: full autonomy is an ideal that does not correspond to our experience. In reality, "our autonomy fluctuates from context to context. . . . Compromises to our autonomy are the norm, not the exception."[27] Put another way, the fact that our desires and pleasures are shaped by patriarchal, racist, and classist gender norms does not mean we are absolutely sexually unfree. It means, however, that our sexual autonomy is limited—that we are neither completely free nor completely able to understand what we want and where our desires and pleasures come from.

The overall problem is this: What should be our sexual ethic if we want, on the one hand, to avoid gender injustices and, on the other hand, to respect and recognize people's autonomy? Can the concept of consent be the keystone of such an ethic and, if so, how?

Consent and Violation

The most pressing problem facing a moral and political analysis of sexuality is to ensure that injustice and violation do not happen during sex. We are testing the proposition that consent is a useful tool in this regard: useful for establishing what rape is and for identifying sexual violations. Is consent in fact so useful?

To answer that question requires first that we understand the distinction between rape and sexual violation. These may sound like the same thing, or rape may appear to be a subset of sexual violation. But it makes more sense to think of rape and sexual violation as categorically distinct. Following the philosopher Linda Alcoff, I use the term "sexual violations" instead of "sexual violence" here to highlight what happens from the standpoint of the victim of such violations.[28] A considerable part of the violations of autonomy and sexual integrity are not violent in the physical sense of the term. Our understanding should be that rape is what rapists *do*, while sexual violation is what happens to the people who are abused.

It is important to draw the distinction because conflating rape and violation serves to hide the reality that rape is *not* sex minus consent; rape is sexual violence and coercion. The problem of sexual violence and coercion is not that abuse victims failed to express their refusal clearly enough; it is that someone, probably a man, sexually abused them. Consent can be a useful tool for victims to identify an element of their violation: someone did not listen to them, their nonconsent was not taken into account. But if we hold that what constitutes rape is just sexual interaction— of any sort—in the absence of consent, then we are downplaying the role of the agent of sexual violence and coercion. Drawing a bright, consent-colored line between sex and rape means that whether rape has occurred is entirely determined by who said what and whether they were listened to, and not at all by the facts of sexual violence and coercion.

Let's note as well the difference between violence and coercion. A considerable proportion of sexual abuse is not violent in the sense of causing physical injury. For a long time, however, both in the legal and moral spheres, it was thought that sex could only be problematic when it involved physical injury. This has contributed to the lasting invisibility of the harm produced by sex obtained through subtler means of coercion. One can be sexually abused without a gun to one's head and even in the absence of the threat of physical violence.

In distinguishing between abuse and violation, we are better prepared to think about sexual violation as a gendered social problem. Anyone might be a sexual abuser, but overwhelmingly they are men, and overwhelmingly their targets are women. As a result, sexual abuse affects all women, not just those who are direct victims. The lessons of violation are experienced across society, influencing the consciousness of women generally. This is why rape and other forms of sexual abuse are a problem for women in particular, even as men and children are also victims of rape: the threat of rape shapes the lives of all women and produces injustices for all women; the same cannot be said of men and of children. As philosopher Ann Cahill shows, the threat of rape places women, by default, in a "pre-victim" status that influences what they can do and can desire.[29] Women are raised with the knowledge that they are perpetually in danger of being sexually abused and that they must constantly adapt their behavior to this threat, whether that means not going out alone at night, refusing to travel solo, staying off of empty subway cars, or avoiding the gaze of a male stranger on the street—even as, in reality, rapes most often are committed at home by people known to the victim. The threat of rape contours women's bodily habits, their movements; women's lived experience is the experience of knowing they are rapeable and, in a way, of expecting to be raped. The philosopher Susan Brison, in her remarkable book about her experience of rape and life afterward, notes the following thought that ran through her mind while she was being raped: *this is what I was warned against since childhood*.[30] Through the lessons that mothers teach their daughters, that older sisters teach younger, that friends teach each other, and that women take from media and the men around them, a part of the violation of rape is experienced by all women. Rape is the danger that all women must prepare for and resign themselves to, and thus all women suffer harms caused by rape, even as not all women have been raped.

This has always been true: there has never been a time when women, including women who have never been raped, have not feared violation by abusive men. But understandings of rape are not static; as we saw, the 1970s brought a massive change in understandings of rape, which produced new conditions for thinking about what rape means politically and how it might be prevented in the lives of individual women. The discovery that rape is not a rare act of barbarism committed by isolated, desperate strangers, but rather a common crime committed by "normal" men—often with fulfilling sexual lives, who are close to their victims—has forced societies to reckon with the absence of a clear and complete distinction between rape and normal sex. The problem is this: If rape is routinely committed by people with whom one can have, and sometimes does have, normal sexual relations, and if these normal relations can include those obtained through pressure and emotional blackmail, how to distinguish between sex and rape?

The answer might be that we can't really—that there isn't some obvious line separating rape and sex. That instead there is a spectrum of behaviors lying between rape and the best, most pleasurable and desired sex, and that, at numerous points on this spectrum, one might experience violation without having been raped. But this is very much a minority view, held mostly by a segment of the philosophers who have tried to think as rigorously as possible about the meaning of sex under conditions of patriarchy. Instead, within the broader discourse—and, in many jurisdictions, in law—it is self-evident that rape is nonconsensual penetrative (or oral) sex. But, as I demonstrate next, relying on consent alone—whether passive or active—to distinguish between sex and rape results in contradictions and confusions, questionable challenges to our intuitions, and even injustices to women.

Consent to Do What?

When people claim that all nonconsensual sexual intercourse is rape, a key problem that arises is the challenge of knowing what is meant by consent in any given instance. When a person consents, what are they consenting to? When a partner consents to sexual interactions, how far do they agree to go? This problem is especially tricky when consent is understood to be passive rather than affirmative. Consider the widely publicized 2018 case of comedian Aziz Ansari, who was accused of sexual misconduct by a woman using the pseudonym "Grace." According to the report breaking the story, Ansari invited Grace to his home after a date and pressured her into giving him oral sex.[31] Reactions to the story were divided, with some arguing that Grace was raped and others that, by accepting the invitation, she had consented to a sexual interaction of some sort. The same difference of opinion surfaced in comments about the victims of movie producer Harvey Weinstein: Why on earth did these women go to his hotel rooms if they did not agree to have sex with him?

Defenders of Weinstein and Ansari were not arguing that these women consented in the Kantian sense. Rather, the defenders claimed that the women who later accused these men of abuse had given permission in the liberal sense. But what was the content of that permission? What were its limits—or were these men permitted to do anything? Could these men also take and sell these women's clothes, for instance? In thinking about the breadth of permissions, philosopher Tom Dougherty uses the example of a host who invites a guest to "make yourself at home."[32] The guest knows intuitively that they have been given permission to, for example, pour themself a glass of water, but they do not have permission to sell the host's furniture. Likewise, we can readily appreciate that whatever permission was implied by Grace and by the actresses who visited Harvey Weinstein's hotel rooms was not without limits. Indeed, even consenting explicitly to sleep with someone does not mean consenting to just any sexual practice that person might wish to engage in.

Clearly, the inferences that people make about the meaning of consent are revealing. It seems to be widely—though certainly not universally—understood that entering a man's bedroom constitutes consent to sex, yet the vast majority of men do not believe, for example, that their partner has the right to digitally penetrate their anus on the grounds that both parties have agreed to sex. A finger in a man's anus, notwithstanding how good it may feel, is something that needs to be consented to verbally, whereas a penis in a woman's vagina could be permitted by the very fact of having entered the penis owner's bedroom. This discrepancy gives us reason to believe that, first, most men know how to give and receive consent when their bodily integrity is at stake, and second, that we are supposed to intuitively know what sex is, which steps it involves, how it starts, and how it ends. Thus when a women consents to sex with a man, this supposedly means that she gives the man permission for penile penetration of her vagina until he achieves orgasm, at which point sex will end. Consent to sex is, for women, consent to a chain of events fully scripted and oriented toward men's pleasure.

Another problem with the equation between rape and nonconsent lies in the fact that consent arguably need not be explicitly stated. Do I consent by virtue of the fact that I want to have sex with someone? If consent is a matter of personal autonomy, then an expression of consent is just that—it is a statement of consent, but the statement is not the substance of consenting. That substance is in my head and doesn't need to be vocalized. In philosophical terms, the problem is whether consent is produced by a mental attitude or by some form of communication. When we think of consent as the manifestation of the autonomy of the will, we think of it as a mental attitude—that is, the fact of making a choice mentally. To consent, therefore, would be to think that one agrees without necessarily saying so. However, it seems obvious that even if I agree in my head to let a friend borrow my bike, they do not have the right to take the bike until I explicitly give my permission.

From here, consider another informational defect that may influence whether consent has been given and therefore whether sex is permissible. If consent requires intention to agree, what happens when consent follows upon some kind of deception? Let's say I consent to sex with a partner whom I believe is single, but it turns out that person is in fact married. Let's say, further, that I would not have consented to sex had I known that the person was married. Does this mean that I did not consent to this sex and have therefore been raped?[33] If the answer is yes, then it might be the case that there can be no consent wherever seduction involves lies or omissions—which is usually the case! For instance, one can easily imagine that a date might lie about their political views for fear of giving offense that would scupper the possibility of sex. Is any sex that follows such a lie nonconsensual and therefore rape? This seems a very strict view. While it may be legitimate to consider that the discrepancy between reality and my beliefs has an impact on the moral quality of the sexual relationship (especially in the case of lies aimed at obtaining consent, like the lie that one is single when one actually is married), surely this discrepancy alone is not sufficient to assess that rape has occurred.

This supports the idea that consent must be *communicated:* the person consenting must express consent, whether they do so verbally or through some other conduct, and consent must be received, as such, by the person to whom it is directed.[34] As Dougherty puts it, consent "involves deliberately engaging in conduct that expresses one's will."[35] If one accepts that consent cannot be only a mental attitude and that it must therefore be communicated, one necessarily recognizes that passive consent is not valid consent: the commonly accepted idea that doing or saying nothing can constitute consent is flawed.[36] A specific expressive action must take place in order that there be consent. This means, at the very least, that sexual consent must be conceived as *positive* or *affirmative*. This does not imply, however, that the expression of consent must be verbal.

Importantly, communication is not just expression; it also involves *reception*. This aspect of consent tends to be overlooked in a discourse that understands consent as a permission given by women to men. In order for consent to truly exist, the will of the consenting person, manifested through active expression, must be adequately received by the person for whom it is intended. This requires two things: that the recipient interprets the expressive behavior in terms of the information available to them, and that the recipient inquires about what they may be missing in order to interpret the situation adequately.[37] Dougherty uses the example of a patient's consent to a medical procedure: in order that a patient's signed consent form be valid, the doctor must have good reason to believe that the patient has understood exactly what the procedure is, understanding that can be fostered by, for instance, describing the procedure to the patient and asking the patient questions about their understanding.

Nonconsent and Rape

So, is affirmative consent the solution to distinguishing permissible sex from rape? If it is, then we are in serious trouble. If only affirmative consent is valid consent—and in particular if affirmative consent must be verbal, enthusiastic, and provided while at least mostly sober, as required by many affirmative consent policies—then most of our sex lives are nonconsensual. People routinely have sex without talking before, or during, about what they want, and many people have sex while intoxicated. Are all parties to this sort of sex being raped? This question is purposefully provocative, intended to inhabit the mindset of conservatives who accuse feminists of ruining sex by pretending our sex lives are nothing but rape.

Indeed, the representation of most of our sex lives as rape goes against the experiences of most people. Active expression of consent to sex is not—at least, not yet—part of the typical unfolding of the sexual script. When it does occur, it has the form of a rupture, an interruption of the continuity of the amorous and sexual encounter.[38] That is, lack of affirmative consent is the statistical norm. Setting aside the arguments of MacKinnon and Dworkin, who equate sex with rape only within a specific political framework, it is simply unfair to say that the vast majority of sexual encounters are rape. It is unfair to those who strive to choose their sexual practices, and it is especially unfair to rape victims, whose specific experience is drowned out by the assertion that even nonviolent, noncoerced, mutually desired sex is—in the absence of affirmative consent—also rape.

We are left, then, with two possibilities. First, all penetrative sex to which neither partner objects is considered to be consensual, in which case it seems likely that any nonconsensual interaction—that is, an interaction in which one of the parties explicitly refuses—is rape. Or, second, consent is considered to be more than nonresistance or passive acquiescence and must be communicated. But, in this case, there is a difference between nonconsensual sex and rape, otherwise statistically normal sex, including sex that is wanted and enjoyed by partners who do not affirmatively consent, would be rape.

The first of these options is untenable because it requires that rape only occurs if a person firmly and explicitly rejects sex and yet has sex imposed on them. This is not satisfactory for several reasons. One, underlined by many psychologists, physicians, and feminists, is paralysis: many victims of sexual assault become paralyzed in the moment, physically unable to respond to what is happening to them. Paralysis is a basic human defense reflex; it cannot simply be overridden.[39] And even a woman who does not experience paralysis may be unable or unwilling to refuse undesired sex with a man. The most obvious reason is the threat of physical violence. Women know how prevalent male violence against women is, and women know that many men respond violently when denied the sexual gratification they feel they are entitled to. What women often don't know is whether they are dealing with a violent man. Between what they do and do not know, women have good reason to fear not only that they will be raped but also beaten up if they object to a sexual encounter.[40]

We also should acknowledge that social training makes it hard for women to say no, so demanding that they do so imposes a burden. Requiring a woman to explicitly refuse sex goes against social norms of both communication and femininity. Nicola Gavey describes an interview in which a woman tells her, "Why can't I say no? . . . I have in the past found it very difficult to say no to a guy who wants to go to bed with me. Very difficult. Practically impossible, in fact."[41] This woman is not alone. Studies using techniques of conversation analysis show that urging women to "just say no" fails to take into account how refusals are usually communicated in normal life.[42] In our everyday interactions, "no" is not the normal response to a proposal one wishes to reject. Silences, compliments, weak acceptances ("hmmm . . . why not?") are generally preferred over simply saying no, and saying no is therefore likely to be perceived as an abrupt or even hurtful response, reinforcing both the risk of violence and the contrast between such a response and norms of femininity. Indeed, clearly refusing sex implies putting forward one's will, one's physical integrity, and not behaving in a kind and accommodating way, which goes exactly against the way women are educated to behave.[43] In other words, directly and unequivocally saying no is itself costly. Therefore, expecting women to do it is unreasonable.

For all these reasons, there is great risk that a woman will not be able to refuse sex that she does not want. This points to a further reason why it is wrong to discern rape only when a person says no: such a conception of rape implicitly places responsibility for many sexual violations on the victim. To suggest that there is rape only if the victim said no means that if a person experiences a violation without having said no, this violation is caused by her weakness and therefore is her responsibility. And if the victim did say no, then the quality of her refusal is subject to evaluation: Was her "no" clear enough? Did she also push him away? Could it be that he didn't hear it? One way or another, the focus is on the victim's reaction and her possible weakness as the cause of the crime, and not on the criminal intent of the person committing it, which adds to the injustice of the crime itself.

One of the reasons women are told to say no is that this is the best way to avoid misunderstandings, which supposedly are a common cause of rape complaints. Expressions of consent and nonconsent should therefore be as clear as possible to avoid misunderstandings.[44] However, laboratory studies show that men and women faced with the same scenarios interpret them in the same way; men do not fail to understand refusals.[45] Moreover, the fact that a considerable proportion of rapists are repeat offenders and have raped multiple victims goes against the hypothesis that rape is a product of misunderstanding.[46] There really is no problem of misunderstanding; rather, sexual violations occur when men choose to ignore the nonconsent of the people of whom they demand sex.[47]

So it is clearly unacceptable to consider as consenting any partner who does not explicitly object to sex. What, then, of option two, whereby consent must be understood as more than nonresistance or passive acquiescence—consent must be communicated. There is considerable merit to this view, but many of the people who hold it also hold a further view with which it is not compatible: the view that all nonconsensual sex is rape. Consider the following hypothetical. Sam and JC meet at a party, leave the party together, go to Sam's house, and have sex initiated by JC. Sam goes along with it, and shows no reluctance, but also shows no enthusiasm. JC is in control throughout. It may be considered—and we will come back to this—that JC is wrong not to ask Sam for their consent and that Sam may experience this as a violation. Yet such a situation is far removed from what would commonly be understood as rape.

There is a simple, pragmatic reason why many feminists defend the idea that sex is rape when any party does not actively consent. Feminists understand that gender inequities permeate sexuality, that men harm women (and many other people) in the context of sex, and that this harm done by men has historically been silenced, even as rape has long been recognized as a very serious crime. Therefore, the hope is that by characterizing as rape all sex lacking active consent, feminists can ensure the experience of violation is recognized for its seriousness.

Yet there are several problems with this notion that sex without active consent must be rape. First, understanding rape as any sex without active consent has the effect of making rape seem less serious. The seriousness of rape stems in part from the perception that it is rare, whereas sex without active consent is not just common but standard. Furthermore, it has never been the case that the seriousness of rape derives from recognition of the harms of male domination or women's victimization. As Georges Vigarello shows, the reason why rape has historically been recognized as a serious crime has much to do with the desire of rich men to ensure that their children are theirs and that they do not risk passing on their wealth to someone else's children.[48] Today, the victim of rape is understood to be the person violated, but this sense is based less on recognition of the problem of male violence than on gendered representations of the harm done to rape victims, including the idea that a rape victim can never recover and will, implicitly, be forever lost as a sexual object.[49] Moreover, the fact that many people see feminist discourses on rape as a sign of a puritanical struggle against sex in general, where affirmative consent is the weapon of women seeking revenge for a sexually disappointing night, suggests that equating rape and sex without active consent is a flawed activist strategy.[50]

More generally, it is not necessary to say that all sex lacking active consent is rape in order to say that all such sex is morally wrong and therefore morally impermissible. Consent provides an effective tool for distinguishing between morally wrong and morally permissible sex, and this distinction is to some extent separable from the question of how best to define rape. (The shift from moral impermissibility to legal prohibition is not self-evident, and the analysis here is still in the moral register, although it has implications for the legal conception of rape.) Indeed, it is important to recognize that the moral evaluation of sexuality is not binary and that not all instances of morally wrong sex necessarily are equally wrong.

To take concrete examples, let's imagine some different versions of the night JC and Sam spend together once they arrive at Sam's house (characters are gendered when their gender affects the course of the scenario):

(1) JC initiates sex and Sam does not want it to happen. Sam pushes JC away. JC gets angry and yells that Sam invited him and he would not have come except to have sex. JC then forces Sam to have sex.

(2) JC initiates sex and Sam does not want it to happen. Sam pushes JC away. JC gets angry and yells that Sam invited him and he would not have come except to have sex. Sam, feeling guilty, lets the sex happen.

(3) JC initiates sex and Sam does not want it to happen. Sam pushes JC away and says they should just go to sleep. But JC has no intention of sleeping and repeatedly tries to initiate sex with Sam. Exhausted, Sam finally lets JC proceed in the hope of eventually getting some sleep.

(4) JC initiates sex and Sam does not want it to happen. But Sam tells herself that she has invited JC to her house and now it is too late to refuse him, so she does not. She doesn't do anything to suggest that she consents, and JC penetrates her.

(5) JC initiates sex and Sam does not want it to happen but is afraid that JC will react violently if she pushes him away. She doesn't do anything to suggest that she consents, and JC penetrates her.

(6) JC initiates sex and Sam does not want it to happen. But she figures that JC is a nice guy, and she should have known that if he came over, it would be with the intention of having sex with her. She feels she can't afford to refuse. JC asks her if she wants to have sex, she says "yes," and they have sex.

(7) JC initiates sex and Sam does not want it to happen. But she likes her reputation as a fearless seductress, so she verbally accepts JC's offer of sex.

These scenarios are all realistic and all could be considered problematic. However, it is reasonable to believe that they differ in severity. In the first two scenarios, JC coerces Sam, even according to the strictest legal sense of coercion. In the third scenario, JC may be seen as coercing Sam, but the law would likely not consider this scenario to be coercion, because JC's harassment does not, strictly speaking, prevent Sam from refusing sex. In scenarios (4) and (5), JC does not care about Sam's wishes, and can be seen as taking advantage of the unjust norms that govern gender relations and the fear that men's violence rightly instills in women. In scenarios (6) and (7), it seems difficult to assign any responsibility to JC. Critically, in none of these cases does Sam want sex, even as in some of them Sam verbalizes consent.

These scenarios show that, instead of opposing legitimate and nonconsensual sex in a binary fashion, we should conceive of a continuum of consent. It should be possible to distinguish, for example, between positively nonconsensual sex, which would include all cases of sex obtained through coercion in the broad sense, and sex that is not actively consented to, in the sense, for example, that the consent given would not be valid because it was not freely given.[51]

To say that these scenarios present cases of nonconsensual sex of unequal severity does not mean that Sam cannot suffer from the less severe cases. To put it simply, a person can feel violated even though their partner has not raped them. Still, it is important to distinguish among the situations because they are not all subject to the same methods of prevention. It seems clear that the way to combat gender norms that press woman to accept sex is probably, at least partially, different from the way to combat the male propensity to obtain sex through violence.

The distinctions among these scenarios highlight what Cahill has called "the heteronormative sexual continuum."[52] This continuum includes the "gray zone" between rape and good sex. The gray zone presents revealing moral problems, to which I now turn.

Gray Zone

The term "gray zone" has emerged in media discourse in the post-#MeToo era to describe those sexual experiences that are not strictly speaking rape or punishable by law yet are potentially traumatic as well as morally and politically problematic. The term comes from the work of Nicola Gavey, in particular her extremely important book, *Just Sex?: The Cultural Scaffolding of Rape*. In this book, Gavey reviews the way rape has been conceived by philosophers, sociologists, feminist theorists, and psychologists. Her research includes illuminating interviews concerning the psychology of sexuality. Gavey shows that, while heterosexual women differentiate between rape and consensual sex—an objection to MacKinnon and Dworkin—the mundane heterosexual experience of sexuality includes incidents that lie in between rape and consensual sex and that help to erect what she calls "the cultural scaffolding of rape." This approach emphasizes the co-constructed nature of patriarchy and sexuality. Gavey writes:

> Many women have talked to me about experiences that they didn't call rape but that I found difficult to see as

just sex. They include stories of situations in which a man applied pressure that fell short of actual or threatened physical force, but which the woman felt unable to resist, as well as encounters where a man was rough and brutish, and the woman described letting sex happen because she felt unable to stop it. They also include stories of situations where a male partner was not directly coercive at all, but where the woman nevertheless found herself going along with sex that was neither desired nor enjoyed because she did not feel it was her right to stop it or because she did not know how to refuse. All of these accounts, in different ways, point to a complex gray area between what we might think of as mutually consenting sex, on the one hand, and rape or sexual coercion on the other.[53]

The delimitation of this gray area is very important. To begin with, we should recognize that having sex despite lacking sexual desire is not itself morally problematic. There are morally acceptable, even morally good, sexual relationships that are not motivated by sexual desire. For example, a person in a loving relationship may wish to show their love for their partner by having sex, even if, strictly speaking, they do not experience sexual desire. One might also achieve desired nonsexual satisfaction—for instance, narcissistic satisfaction—through undesired sex. It is common, of course, for sexual giving to be problematic (for example, when such giving is based on the idea that women should give sex to men, or in cases of emotional blackmail), but to believe that sexual practice must necessarily be motivated by sexual desire or arousal in the moment implies a reductive view of sexuality and its meaning in human lives and experiences. So the problem of the gray area is not that of sex without sexual desire; it is that of sexual interactions that are themselves *unwanted* by women and yet can be considered *consensual* in the sense that they are accepted.[54] These interactions highlight what legal scholar Robin West has called the "harms of consensual sex."[55]

Gavey offers a typology of reasons women may have for not preventing unwanted sexual interactions: dominant discourses of heterosexuality are such that women feel a sense of obligation to men (for example, a married woman might feel that she owes her husband sex, or a young woman may feel that she must agree to sex if she hopes for a romantic relationship); as discussed above, saying no would involve behaving in a way that would break too much with norms of femininity and polite refusal; refusing would incur reputational damage (a woman might become known as a "frigid bitch"); refusing would damage an otherwise-wanted relationship; and finally fear of the possible consequences of refusal, in particular fear of being raped. This last case—allowing sex in order not to be raped—may seem paradoxical in theory, but it is not at all in practice: the fear of male violence as well as the fear of the traumatic consequences of a clearly coerced sexual encounter are such that women prefer to give in to a sexual interaction that they absolutely do not want rather than take the risk of being raped. Contrary of what some may think, these dynamics are also at work in nonheterosexual sexual interactions: gender norms, and the specific norms of heterosexuality as a social system, influence everyone's sexual relationships.[56]

Two lessons can be drawn from the existence of this gray area and the typologies proposed. The first, which is already familiar to us and which has very important consequences, particularly in legal terms, is that the prism of individual responsibility is not sufficient to account for or combat the moral problems of sexuality. In some of the real-life cases Gavey describes, women had unwanted sex without being coerced or prevented from refusing. In these cases, the male partners may have had the benefit of a sexual script, gender norms, and social realities (including men's violence) that favored them, but they did not intend to force or even push the woman to agree. These women were often in situations where it was too costly or simply impossible for them to express refusal. One cannot, therefore, think about the morality of sexual conduct without considering patriarchal structures and how they influence the choices available to women. And it must be possible to accept that unwanted sex can occur even as the partner who initiated it is not culpable for lack of consent.

The second lesson stems from the very fact of the gray zone: it reflects, on the one hand, a continuum rather than a clear binary between normal sex and rape, and, on the other, the existence of a clear difference at the individual level between actively intended or consensual sex and unwanted or nonconsensual sex. Instead of a distinction between normal sex and rape, where normal sex is what happens in the vast majority of sexual interactions and rape is a serious and rare crime, easily defined in its exceptionality, rape is understood to be an extreme case in a continuum of unintended sex, which presumably accounts for a considerable part of sexual relations. Clearly identifying the difference between morally good sex and other sex is thus more difficult than one might think. Against a vision of sexual intercourse as involving the partners and their simple choices based in sexual desire, we see the diversity of motivations for sexual activity and the difficulty of establishing a clear difference between social pressure, negligence, coercion, and threat. And we understand that if the criterion of legitimacy of sexual relations is that they are absolutely and positively consensual, it is quite likely that a considerable part of everyday sex is illegitimate: it is wanted sex rather than nonconsensual sex that seems to be the exception.

At the same time, the women Gavey interviews show that everyone—and women in particular—makes a distinction between sex that is wanted and sex that has been imposed on them. For these women and many others who have shared accounts of their experiences, sexual acts can be wanted and enjoyed, and eroticism can be part of the great joys of life, even in a patriarchal context. The normal experience of sex is often one of nonconsent, yet sex is still an experience that can be not only pleasurable but also profoundly structuring for the human experience. And so the central questions remain: What is morally good sex? And how do we make the experience of sex overwhelmingly good?

7

SEX AS A CONVERSATION

IF THE PICTURE painted in this book so far seems quite grim, there is hope on the horizon. The mainstream conception of consent does not live up to its promises: it does not allow us to make a clear distinction between sex and rape, and the liberal intuitions at its foundations are part of the "cultural scaffolding of rape." But, in the light of the preceding analysis, we can develop a new understanding of consent, creating a tool for understanding what good sex is and how we can seek it.

The goal of this moral and political study of sex is to know how to have good sex, in the double sense of sex that is not impaired by unjust social norms—such as the norm of female submission, which prevents women from asserting what they want and like—and sex that fosters a good life. Consent cannot automatically provide us good sex in either sense, and, when understood on conventional terms, it actually reinforces unjust social norms. But a different, contextually sensitive approach to consent can accomplish what mainstream ideas of consent fail to. If consent is going to be our aid, then it cannot be liberalism's abstract vision that we rely on. Rather, we need a model of consent that is embedded in the real world—and the bedroom: consent that responds to the *specifics* of sexual situations.

Throughout this book, I have used detailed case studies and hypotheticals because, in these details, we find the realities of sex that we need consent to respond to. We must be attentive to the details of the situation, as well as to the broad organization of society, in order to understand what is going on between partners when they have sex. Indeed, the partners must be so attentive, and they can be if they break the silence and mystery, and the sense of antagonism, that surrounds sex. Here is our solution: talk to each other. If the aim is to contest gender injustices while preserving the sexual autonomy of all—if the aim is, in the words of the feminist icon Gloria Steinem, to "eroticize equality" rather than domination—then sexual consent, conceived as an erotic conversation, is the future of love and sex.[1]

There is a third way of conceiving consent, one that is neither the traditional sexist model in which women are prey who consent by giving in, nor the liberal notion of authorization to use each other's body parts. The third way understands consent as respect, affirmed in the context of an erotic conversation. The focus is less on how consent is given—what facts must be in place so that we can know, in the legal sense, that a party has consented—than on the conditions that enable consent. Instead of wondering if women have said yes or no, we ask what the partners can and should do for each other in order to build pleasure together.

I am placing consent in a novel register: that of all partners. Today, women, insofar as they are structurally at risk of having sex imposed on them, are understood as the ones who should give or refuse their consent. In other words, consent as commonly practiced presumes that the partner having less power, who does not take initiative, is obligated to consent or withhold consent. Against this view, which places the whole responsibility for consenting on one person, I argue for a relational understanding of consent: in sex, consent is created by the partners through the ongoing exchange of agreement with one another.

In a just world, this exchange would be perfectly symmetrical. But we do not live in a just world. Our world is riven with social inequalities; we cannot usefully think about consent outside of the social situation of the partners and outside of the power dynamics at play. This means that the more powerful party in the dynamic—often the man in a heterosexual context, but not always, considering the roles of race and class—is the one with primary responsibility for building consent. Consent is a collective effort, but as long as we live in such an unequal society, the powerful must take the leading role in ensuring that mutual respect is possible. Therefore, in most circumstances, men have a greater responsibility in fostering the conditions for an egalitarian sexual conversation.

Sex Should Not Be a Battlefield

The consent of mainstream discourse is grounded in the idea that, by definition, relations between sexual partners and between genders are conflictual. Sex is seen as a sort of compromise between partners with diverging desires and interests. This is as true in the eighteenth-century model of man as hunter and woman as prey as it is in the contemporary assumption that it is women who need to consent.

Liberalism has not swept away the old model; it is still with us. In this world, women are passive, they consent; men do not consent, they act (and they fuck, as MacKinnon would say). As such, making consent the touchstone of sexual ethics implies that it is up to women to intervene against the insatiable and uncontrollable desire of men. Men want sex all the time—and therefore can never themselves be raped—and women, whether they want it or not, must say they don't, until a man makes them give in.

To contain the ill effects of this sexist framework, many of us have turned to consent-as-contract. Here, the partners consent in the sense that they renounce their right to the guarantee of their physical and sexual integrity. Intercourse appears as a quasimarket transaction: it is not a matter of love or desire but rather of exchanging sexual services with minimal risks and surprises. This is the sex of Tinder and Grindr, in which one hedges against the unknown by sending detailed photographs and agreeing ahead of time on everything that will happen. It is an efficient process, as if to make sure of losing as little time as possible, gaining as much pleasure as possible, and giving as little as possible in exchange. It is as though pleasure were scarce and subject to a zero-sum logic: if you get more, I get less.

Consent is caught between the sexist model of old-fashioned love and a capitalist model of exchange among absolutely independent individuals who do not wish for and probably will never experience any emotional bond. In these two models, the relationship between the partners is implicitly understood to be antagonistic: it is necessary that the husband triumphs over his wife; I need to be sure to optimize my practices to give as little as I can to the other while taking as much pleasure as I can from them.

This competitive approach, in which the desires of the parties are conceived as fundamentally their own, without reference to each other's pleasure, is the foundation of continual misery. Indeed, as we have seen, one of the main sources of violence and suffering in sexuality is that it is seen as a sphere in which men want one thing (orgasm), women want something else entirely (marriage), and men do something to which women respond. As Nicola Gavey has shown, three major theses undergird this state of affairs: (1) the idea that men always want to have sex; (2) the idea that women do not want sex for its own sake but as a means of obtaining a stable, monogamous relationship; and (3) the idea that sex is the penetration of a woman's body by a man's penis. In short, women want love, men want sex, and the price women would pay for love is that sex is imposed on them. These ideas constitute the cultural scaffolding of a sexual order in which men violate women and in which women have great difficulty refusing men's desire.

But of course these three theses are not facts of nature; they reflect and shape cultural tendencies, and yet real people defy them. Men may lack sexual desire.[2] Men may be coerced into sex, by other men as well as by women.[3] Men may want romantic relationships; women may want sex for its own sake and not as a bargaining chip. And sex is not just penile penetration.

Instead of recognizing these realities and allowing them to influence how we have sex, we persistently assume that the partners in a sexual relationship cannot want the same thing and therefore are fundamentally engaged in an exchange in which they must give up something in order to obtain what they desire. For the man, what must be given up is freedom: he is at risk of being confined in monogamy by a woman in love, who would prevent him from having the sex and the life he wants. The woman, meanwhile, is at risk of granting sexual favors without obtaining the social and moral stability of marriage—hence injunctions to make the man wait, repeated over and over again in manuals that pledge to help women "hook" men once and for all.[4] In such an antagonistic context, respect, politeness, and love are the prerogative of women, while men often steer clear of being respectful, lest they be trapped by it: a man may worry that being courteous and considerate will make him appealing to women seeking a husband, so that respectful behavior is a threat to himself. Paradoxically, the gender norms of a society obsessed with sexual morality serve to distance sexuality from morality, asserting that sex is a battlefield on which men serve their own interests by avoiding considering women as partners, equals, and friends, and the only regulation is legislation against sexual violence.

Another way is implicit in the very etymology of "consent"—*cum sentire*, literally to *feel with*.[5] Feeling together can be an avenue toward respect for the other. The deep, genuine promise of consent lies in the possibility of an eroticism that builds equality through the sexual relationship instead of presuming equal and independent partners. Here consents are exchanged rather than given unilaterally. In this view of consent, what matters is not isolated individuals using each other toward their potentially incompatible private ends but rather the relation built through sex, whether this relation lasts minutes or years.

Sexual Intersubjectivity: Consent as Respect

To not be raped or assaulted does not suffice to have a fulfilling or joyful sexual experience. Yet the moral question of what is positively *good* sex tends to go missing from debates about consent, which overwhelmingly focus on preventing bad sex. The secondary importance granted to thinking about good sex has undoubtedly contributed to the sexual revolution's failure to fulfill all its promises for women. We still live in a world where men use women as objects of their pleasure rather than as subjects with whom to have a real sexual relationship.

By "relationship," I don't mean a long, monogamous pairing based on love. I mean any encounter in which the participants focus on the fact that they are doing something together, cooperatively. They are not just "having" sex, an expression that tends to erase the partner. They are deciding together on which sexual activities to do with one another, and their own satisfaction cannot be conceived outside of a common satisfaction. There is no such thing as "sex" that one can "have"—no predefined set of practices. There are sexual activities to do together. And there is no singular model of the sex relationship. A one-night stand can be a relationship, provided that the other is treated with respect. A friend-with-benefits is by definition a relationship; this is what the word "friend" signals. A booty call could be a relationship if it were understood as cooperative, but the sexual objectification at play in the name itself suggests that this is improbable.

What do people need in order to have good sex? In the present context, with the representations and social dominations that structure our sexuality, individuals are not fully autonomous and equal, so consent-as-authorization cannot by itself get us to good sex. Consent understood as verbal agreement helps to prevent rape and keep sexual interactions outside the most problematic areas of the gray zone, but it doesn't make for positively good sex. So what does? What, at last, are the predicates of positively good sex?

Sexual Desire Is Not Enough

At first sight, it seems that good sex is sex that is both motivated by and satisfies physical desire. But this is a misleading intuition. For one thing, it is quite possible to experience sexual desire and yet not want sex and be unwilling to consent to it. This is what happens when a person in a monogamous relationship meets someone to whom they are sexually attracted and yet honors their commitment to their partner. For another thing, as we have seen, patriarchy shapes our desires so that we might experience wanting certain experiences—for example, sexual submission—without wishing to act on these desires.[6]

Furthermore, it is not the case that the only good sex is sex we desire. Consider the following comparison: it is universally recognized that, in everyday life, people take actions they do not wish to because these actions, though themselves unwanted, are means to desired ends. For example, I don't enjoy cleaning my apartment, but I do want to have a clean apartment, and because this is a worthwhile end, I am willing to undertake undesirable activities to obtain it. Although, as noted elsewhere, it is widely appreciated that sex is special in some ways—distinct from mundane activities—I see no reason to believe that sex should be thought of differently in this context. It is not clear why it would be morally unacceptable to engage in sex for a morally good purpose other than sex itself—for instance, in order to please someone or to relax. Perhaps especially in cases of long-term, loving relationships, there should be little controversy over this point. One can easily imagine a case in which Toni, observing that long-term partner Jo is stressed out, and knowing that Jo will feel better after sex, chooses to have sex with Jo in order to improve Jo's mood. Because Toni knows and loves Jo, Toni can decide to have sex with Jo whether or not Toni feels physical desire during the moment of sexual interaction. If, in Jo and Toni's relationship, this kind of care goes both ways, then Toni's choice to have sex with Jo not only is morally permissible but may be morally good.

Having studied the widespread motivations underlying sex—and abstinence—sociologists Jennifer Hirsch and Shamus Khan encourage us to think about what they call a "sexual project":

> A *sexual project* encompasses the reasons why anyone might seek a particular sexual interaction or experience. Pleasure is an obvious project; but a sexual project can also be to develop and maintain a relationship; or it can be a project to *not* have sex; or to have sex for comfort; or to try to have children; or because sex can advance our position or status within a group, or increase the status of groups to which we belong. A sexual project can also be to have a particular kind of experience, like sex in the library stacks; sex can be the goal rather than a strategy toward another goal. People don't just have one sexual project. They can have many. Wanting intimacy doesn't mean not wanting other things, like to hook up from time to time.[7]

One might add to this list the controversial project of making money. While there is no doubt that sales of sex are steeped, in practice, in patriarchal norms of sexuality, it is reasonable to argue—without resolving once and for all the question of what position the state should take on sex work—that exchanging sex for money is one sexual project among many. This brings us back to the agency dilemma discussed above and to the importance of a struggle against patriarchy that is not opposed, in a paternalistic way, to the preservation of sexual autonomy.

Consent Is Not an Admission Ticket

The fundamental question, then, is not how to ensure that everyone takes only pleasure from sex but rather that each of us has only sexual experiences that are wanted and valued. Consent can help us in this regard.

Consent in the sense of surrendering one's rights to physical integrity is of little help here; this definition is far removed from what partners experience in a fulfilling sexual relationship. But we can learn something from the push for affirmative consent and the debate surrounding it. Here is how California defines affirmative consent in its 2014 law implementing an affirmative consent standard on university and college campuses:

> "Affirmative consent" means affirmative, conscious, and voluntary agreement to engage in sexual activity. It is the responsibility of each person involved in the sexual activity to ensure that he or she has the affirmative consent of the other or others to engage in the sexual activity. Lack of protest or resistance does not mean consent, nor does silence mean consent. Affirmative consent must be ongoing throughout a sexual activity and can be revoked at any time. The existence of a dating relationship between the persons involved, or the fact of past sexual relations between them, should never by itself be assumed to be an indicator of consent.[8]

Although I do not believe this law guarantees that all legally compliant sex on California college campuses is good sex—indeed, no law, in any circumstances, could guarantee good sex—it does point to something crucial concerning the relationship between consent and good sex: in the case of good sex, and not just sex subject to affirmative consent, consent is "ongoing throughout the sexual activity." Some conservative commentators have replied that this is an onerous demand that undermines pleasure. They argue that it is ridiculous to imagine that consent could be secured at, say, every change of position. On this view, consent must occur, once and for all, at the threshold of sexual activity; anything else is not only unrealistic but perhaps impossible. As philosopher Vanina Mozziconacci and sociologist Cécile Thomé show, the idea of consent as a "love-killer" that would interrupt the "natural" unfolding of the sexual act is widespread. According to this view, the demand for consent is analogous to the demand for using condoms: it can be justified for safety reasons but is an unpleasant formality that goes against the impulses of desire and pleasure.[9] The conservative opposition to ongoing consent is therefore understandable even if conservatives agree that consent is important (which not all do): if consent kills the mood, we should want to minimize it. In that case, a single expression of consent, before sex begins, is the most that can be tolerated.

But consent is not like an admission ticket—a toll paid for entry to the highway of sex. Such a representation is problematic first of all because it wrongly naturalizes a social fact: seeing consent as only a threshold matter implies that once the partners say yes, all know where sex is going because sex inevitably follows its preordained course. In truth, the presumed "natural" course of sex is determined by social norms and cultural practice. Discomfort with the idea of establishing ongoing consent is rooted less in concerns for interrupting a natural process than in patriarchal cultural representations according to which the man should triumph over the woman's resistance and unleash his natural drive. After all, verbal exchange during sex often enhances the excitement; yet talking about consent during sex is supposed to be an insurmountable cure for desire?

This representation is especially problematic because it implies that respect for and attention to the other, though necessary in nonsexual interpersonal relationships, is not necessary in sex and should even be absent. Being polite and caring, and asking people what they want and like, would seem to be the right way to behave in every human activity except sex. We are dealing here with a puritanical reflex that seeks to preserve the mysteries of the natural and possibly sacred against heretics who would profane it with their words.

Reason counsels against this position. If we understand morality as a function of evaluating the quality of our actions, then why should the usual moral standards not apply between people who love each other or who have intimate relationships with each other? On the contrary, the vulnerability created by feelings of love and affection requires heightened moral care. Our actions are not necessarily good, nor are we absolved of moral responsibility, in the name of intimacy. Indeed, if we take seriously the vulnerability involved in sex and in loving feelings, if we give credence to sex as a source of both immense joy and great suffering, how can we not make the effort to care for our partners?

Sex as a Relationship among Equals

The fundamental problem with so much consent talk is that it treats autonomy as something that must be protected against attacks but not as something that needs favorable conditions for its development. The mutual care I have just referred to is a part of these conditions. In order for sexuality to fulfill its promise, partners must be allowed to flourish as persons and as embodied subjects, who desire, think, and want. As Ann Cahill, one of the philosophers we've previously encountered, puts it, the problem that patriarchy poses to our sexualities is that it prevents them from being lived as experiences in which the subjects recognize each other as subjects of desire and pleasure.[10] Such recognition is at the heart of a Kantian vision of good sex. To realize this vision requires a form of consent whose ambition is not to prevent negative outcomes but to respect the person as a person. In sexual interactions, as in all other circumstances, the other person cannot be treated only as a means; they must be an end in themselves.

A positively moral sexuality requires first the development of a sexual subjectivity, which philosopher Linda Alcoff describes as follows:

> This involves more than our arousal patterns and our conduct or sexual choices. It also includes a complex constellation of beliefs, perceptions, and emotions that inform our intrapsychic sexual scripts and affect our very capacity for sexual agency. Because our sexual subjectivity is interactive with others and our social environments, it is always in process, changing in relation to our experiences. For this reason, our sexual subjectivities are constitutively or intrinsically vulnerable.[11]

The crucial question for my sexual subjectivity is "whether I have the ability to participate in the making of my sexual self."[12] Sexual autonomy is therefore important here, and—among women in particular, but not only among women—it is endangered by gender norms. This idea of sexual subjectivity echoes the important place that Simone de Beauvoir gives to erotic experience in *The Second Sex:*

> The erotic experience is one that most poignantly reveals to human beings the ambiguity of their condition. They feel there as flesh and as spirit, as the other and as subject. Woman experiences this conflict at its most dramatic character because she seizes herself first of all as an object and does not immediately find a confident autonomy in pleasure; she has to reconquer her dignity as

transcendent and free subject while assuming her carnal condition: this is a delicate and risky enterprise that often fails. But the very difficulty of her situation protects her from the mystifications by which the male lets himself be duped; he is easily fooled by the fallacious privileges that his aggressive role and the satisfied solitude of the orgasm imply; he hesitates to recognize himself fully as flesh. The woman has a more authentic experience of herself.[13]

This passage testifies to the fact that subjectivity is corporeal: to be a subject, and in particular a subject of desire, is both to be and to have a body—that is, both to be a subject in a body and to have a body that is an object for others. For Beauvoir, authentic existence involves recognizing this ambiguity of being both subject and object, both autonomous and caught up in gender norms. This ambiguity is part of the human condition, so it affects us all. But men have the power to represent women in a way that allows men to avoid confronting this ambiguity. Beauvoir's highly original analysis reverses the usual perspective: it shows that fulfilled sexual life is not on the side of men. On the contrary, male domination deprives men of a fulfilled sexuality by proposing to them a self-centered, inauthentic conception of their own eroticism. Men are compelled to conceive of women in a way that deprives men of an authentic relationship with women.[14]

Beauvoir's analysis is important for us because it helps to specify what a successful erotic experience should look like from the point of view of the individual's relation to themself. A successful erotic experience is not simply one in which pleasure is maximized, although maximizing pleasure is often desirable. Rather, a successful erotics is one in which the human being experiences corporeally, carnally, what they are in all their ambiguity. And in this experience, the relationship with the other is absolutely essential. It is alongside the other, because I conceive them as *another,* that I recognize myself as a subject. It is through the view of the other that I know myself as an object and therefore discover myself as essentially both subject and object. And what gives dignity and freedom to the subject is precisely their holding together this ambiguity of being at the same time subject and object. This ambiguity is a source of vulnerability but also the very condition that enables the joys of the erotic experience.

Now, crucially, this ambiguity is possible only in the condition of *relation,* and it is for this reason that Beauvoir finds the feminine experience more authentic than the masculine: in sexuality as elsewhere, men can avoid the relation—they are able to believe themselves alone and independent. However, according to Beauvoir, this is a lie men tell themselves because our being-in-the-world is a being-with-others, and it is in our relation to others that our subjectivity is constructed, progressively and mutually.[15] Thus, for Beauvoir, male domination is an obstacle to erotic fulfillment, and even more so for men than for women, because it leads men to deny what they really are.

But if a man renounces domination, if he accepts the true realization that he is essentially in relation to others, then erotic fulfillment is possible both for him and for his female partner, no matter that female sexuality is shaped by gender norms. Beauvoir writes:

> The asymmetry of male and female eroticism creates insoluble problems as long as there is a battle of the sexes; they can easily be settled when a woman feels both desire and respect in a man; if he covets her in her flesh while recognizing her freedom, she recovers herself as the essential in the moment she becomes an object, she remains free in the submission to which she consents. Thus, the lovers can experience shared pleasure in their own way;

each partner feels pleasure as being their own, while at the same time having its source in the other. The words "receive" and "give" exchange meanings, joy is gratitude, pleasure is tenderness. In a concrete and carnal form the reciprocal recognition of the self and the other is accomplished in the most acute consciousness of the other and the self . . . the dimension of the *other* remains; but the fact is that otherness no longer has a hostile character; this consciousness of the union of the bodies in their separation is what makes the sexual act moving; it is all the more overwhelming that the two beings who together passionately negate and affirm their limits are fellow creatures and are yet different. . . . What is necessary for such harmony are not technical refinements but rather, on the basis of an immediate erotic attraction, a reciprocal generosity of body and soul.[16]

Against the idea that a good erotic experience is an experience of using the other, which corresponds to the model of male sexuality, we see that the moral quality but also the joy and pleasure of good sex comes from giving—giving of oneself—and receiving. Women, then, have easier access to fulfilling sex than men do. The main barrier to women's fulfillment is men who, because of the norms of masculinity, deprive themselves and women at the same time. It is clear that a fulfilling erotic experience on these terms requires not romantic love but "reciprocal generosity"—the mutual, or intersubjective, recognition that is the basis of treating the other as a person.

This intersubjective recognition is difficult to acquire. Gender norms generate epistemic inequities whereby men are invited to actively ignore the subjectivity of their partners and see them as occasions for sexual pleasure, while women are discouraged from expressing and even conceiving their pleasure and desire. Intersubjective recognition is also difficult to acquire because sexuality tends to be conceived as an economic terrain in which one maximizes one's pleasure at the least possible cost. But such recognition is indeed the condition of an authentic sexual *relationship* in which partners engage as equal human subjects committed to reinforcing their equality. And this recognition absolutely can be achieved when consent is understood as conversation.

For an Erotic Conversation

In the face of all the difficulties imposed by patriarchy, it seems that the solution to good sex is to be found not in the exchange of consents once and for all but in a conversation between consenting subjects about their consent. In such a framework, consent is no longer to be understood as a formal agreement reached all at once but as the manifestation of the sexual autonomy of the partners, which must occur continuously during the sexual encounter. This brings us closer to the Kantian idea that taking into account the consent of the other is inseparable from treating the other not only as a means but also as an end. Such treatment, as we have seen, implies respect for and attention to the other, their present situation, their limitations, and the power differentials that may exist between the other and oneself.

The patriarchal approach to sex, including the forms of consent available to it, are arrayed against this Kantian approach. While there are few studies of female desire, those that exist suggest the very idea of consent being exchanged before the sexual encounter is based on a masculinist model of sexual desire. According to this model—which describes the experience of many men, but not all—arousal and desire are effectively the same. Both are present prior to the encounter, through which arousal is discharged. In contrast, women more often experience a distinction between desire and arousal. Desire is present before sex, but arousal occurs gradually in the midst of it.[17] This difference between arousal and desire suggests that the presence of sexual

arousal at the outset of sex is not enough to determine that partners want it. In addition, sociological studies show that the conception of sexuality as something intimate, private, and possibly
dangerous or shameful results in people tending to ask few questions about their "sexual projects," which makes it hard for
people to know what they desire and what they want.

If we want to recognize the complexity and unpredictability
of desire, the fact that we may not know exactly what we want
or don't want until the moment presents itself, and that we may
be unsure of whether a practice is pleasurable until we have tried
it, then we must create the best possible conditions for erotic experimentation. Analyzing sex through the prism of the philosophy
of language, the philosopher Quill Kukla proposes conceiving
of sex as a series of negotiations that take into account the indirect quality of erotic language: we rarely say simply yes or no,
and some erotic language is metaphorical. In particular, Kukla
proposes that we understand the initiation of the sexual act on
the model of an invitation or gift. In everyday life, invitations and
gifts involve speech acts governed by very precise rules. There
are particular kinds of language we are expected to use when
offering invitations and gifts, when accepting or declining them,
and when responding to acceptance and refusal. For example,
one can be disappointed at the refusal of one's invitation, but
one cannot be offended. And there are more and less polite ways
to refuse an invitation. Kukla shows convincingly that there is
value in understanding the initiation of sex outside of an ongoing relationship as an invitation and, in some established relationships, as a form of giving. Kukla also shows that BDSM's
system of safe words could be productively introduced to the
wider world of sex, where it could be used to accept and refuse
propositions and practices during intercourse. Such a system both
prevents miscommunication stemming from the indirect nature
of erotic language and provides tools that positively facilitate
sexual experimentation. Finally, Kukla's view of sex as negotia-

tion emphasizes that only the collaboration and communication developed between partners can allow for the exploration of sexual submission, for instance the rather complex BDSM practice of voluntary temporary nonconsent.[18]

These proposals are extremely useful in conceiving of what a moral sexual relationship might look like, serving not only to protect sexual autonomy and integrity but also nurturing the development of subjectivity and autonomy. This places sexual morality in the register of personal choice and growth, rather than straitjacketing it behind claims that, for instance, only sex between people who love each other could be moral. On the contrary, the goal is to create conditions allowing for the greatest diversity of sexual practices, because the development of personal autonomy requires the possibility of experimentation.

However, rather than conceive of these exchanges as a negotiation, it is more fruitful to consider them a *conversation*. Negotiation puts one in mind of sexuality as a battlefield—the model in which each person maximizes their individual pleasure, even at the expense of the other. Negotiation also implies that collaboration occurs at some stage of the process—probably the beginning—and then is meant to end once agreement is reached. In contrast, conversation implies no end state. In a real conversation, not "talking at" but "talking with," interlocutors pay attention to each other throughout. In the sexual conversation, the participants note each other's potentially shifting desires, movements, and situations. Throughout, the focus is on the deeply relational character of sexual *practice*. One can come to sex as an individual, only to discover that one of the great joys of sex is undoubtedly the relationship that develops, even if it does not last and is not a relationship in the romantic sense of the term.

To understand good sex as a conversation is also to distinguish it from a dialogue or a discussion. The term "conversation" emphasizes collaboration, the fact that the partners work together toward a common goal rather than possibly talking past each other or trying to advance their own arguments. In a conversation, we progressively lose track of the authorship of ideas, as the conversation itself becomes something generative that steers participants in unforeseen directions.

To understand sex as a conversation also means attending to the different temporalities of consent: people need to agree to start this conversation, but they also need to agree, as the conversation progresses, to keep the conversation going. Let's recall the idea, developed by BDSM practitioners, that consent occurs before, during, and after sex: a conversation is a better model than a negotiation if we want to accommodate this temporality. We can look back on a conversation to elucidate its qualities and its weaknesses. Finally, the image of the conversation emphasizes skill-building, which is also relevant to good sex. One is not born a good conversationalist; good conversation is a practice that develops with experience, as we learn to use words and gestures, to attend to silences and hesitations. Likewise, developing sexual skills—which also involve words and gestures, silences, and hesitations—takes time and experience.

Here, a worry arises: How can we have good sex if good sex requires an art of erotic conversation that we do not already possess? I believe that this is where consent could be emancipatory. When we practice this erotic conversation, we are not only practicing better sex, we are also learning about our desires and our pleasures and those of our partners, thus creating conditions for better sex in the future. Most importantly, we are progressively inventing a way to talk about these pleasures and desires, and this way of talking can be transmitted to others. My hope is that the more people practice erotic conversation with partners, the more comfortable they will become at talking about sex, during sex and outside of it. When we talk comfortably about sex, we are breathing new language into the world, which others can use to help themselves have better sex, know themselves better, and in turn contribute to a collective capacity to talk about sex. One of the important obstacles to good sex is the discomfort most of us feel when talking about sex and the lack of vocabulary that goes with it: we need language to describe what feels good and what doesn't so that we can achieve knowledge of ourselves and of others as sexual people. With better conversational skills at our disposal, we may attune our capacities to interpret and understand what others are saying or showing about they want. In this way, consent that really gets at the heart of our wants and desires is bound up in erotic conversation.[19]

Given the state of our world, this conversation is unlikely to be among equals. But the idea of a conversation helps us to identify the practical consequences of this fact: we know from our daily life that when a professor has a conversation with a student, a parent with their child, a boss with their employee, a socially privileged person with an oppressed person, the person in the position of power has an ethical responsibility to make sure the person who has less power can express themselves without fear. It is to some extent possible, through this care of the powerful person, to create from a situation of inequality the conditions for a conversation between near-equals. In the context of sex, too, this is possible—the powerful person can make an effort to create conditions for equality. For instance, a heterosexual man is responsible for recognizing the threat that male violence constitutes to women's autonomy and for doing something about this, in his own life. His duty is to bring comfort to potential sexual partners so that they need not fear rejecting him and incurring a wrathful response.

Sex as an erotic conversation corresponds with what sex is when it takes place in a respectful way between equals. It is also what sex should look like if it is to be a practice of the larger social equality that egalitarian-minded people call for. Such a conversation implies that partners have enough mutual respect to recognize each other as subjects of desire and pleasure who seek, together, to give each other pleasure (and possibly pain) and to explore their desires. But these practices of erotic conversation are also emancipatory in that they are about practicing equality and, through this practice, challenge gender norms. In essence, they achieve what has been identified as liberating in BDSM relationships while fighting against the reinforcement of gender hierarchies.

What Comes Next

How, in concrete terms, can we promote this understanding of consent as an erotic conversation with emancipatory potential for sex, love, and therefore our lives in general? Can we somehow make it into law and change society that way? Should we trust individuals to take up the call and then hope for the best?

With respect to law, there is not a lot that it can, or should, do to promote a new sexual order. Law can be used to prosecute rape and other forms of assault but it cannot inspire or incentivize us to achieve emancipation through good sex. A first issue is that people commonly conceive of consent in its liberal, non-emancipatory form and will bring this conception to their application of consent law. Indeed, it is already the case that consent law is interpreted along liberal lines even when the language of it diverges from liberal commitments. Legal philosopher Roseanna Sommers has established from empirical investigation that people's moral intuitions about consent are completely different from the legal (and philosophical) understanding of consent, to the point that the commonsense understanding consistently fails to consider that deception invalidates consent.[20] She assumes that this common-sense understanding explains, for example, why judges have difficulty considering that, in the sexual realm, deception can invalidate consent and thus that someone who obtained sex by lying could be prosecuted for rape.[21] Put in general terms, the law needs to be applied in order to have an effect on the social world, and this application is done by people who have representations about what the words comprising laws mean. It follows that a law that introduces views far from the commonsense view risks being ineffective.

Second, it is not clear that criminal law is able to marshal any version of consent toward even the protection of autonomy, much less the development of autonomy and subjectivity. The figures are striking: less than 3 percent of sexual assaults lead to a felony conviction.[22] This is partly due to the fact that victims are not listened to or taken seriously. Pursuing charges against an abuser can also lead to secondary victimization: the abused person's life is questioned by investigators and during trial; if they do not fit the image of the "good victim," it is unlikely that the perpetrator will be convicted. And so victims often stay silent rather than suffer a second injustice, this one created by the criminal process itself. Indeed, society as a whole suffers, because impunity maintains rape culture. And even when investigators and prosecutors want to do right by victims of sexual violence, they are often stymied during the criminal process. The fact is that criminal defendants have rights, as most of us believe they ought to. Where consent is the difference between rape and sex, a prosecutor cannot just say that consent was not provided—they must *prove* it with evidence that meets demanding standards. This is often impossible, given that typically there are no records of what goes on in the context of intimate relationships. Moreover, in the United States, attempts to write consent, and in particular affirmative consent, into law as a criterion for defining sexual assault have left much to be desired. The statutes lack definitional clarity about consent, a problem that has worsened over time.[23]

The law as it exists incorporates two forms of nonconsent, both of which are problematic. There is statutory nonconsent, which holds that certain individuals lack the capacity to consent because their youth, mental capacities, or some other status that renders them insufficiently autonomous. And there is situational nonconsent, which is invoked when a person deemed capable of consenting is determined not to have done so in a particular instance.[24] Statutory nonconsent poses moral problems in that it excludes, even if for excellent reasons, from the capacity to consent some people who ought to be granted that capacity. For example, one would ideally want a person with severely diminished mental faculties to be both protected from violence *and* have some of the joys of erotic experience.[25] As for the situational conception of consent, it is easy to see how this fails to protect people. The law usually presumes that there is consent when the victim fails to actively consent but also faces no active moral constraint to consenting—constraint implying that it must be proved that the victim could not but obey. This leads to injustices whereby victims of rape and sexual assault are considered by the justice system to be consenting when they are not.

There is a fundamental point on which the law could and probably should intervene, and that is the moral element of rape and sexual assault. As I noted earlier, a crime is characterized by the concurrence of prohibited voluntary conduct (*actus reus*) and the individual's intention to commit wrongdoing (*mens rea*): in order for a crime to be established, the perpetrator must have acted with intent. However, a considerable number of rape and sexual assault proceedings stumble on this question of intent, on the grounds that the aggressor thought the sexual intercourse was consensual.

Courts could adjudicate intent in ways that reduce impunity. This is so because courts don't just listen to defendants' claims. For example, it is not enough that a defendant argues he believed that the alleged victim consented; this alone is insufficient to exonerate. Rather, the court establishes intent in an objective way, according to the evidence present and methods of reasonably interpreting that evidence. Often courts consider that it may be reasonable to infer consent from a situation in which the victim has given no positive indication of consent, which allows perpetrators to escape accountability.

This could change, and indeed has changed in some jurisdictions. In 2018 the Swedish legislature, responding to a strong social movement against sexual violence, passed a law specifying that sexual intercourse must be voluntary—defined as active participation that is communicated either by word or deed—and creating a crime of "negligent rape." Of lesser severity than rape, negligent rape was established to penalize individuals who are grossly negligent in seeking their sex partners' consent. For instance, if a person is aware that their partner might not be voluntarily participating in intercourse but, without intending to rape, does nothing to ensure consent, that person may be guilty of negligent rape. Opponents, including many critics outside Sweden, argued that the law will punish people whose partners decide after sex that the act was not consensual, but a detailed scientific paper reviewing actual cases of negligent rape tried by Swedish courts shows that this is not the case: findings are based on what goes on during the sex act, and guilt has been assessed only when it is established that the guilty party has in fact neglected to ensure that the consent of the other partner was valid.[26]

An interesting aspect of this law and its application is that it implicitly recognizes that one can experience violation even when one's partner has committed no wrongdoing, although this is not the most common case. The courts evaluate "the situation as a whole," which means that they consider what the accused person could infer from the victim's behavior; this has led to some cases in which the victim gives signs of "external voluntariness"—and therefore the accused party is not negligent—and yet the intercourse that happens is nonconsensual.

The idea of a crime of nonconsensual sex, as distinct from a crime of rape, is hardly outrageous. (For the reasons I developed above, however, I think it would be better not to call it "negligent rape" and to retain "rape" only for cases of coercive intercourse.)

Such a legal distinction was proposed decades ago by the legal scholar Stephen Schulhofer, and now we see that it is functioning as intended in Sweden.[27] It could work elsewhere, too. This is a promising method for addressing intent as an obstacle to accountability in a society where much nonconsensual sex occurs because men are grossly negligent and are responsible for their negligence. Men who do not have a clear intent to rape can still be responsible for holding patriarchal beliefs on the basis of which they feel they do not need to seek consent. Exposure to criminal prosecution for nonconsensual sex would encourage men to actively pursue consent and would suppress the possibility of pleading a misunderstanding.

But such legal change is not even close to a panacea for the problem of sexual violence, and we should be wary of tacking too far in the direction of criminal prosecution as our remedy. Today, many feminist activists and scholars of law, sociology, philosophy, and political science argue against placing our hopes in the criminal justice system, and with good reasons. Explicating all of them would be beyond the scope of this book, but allow me briefly to list a handful. First of all, critics question whether the legal system really can do better on behalf of women, given that complaints of rape so rarely result in convictions.[28] Of course, the hope is that legislative change might change this dynamic. Yet, would we really want it to, given that the rare convictions obtained already are usually of poor, racialized men, whereas victimization figures do not show that rapists fall into any particular class or race?[29] This gives reason to worry that laws differentiating rape from nonconsensual sex would provide a racist and classist justice system new avenues for prosecuting oppressed men, while others retain impunity. Perhaps more importantly, research shows that convicting rapists does not deter them from raping in the future; the recidivism rates among perpetrators of sexual violence do not seem to be reduced when they spend time in prison.[30] So there is some question as to whether increasing the rate of successful prosecution actually would serve to protect women from aggression, whether intentional or merely negligent. And again, criminal trials risk secondary victimization, a problem that would not be addressed by creating a structure of culpability for negligent rape.[31] Finally, we know that the gender stereotypes permeating society intervene strongly to the disadvantage of sexual assault victims in criminal trials.[32] For example, women's sexual history is almost always scrutinized in rape trials, and a woman who has had several sexual partners in her life is likely to be perceived as a woman of easy virtue, who, therefore, is not rapeable. These stereotypes and their ill effects won't necessarily recede just because jurisdictions adopt a law against nonconsensual sex.

Beyond the criminal justice context, nonstate actors are also using the norm of consent to create quasilegal instruments that are not necessarily protecting anyone, even as they punish wrongdoing and negligence. On US college campuses, in particular, well-intentioned policies to combat sexual violence through consent rules have arguably given rise to repression, without demonstrating clear success in terms of protection. Legal scholars Jacob Gersen and Jeannie Suk Gersen have highlighted the "sex bureaucracy" generated by the desire to prohibit and punish all forms of nonconsensual sex on campus, and the way in which the institutionalization of consent has left the concept more vague, not less. They argue that in many contexts where authority figures rely on consent to distinguish permissible and prohibited sex, the concept is now so contested and so marred by ambiguities that it is no longer useful in practice.[33] Thus there is reason to fear that both the legal and administrative prosecution of sexual assault does not reduce incidence of sexual violence.

But let us say that legal change could be successful in improving conviction rates in cases of sexual assault. Do we really want the solution to sexual violence to be more men in prison? Amid mass incarceration in the United States, and given how widespread rape really is, it is arguably both unrealistic and undesirable to send all rapists to prison. Consider that, by the most modest estimates, doing so would mean imprisoning hundreds of thousands of additional men every year in the United States, bearing in mind that the current prison population is about 2 million. What is more, an estimated 80,600 inmates each year experience sexual violence while in prison or jail.[34] It is undeniable, moreover, that the anti–sexual violence agenda has, in recent decades, been instrumentalized by those seeking a larger criminalization of sex.[35] For instance, as Joseph Fischel has shown, the notion of consent has played a key role in the construction of the image of the sex offender and of sex-offender registries, with catastrophic consequences. At the same time, interest groups pushing sex-offender registries have used consent to render certain forms of sexual violence, notably sexual violence committed by adolescents, invisible.[36]

More fundamentally, there are those who argue against the idea of punishing our way out of sexual violence. In recent years, and especially in the wake of #MeToo, advocates at the intersection of antiprison and feminist politics have developed a powerful critique of what they call "carceral feminism."[37] These activists—who include many feminists of color—criticize the tendency, which they identify in corners of the feminist movement, to seek the incarceration of violent men without sufficient concern for the unjust consequences of this incarceration. Those consequences affect the incarcerated, to be sure, but also their loved ones, in particular women.[38] These critics are not against accountability, but in place of imprisonment, they propose transformative and restorative approaches to justice, designed to aid victims and reduce violence using methods available outside the criminal justice system. Such an approach might escape the criminal justice system's bias against those who do not fit the image of the "good victim," while allowing victims to seek protection and support without exposing their abusers—who may be loved ones and, again, are likely known to them—to a justice system that puts them at risk.[39]

Given that criminalization is itself so destructive, we should question the idea that more punishment will lead to more justice. Even if every jurisdiction adopted Sweden's law, their criminal justice systems would still operate in politicized environments where poor and racialized men are punished with greater severity. Women would still be revictimized during the criminal process. Women would still be relying for protection on police, prosecutors, judges, and juries beset by sexism. And there is no guarantee that the puny resources provided for investigations of rape allegations would be expanded, making even well-crafted law a dead letter.[40]

Let us not forget that rape is already a serious crime, carrying crushing penalties for convicted offenders. And yet rape happens often. That alone is reason to believe that the criminal justice system is not going to protect women, let alone contribute to an efflorescence of good sex.

Social Change and Nonideal Sexuality

If not by law, then how can we hope to put an end to sexual violence and to promote the erotic conversation that can help build a more egalitarian sexual future? The solution cannot be simply at the individual level, because, as we saw, the main obstacle to sexual autonomy is gender norms.

People need to practice erotic conversation with each other because the more we talk about sex, the better at it, and less embarrassed about it, we become. And such a practice can be fostered at the social level through broad discourse and sex education for young people and for adults. The #MeToo movement, though its effects have been modest, has done more than decades of legal change to respond to the question of how we get men to stop raping. Moreover, whatever one thinks of using the criminal justice system, two things are clear: first, the injustices of the gray zone can never be solved by criminal justice; and second, the law will do nothing to advance the kind of sexual conversation that is necessary for a moral, joyful, fulfilling sexual life. Sex and rape constitute a political problem that affects all people; the solution will have to involve the public at large, not just what goes on in courtrooms.

As for sex education, it should be both more detailed—discussing specifics of sexuality—and broader, encompassing the subject of gender equality.[41] Hirsch and Khan, the sociologists who developed the notion of the sexual project, found in their study of college students that "almost no one reported an experience in which an adult sat them down and conveyed that sex would be an important and potentially joyful part of their life, and so they should think about what they wanted from sex, and how to realize those desires with other people in a respectful way."[42]

The exact form that sex education should take is a matter of debate and, ideally, work—we should want it to improve. But we know that when sex education looks like an awkward eighth-grade biology class, and when it teaches sexism, homophobia, abstinence, and the shame of sex—that is, when it looks like the sex education typically found in schools—it only promotes and preserves rape culture.[43]

Beyond schools, we need sex education for adults—we should not give up on good sex for everyone above the age of twenty. Adults, too, are part of humanity's sexual future, both their own and those of young people who learn from them. Right now, adults need to learn how to hold the erotic conversation. Some activist books, like the old *Our Bodies, Ourselves,* can help.[44] But as a policy matter, there is much to be said for a large-scale public commitment to promoting a positive norm of sexual consent through popular education and well-conceived sexual violence–prevention campaigns. These campaigns could take advantage of popular culture, including television series such as

Sex Education, Normal People, The Sex Lives of College Girls, and even *Grey's Anatomy,* which normalize positive consent and illustrate its erotic potential. Public-health campaigns are common, of course—they have been used against HIV, COVID-19, gun violence, and even sexual violence. But such campaigns are rarely oriented toward positive goals. We could continue public campaigns for punishing abusers, with middling success at best, or we could try something new: a campaign promoting the flourishing that can be attained by talking about sex and thinking about the kind of sex lives we want.

Sex education should incorporate consent education, which could draw on practices developed in the field of bioethics. Bioethicists have developed useful solutions for guaranteeing autonomy in another situation of strong imbalance: that of patients responding to doctors who have both power and knowledge that patients lack. Consent discourse in medicine recognizes even caring physicians struggle to behave morally given the pressures of real life; they may be tired or overworked or, for any number of reasons, unable to put themselves in the shoes of the patient and their family. This makes it hard to ensure genuine consent to medical decisions. In response, bioethicists have developed resources such as Vital Talks, a compendium of advice for doctors struggling to convey sometimes-discouraging information to patients. Meanwhile the Conversation Project suggests questions that medical professionals should ask or encourage patients to ask and even provides conversation scripts that support patient education and help to ensure that physicians understand what patients really mean when they give consent.[45] Scripts could also improve our approach to sexuality, whether they are conceived as educational materials or as the words we might use in the heat of the moment, if we find ourselves struggling to talk about consent. Lots of us, including adults, would benefit from simulated encounters with concrete sexual situations, so as to learn how to address them. We could use scripts to gain skills in erotic conversation, for instance by distinguishing the kind of erotic conversations one might have with a stranger from those with a long-term partner.

Scripts might also be useful in creating conditions for more people to have sex lives. As it stands, people who are socially awkward or cognitively different from the norm are often unable to experience the joys of sex because they are not perceived as potential partners, because they perceive themselves as unworthy of sex, because they have never been introduced to sexual practices, or because they are uncomfortable pursuing sex. Such people, to the extent that they want sex, could benefit from access to education within a society that provides opportunities for sexual autonomy.

To date, consent discourse has been obsessed with law. Reflecting our liberal intuitions concerning the rights of individuals, we have sought to create both laws and—their relative—rules of conduct that firmly distinguish sex from rape, so that violators may be criminally punished and socially shamed and women thereby protected from assault. Ironically, liberal convictions that strongly constrain state action leave us demanding the protection of states—states built by men who often advance male prerogatives.

Because the primary obstacles to a chosen, moral, and joyful sexuality are the social norms that uphold the politics of patriarchy, the best solutions lie in broad social change and in challenging the social domination of men over women—not in criminalization, with consent as the dividing line between licit and illicit sex. This is not to say that law is irrelevant, but legal change follows cultural change. As philosopher Sally Haslanger shows, legal activism tends to be ineffective when it is not grounded in the collective action of social movements and political advocacy.[46] Sweden's law could not have come about prior to the sexual revolution, and indeed was passed decades later. France's recent legislation adopting a firm age of consent was a result of mobilization by feminists and child-abuse activists.

It is undoubtedly in the feminist movement that the first response to the struggle for better sexualities can be found. But, once again, BDSM participants can lend a hand. Having discovered the scope of sexual abuse within their own community, BDSM practitioners no longer focus strictly on the responsibility of the partners in given scenes—including responsibilities to exchange consent and be limited by the terms of the exchange. Instead, the BDSM community as a whole is now working to foster the circumstances that enable genuine consent—consent among equals—by promoting collective responsibility for what transpires in intimate settings.[47] Even in communities marked by the most liberal, individualistic conception of sexual consent, consent is increasingly understood as conditioned by social situations steeped in gender norms and power relations.

As Simone de Beauvoir so eloquently demonstrated, no individual liberation is possible without a social transformation produced by large-scale movements. But at the same time, movements comprise individuals. We can, in our own lives, recognize the imperfect but real emancipatory potential of consent by treating it as an invitation to an erotic conversation between equals. And we can encourage others to do the same because this is the version of consent that can not only protect vulnerable people but allow all of us to achieve lives of sexual thriving.

CONCLUSION

AT THE END OF THIS JOURNEY, it is worth returning to the questions that Sally Haslanger puts at the center of ameliorative conceptual analysis: "What is the point of having these concepts? What cognitive or practical task do they (or should they) enable us to accomplish? Are they effective tools to accomplish our (legitimate) purposes?"[1] In this book we have developed a concept of consent that allows us to think about erotic relationships in their complexity—to effectively identify and hopefully combat sexual violence but also to seek a future that is at once egalitarian, liberated, and joyous.

Whereas sexual consent in the intuitive, liberal mode is a source of permission, this alternative vision of consent is refracted through a Kantian prism of respect and autonomy. Whereas liberal consent is a woman's problem, consent in the Kantian mode is the responsibility of everyone—especially the most powerful among us. Consent is not given once and for all; it needs to be exchanged, built, and recognized continually. It needs to be grounded in a conversation between, if not equals, then people who aspire to be equals. Consent needs to happen through the progressive acquisition of a new language of sex, a language in which we will over time feel at home and not embarrassed and in which we will be able to express our own sexual projects and shape our own sexual scripts.

Our approach to consent should not presume that we actually live in freedom and equality, nor should it presume that erotic pleasure is unavailable to heterosexual women under patriarchy. We are best served by concepts that acknowledge the reality of how we live, including the multiplicity of our sexual lives and their entanglement with politics, money, and social norms. In this respect, our thicker version of consent is not just a tool for improving people's lives but also a means of thinking through the hard questions posed by sex in its abundant forms. It allows us to understand that prostitution is neither "paid rape" nor a job like any other; that pornography can give pleasure to the men and women who watch it, even as it offers representations of men, women, and sexuality that harm women as a group and human beings in general. An emancipatory consent can distinguish having sex after a few drinks from using the body of a person so drunk that they are barely conscious. And, contrary to what some critics of consent would have us believe, an ethics of consent can recognize the difference between sex that is bad because it is disappointing and sex that is bad in the sense of failing to respect autonomy and integrity. Finally, the emancipatory model of consent is implemented with the understanding that women are particularly vulnerable in sexuality and that heterosexual men therefore bear special responsibility to ensure their partners' consent. Women are not the only ones whose consent matters, and no one's consent can be taken for granted.

Sexual consent is a concept to be handled with care. It is easily co-opted by patriarchy—indeed, it is patriarchy that consent has primarily served for centuries. But consent can instead serve freedom and autonomy. Within it lies the promise of a sexual revolution that, this time, could be a liberation for all.

Notes

Introduction

1. This position is defended in, for instance, Martha Nussbaum, "'Whether from Reason or Prejudice': Taking Money for Bodily Services," *Journal of Legal Studies* 27, no. S2 (1998): 693–724.

2. "Les chiffres de référence sur les violences faites aux femmes," Arrêtons les violences, Government of France, n.d., https://arretonslesviolences.gouv.fr/je-suis -professionnel/chiffres-de-reference-violences-faites-aux-femmes.

3. The number of sex offenses tabulated by the FBI can be found in "National Incident-Based Reporting System (NIBRS) Tables" at https://cde.ucr.cjis.gov /LATEST/webapp/#. The relevant table, which may be downloaded by selecting "Offenders" from the dropdown menu, is "Offenders_Sex_by_Offense_Cat-egory_2021" (Microsoft Excel File). Accessed March 1, 2023. The FBI definition of sex offenses includes rape, sodomy, sexual assault with an object, fondling, incest, and statutory rape. For rate of reporting rape/sexual assault: Lynn Langton and Jennifer L. Truman, "Criminal Victimization, 2013," NCJ 247648, Bureau of Justice Statistics, U.S. Department of Justice, September 2014 (rev.), 7, https://www .ojp.gov/ncjrs/virtual-library/abstracts/criminal-victimization-2013.

4. See Kate Manne, *Down Girl: The Logic of Misogyny* (Oxford: Oxford University Press, 2017), 196–205.

5. "Sexual Violence Affects Millions of Americans," Rape, Abuse, and Incest National Network (RAINN), https://www.rainn.org/statistics/victims-sexual -violence. RAINN uses a five-year rolling average to adjust for changes in the year-to-year National Crime Victimization Survey data (U.S. Department of Justice).

6. S. G. Smith, X. Zhang, K. C. Basile, M. T. Merrick, J. Wang, M. Kresnow, and J. Chen, "The National Intimate Partner and Sexual Violence Survey: 2015 Data Brief—Updated Release," National Center for Injury Prevention and Control,

Centers for Disease Control and Prevention, November 2018, https://www.cdc.gov /violenceprevention/pdf/2015data-brief508.pdf.

7. Annual average calculated from "2019 Crime in the United States," Table 1, Uniform Crime Report, Federal Bureau of Investigation (FBI), U.S. Department of Justice, https://ucr.fbi.gov/crime-in-the-u.s/2019/crime-in-the-u.s.-2019/topic-pages /tables/table-1. Seven-year average calculated from annual number of rapes (revised definition) for 2013 through 2019.

8. The most important of these studies is Nicola Gavey, *Just Sex? The Cultural Scaffolding of Rape,* 2nd ed. (New York: Routledge, 2019).

9. Robin Warshaw discussed this phenomenon earlier, in her popular book that brought to the forefront the problems of acquaintance and date rape. Robin Warshaw, *I Never Called It Rape* (New York: Harper and Row, 1988).

10. The idea of thick description was first developed by Gilbert Ryle and then applied in Clifford Geertz, *The Interpretation of Cultures* (New York: Basic Books, 1973). See also Carolin Emcke, *When I Say Yes,* trans. Tony Crawford (Cambridge, MA: Polity Press, 2020).

11. Methodologically, this book provides the kind of conceptual engineering that the philosopher Sally Haslanger calls ameliorative conceptual analysis, which seeks to respond to the questions, "What is the point of having these concepts? What cognitive or practical task do they (or should they) enable us to accomplish? Are they effective tools to accomplish our (legitimate) purposes; if not, what concepts would serve these purposes better?" Sally Haslanger, "Gender and Race: (What) Are They? (What) Do We Want Them to Be?" *Noûs* 34, no. 1 (2000): 31–55, 33.

12. Cécile Daumas, "Interview: Manon Garcia 'Le mot consentir sous-entend une forme de passivité,'" *Libération,* October 19, 2017, https://www.liberation.fr /debats/2017/10/19/manon-garcia-le-mot-consentir-sous-entend-une-forme-de -passivite_1604293.

1. Saying Yes to Sex Is Not Like Saying Yes to a Cup of Tea

1. Brian H. Bix, "Contracts," in *The Ethics of Consent: Theory and Practice,* ed. Franklin Miller and Alan Wertheimer, 251–280 (New York: Oxford University Press, 2009), 251.

2. Code civil, "The Sources of Obligations: Contract: Chapter 1, Introductory Provisions," Art. 1109, in John Cartwright, Bénédicte Fauvarque-Cosson, and Simon Whittaker, "The Law of Contract, the General Regime of Obligations, and Proof of Obligations," translation of part of the Code civil commissioned by the Ministry of Justice of France, http://www.textes.justice.gouv.fr/art_pix/Translation revised2018final.pdf.

3. Hannah Pitkin, "Obligation and Consent, I," *American Political Science Review* 59, no. 4 (1965): 990–999, 991, 993. Emphasis in original.

4. "Crime in the United States, 2013," Definition, Uniform Crime Report, Federal Bureau of Investigation (FBI), U.S. Department of Justice, https://ucr.fbi .gov/crime-in-the-u.s/2013/crime-in-the-u.s.-2013/violent-crime/rape.

5. Code pénal, art. 222–23, Légifrance, Government of France, https://www .legifrance.gouv.fr/codes/article_lc/LEGIARTI000043409305. My translation.

6. Ga. S. Univ., 2015 Annual Security Report 39 (2015) quoted in Jacob Gersen and Jeannie Suk, "The Sex Bureaucracy," *California Law Review* 104, no. 4 (2016): 881–948, 925–926.

7. Evan Raschel, *La Pénalisation des atteintes au consentement dans le champ contractuel* (Poitiers: LGDJ-Lextenso, 2014). See also Xavier Pin, *Le Consentement en matière pénale* (Paris: LGDJ, 2002); Laurence Attuel-Mendes, *Consentement et actes juridiques* (Paris: Lexis-Nexis, 2008).

8. Jean Carbonnier, *Droit civil*, vol. 4, *Les obligations*, 16th ed. (Paris: Presses universitaires de France, 1992), part 34. My translation.

9. *Tyson v. Trigg*, 50 F.3d 436, 448 [7th Cir. 1995]) (internal citations omitted) cited in Jacob Gersen and Jeannie Suk, "Timing of Consent," in *The Timing of Lawmaking*, ed. Frank Fagan and Saul Levmore (Cheltenham, UK: Edward Elgar, 2017), 149.

10. Raschel, *La Pénalisation des atteintes au consentement*, 41.

11. See, generally, Pin, *Le Consentement en matière pénale*.

12. Pin, *Le Consentement en matière pénale*, back cover and 19.

13. The distinction between contract and criminal law, with respect to the mechanics of obligation, is shared by common and civil law systems. As Brian Bix puts it, discussing a common law system, "Contract law, both in principle and in practice, is about allowing parties to enter arrangements on terms they choose, each party imposing obligations on itself in return for obligations another party has placed upon itself. This 'freedom of contract'—an ideal by which there are obligations to the extent, but only to the extent, freely chosen by the parties—is contrasted with the duties of criminal law and tort law, which bind all parties regardless of consent. We do not individually choose the legal obligations we have not to murder and not to defraud, but we have an obligation to pay Acme Painting $400 to paint our fence if and only if we choose to take on that duty." Bix, "Contracts," 251.

14. See, for instance, Olivia Goldhill, "'Sexual Consent Contracts' Are Now a Thing. Would You Sign?" *Telegraph*, July 15, 2015.

15. While there are not two separate contracts—a pact creating the political society and a pact binding the population to follow its laws—Locke does differentiate between the moment of political association codified by the pact and the act by which the political body, once formed, authorizes a government. "The *beginning of politic society* depends upon the consent of the individuals, to join into, and make one society; who, when they are thus incorporated, might set up

what form of government they thought fit." Locke, *Second Treatise of Government* [1690], ed. C. B. Macpherson (Indianapolis: Hackett, 1980), § 106, 56. Emphasis in original.

16. Locke, *Second Treatise of Government*, § 119, 63. Emphasis in original.

17. Locke, *Second Treatise of Government*, § 119, 63–64.

18. Edward Herman and Noam Chomsky, *Manufacturing Consent: The Political Economy of the Mass Media* (New York: Pantheon, 1988).

19. Emmeline May, "Tea Consent," Blue Seat Studios, May 12, 2015, https://www.youtube.com/watch?v=oQbei5JGiT8.

20. Martha Nussbaum, "'Whether from Reason or Prejudice': Taking Money for Bodily Services," *Journal of Legal Studies* 27, no. S2 (1998): 693–724.

21. Adam Smith, *An Inquiry into the Nature and Causes of the Wealth of Nations*, Bk. I, Chapter X, Part 1, b, §25 (1776; Indianapolis: Liberty Classics, 1981), cited in Nussbaum, "Whether from Reason or Prejudice," 694.

22. In a December 9, 1993, decision, France's high court of appeals, the Court of Cassation, held that the introduction of a stick into the anus did not, in the case in question, have a sexual character and that the act did not therefore constitute a rape. Cour de Cassation, Chambre criminelle, du 9 décembre 1993, 93-81.044. However, in a decision of December 6, 1995, the same court came to the opposite conclusion in a case concerning the insertion by teenagers of a pickaxe handle covered with a condom into the anus of a young man. In this instance, the court ruled that the defendants could be charged with rape. Cour de Cassation, Chambre criminelle, du 6 décembre 1995, 95-84.881. See Simon Auffret, "Affaire d'Aulnay: la qualification de 'viol' au centre de l'enquête," *Le Monde*, March 9, 2017.

2. How Does Consent Make Things "Good"?

1. Samantha Stark, "'I Kept Thinking of Antioch': Long before #MeToo, a Times Video Journalist Remembered a Form She Signed in 2004," *New York Times*, April 8, 2018. For the French response, see, for example, Gilles Lipovetsky, *La Troisième Femme: Permanence et révolution du féminin* (Paris: Gallimard, 2007). Senate Bill 967, Ch. 748, "Student Safety–Sexual Assault," 2013–2014, California Legislative Information, https://leginfo.legislature.ca.gov/faces/billNavClient.xhtml?bill_id=201320140SB967. For a severe yet precise analysis of the adoption of affirmative-consent sex policy, see Janet Halley, "The Move to Affirmative Consent," *Signs* 42, no. 1 (2016): 257–279.

2. Heidi M. Hurd, "The Moral Magic of Consent," *Legal Theory* 2, no. 2 (1996): 121–146. For compelling objections to consent as "moral magic," see Susan Brison, "What's Consent Got to Do with It?" *Social Philosophy Today* 37 (2021): 9–21.

3. The choice of unisex names here and at other points in the text is deliberate, as some of the hypothetical scenarios I include are designed to consider questions of sexual morality without reference to the gendered dynamics of social domination. At other points, I do consider the genders of the parties and elaborate on their impact.

4. Ruwen Ogien, "L'incohérence des critiques des morales du consentement," *Cahiers de recherche sociologique* 43 (2007): 133–140, 137, my translation. See also, Ruwen Ogien, *Penser la pornographie* (Paris: Presses universitaires de France, 2003); and Ogien, *L'Éthique aujourd'hui: maximalistes et minimalistes* (Paris: Gallimard, 2007).

5. The word "puritanism" is itself interesting for understanding the specifically French refusal of a supposed Americanization of morals. The Puritans were a subset of sixteenth- and seventeenth-century English Protestants, who sought to purify the Church of England of its Catholic practices and bring it closer to Calvinist precepts. Some of these Puritans participated in the British colonization of New England, particularly between 1629 and 1640, where they contributed to the shape of American education and moral life. While scholars have shown that the Puritans were less strict in matters of sexual morals than many other religious groups of the time, the crucial role of Puritan ideology in the US temperance movement helped to give rise to the claim that Puritans were obsessed with sobriety, the absence of pleasures, the fight against hedonism, and moral rigor in general. This puritanism became one of the axes of a certain anti-American sentiment in France, as seen, for example, in Louis-Ferdinand Céline's 1932 novel *Journey to the End of the Night:* "Every month Anglo-Saxon puritanism is drying us up a little more; it has already reduced those impromptu backroom carousals to practically nothing." Louis-Ferdinand Céline, *Journey to the End of the Night,* trans. Ralph Mannheim (New York: New Directions, 1983), 60.

6. Georges Vigarello, *A History of Rape: Sexual Violence in France from the 16th to the 20th Century,* trans. Jean Birrell (Malden, MA: Polity Press, 2001).

7. Isaiah Berlin's framework of positive and negative liberty is useful here. Consent is expected to guarantee not only our freedom *from* unwanted sex but also our freedom *to* gain self-fulfillment through sex. See Isaiah Berlin, "Two Concepts of Liberty" (1958), in Berlin, *Four Essays on Liberty* (Oxford: Oxford University Press, 1969).

8. I am taking precautions here, as Kant considers his argument to be formal and not substantive. Kant is precisely trying to elucidate the formal and not the substantive dimension of morality—that is, the *form* of the moral law independent of the goals that an action may pursue. But in doing so, he proposes a *substantive* conception of morality—in the common sense of the term—because the moral law has a formulation and a content.

9. Renée Jorgensen Bolinger, "Moral Risk and Communicating Consent," *Philosophy and Public Affairs* 47, no. 2 (2019): 179–207, 180.

10. John Stuart Mill, "On Liberty," in Mill, *On Liberty, Utilitarianism, and Other Essays,* ed. Mark Philp and Frederick Rosen, 2nd ed., 1–112 (Oxford: Oxford University Press, 2015), 8, 58, 63.

11. Mill, "On Liberty," 13.

12. Mill, "On Liberty," 15.

13. Jeremy Bentham, "Offences against One's Self: Paederasty, Part 1," *Journal of Homosexuality* 3, no. 4 (1978): 389–406; and Bentham, "Jeremy Bentham's Essay on 'Paederasty,' Part 2," *Journal of Homosexuality* 4, no. 1 (1978): 91–107.

14. Immanuel Kant, *Groundwork of the Metaphysics of Morals,* trans. and ed. Mary Gregor (Cambridge: Cambridge University Press, 1998), Ak 4:393–394, 7–8.

15. Kant, *Groundwork,* 4:397, 10–11.

16. Kant, *Groundwork,* 4:421, 31.

17. Kant, *Groundwork,* 4:428, 36–37. Emphasis in original.

18. Kant, *Groundwork,* 4:440, 46.

19. Jean-Jacques Rousseau, *On the Social Contract,* in *The Major Political Writings of Jean-Jacques Rousseau,* trans. and ed. John T. Scott (Chicago: University of Chicago Press, 2012), Bk. I, ch. 8, 446.

20. "*Will* is a kind of causality of living beings insofar as they are rational, and *freedom* would be that property of such causality that it can be efficient independently of alien causes *determining* it." Kant, *Groundwork,* 4:446, 52. Emphasis in original.

21. Kant, *Groundwork,* 4:429, 38.

22. See, for example, Martha Nussbaum, "Objectification," *Philosophy and Public Affairs* 24, no. 4 (1995): 249–291; and Barbara Herman, "Could It Be Worth Thinking about Kant on Sex and Marriage?" in *A Mind of One's Own,* ed. Louise Antony and Charlotte Witt, 53–72 (Boulder, CO: Westview Press, 1993).

23. Onora O'Neill, "Between Consenting Adults," *Philosophy and Public Affairs* 14, no. 3 (1985): 252–277.

24. O'Neill, "Between Consenting Adults," 268, 272.

25. As Michela Marzano shows, Mill's and Kant's views are not necessarily opposed and can lead to similar outcomes. However, in sexual ethics, their positions have commonly been used to distinguish distinct understandings of sexual consent. Michela Marzano, *Je consens, donc je suis: Éthique de l'autonomie* (Paris: Presses universitaires de France, 2006), 68–70.

3. *"Hit Me Baby One More Time"*

1. Brandy Simula, "Pleasure, Power, and Pain: A Review of the Literature on the Experiences of BDSM Participants," *Sociology Compass* 13, no. 3 (2019): e12668.

2. Danielle Lindemann, "BDSM as Therapy?" *Sexualities* 14, no. 2 (2011): 151–172.

3. See Dick Hebdige, *Subculture: The Meaning of Style* (London: Methuen, 1979). For additional discussion of subcultures as sites of resistance, see Stuart Hall and Tony Jefferson, *Resistance through Rituals: Youth Subcultures in Post-War Britain* (London: Hutchinson, 1993). The 2002 film *Secretary*, a darling of the festival circuit, was the first film about BDSM to reach a large audience. Lars von Trier's *Nymphomaniac*, released in 2013—and in particular the bondage scenes in the second volume—is an auteur's take on BDSM. The literary counterpart to this vogue for representations of BDSM can be identified, in France, in the success of Catherine Millet, *The Sexual Life of Catherine M.*, trans. Adriana Hunter (New York: Grove Press, 2002).

4. E. L. James, *Fifty Shades of Grey* (New York: Vintage Books, 2011); James, *Fifty Shades Darker* (New York: Vintage Books, 2012); James, *Fifty Shades Freed* (New York: Vintage Books, 2012); Margot D. Weiss, "Mainstreaming Kink: The Politics of BDSM Representation in U.S. Popular Media," *Journal of Homosexuality* 50, no. 2–3 (2006): 103–132.

5. See Manon Garcia, "BDSM," in *The Routledge Handbook of Philosophy of Sex and Sexuality*, ed. Clare Chambers, Brian Earp, and Lori Watson (New York: Routledge, 2022), 437–451.

6. The word "slave" is widely used in S&M and BDSM literature and is central to the expression of complete submission, but the experience of the BDSM slave bears little resemblance to that of enslaved people historically.

7. Gilles Deleuze and Leopold von Sacher-Masoch, *Masochism: Coldness and Cruelty* and *Venus in Furs* (New York: G. Braziller, 1971; New York: Zone Books, 1989), 292–293.

8. See Darren Langdridge and Meg Barker, eds., *Safe, Sane and Consensual: Contemporary Perspectives on Sadomasochism* (New York: Palgrave Macmillan, 2007).

9. I use the term "scene" because BDSM encounters are often described using theatrical language.

10. For sample and model contracts, which give an idea of the standards of BDSM contracts, see, for example, "BDSM Contracts: Templates and Rules, a Complete Guide," BDSM Contracts, n.d., https://bdsmcontracts.org; Adriana, "Consensual Bondage: The Ultimate Guide to BDSM Contracts," Bad Girls Bible, n.d., http://badgirlsbible.com/bdsm-contract.

11. It is customary, in order to guarantee the health of the submissive, to proscribe any practice that would leave a permanent physical trace or that could have harmful health consequences in the medium or long term. For details see, for example, interviews with Catherine Robbe-Grillet on *France Culture*, Radio

France, June 26–July 1, 2016, www.franceculture.fr/emissions/voix-nue/catherine
-robbe-grillet-la-singuliere.

12. It is common to use two different safe words, described as "orange" and
"red": invoking the orange safe word means that the specific practice taking place
should stop right away. Invoking the red safe word means that the whole scene
should stop right away.

13. Jill Weinberg, *Consensual Violence: Sex, Sports, and the Politics of Injury*
(Berkeley: University of California Press, 2016), 54–61.

14. D. J. Williams et al., "From 'SSC' and 'RACK' to the '4Cs': Introducing a
New Framework for Negotiating BDSM Participation," *Electronic Journal of
Human Sexuality* 17 (2014), www.ejhs.org/volume17/BDSM.html.

15. Code civil, art. 6, Légifrance, Government of France, https://www.legifrance
.gouv.fr/codes/article_lc/LEGIARTI000006419285. My translation.

16. Pierre-Yves Quiviger, "Du droit au consentement. Sur quelques figures
contemporaines du paternalisme, des sado-masochistes aux Témoins de
Jéhovah," *Raisons politiques* 2, no. 46 (2012): 79–94.

17. Roberto Mangabeira Unger, "The Critical Legal Studies Movement,"
Harvard Law Review 96, no. 3 (1983): 561–676, esp. 622–624; Elizabeth F.
Emens, "Compulsory Sexuality," *Stanford Law Review* 66, no. 2 (2014): 303–385,
356. More broadly, on the relationship between law and BDSM in American law,
see Margo Kaplan, "Sex-Positive Law," *NYU Law Review* 89, no. 1 (2014):
89–164; Devin Meepos, "50 Shades of Consent: Re-Defining the Law's Treatment
of Sadomasochism," *Southwestern Law Review* 43, no. 1 (2013): 97–120.

18. US cases relevant to BDSM include *Commonwealth v. Appleby,* 402 N.E. 2d
1051 (1980); *Govan v. State*, 913 N.E. 2d 237 (2009); *People v. Febrissy*, No. C049033,
2006 WL 2006161 (Cal. Ct. App. July 19, 2006); *People v. Samuels*, 250 Cal.
App. 2d (1967); *State v. Collier*, 372 N.W. 2d 303 (1985); *State v. Van*, 688 N.W.
2d 600 (2004).

19. "Nonbinding Bondage," *Harvard Law Review* 128, no. 2 (2014): 713–734.

20. According to Jill Weinberg, BDSM appropriates legal formalism both for the
instrumental purpose of creating rules and in order to signal conformity with the
social order. Furthermore, communicating desires in this arcane way helps to
establish group identity and belonging. Weinberg, *Consensual Violence,*13.

21. For example, sexual sadism and masochism are still classified as psychiatric
disorders according to the fifth edition of the *Diagnostic and Statistical Manual of
Mental Disorders,* the bible of US psychiatry. That said, between the fourth
edition, published in 1994, and the fifth, published in 2013, sexual sadism and
sexual masochism were redesignated from "paraphilia" to "paraphilic disorder,"
implying that they are no longer considered pathological but are viewed as
deviations from the norm. American Psychiatric Association, *Diagnostic and*

Statistical Manual of Mental Disorders, 4th ed. (Arlington, VA: American Psychiatric Association, 1994); American Psychiatric Association, *Diagnostic and Statistical Manual of Mental Disorders,* 5th ed. (Arlington, VA: American Psychiatric Association, 2013).

22. Gayle Rubin, "The Leather Menace" (1982), in *Deviations: A Gayle Rubin Reader* (Durham, NC: Duke University Press, 2011).

23. The most important collection of feminist anti-sadomasochism essays is Robin Linden, ed., *Against Sadomasochism: A Radical Feminist Analysis* (East Palo Alto, CA: Frog in the Well, 1982).

24. Courts do not necessarily accept the argument that consent protects against prosecution, of course. See, for example, Eugene Volokh, "No Constitutional Right to Engage in Consensual BDSM Sex," *Washington Post,* March 4, 2016.

25. *Lawrence v. Texas,* 539 U.S. 558 (2003), is analyzed in depth in Laurence Tribe, "*Lawrence v. Texas:* The 'Fundamental Right' That Dare Not Speak Its Name," *Harvard Law Review* 117, no. 6 (2004): 1893–1955.

26. On the legal dimension of the comparison between BDSM and sports, see Vera Bergelson, "The Right to Be Hurt: Testing the Boundaries of Consent," *George Washington Law Review* 75, no. 2 (2007): 165–236; Cheryl Hanna, "Sex Is Not a Sport: Consent and Violence in Criminal Law," *Boston College Law Review* 42, no. 2 (2001): 239–290; Kaplan, "Sex-Positive Law," esp. 115–141.

27. Weinberg, *Consensual Violence,* 1–3. Weinberg's argument might be stronger: one can readily imagine that the strangulation of a prizefighter involves more risks than does sadomasochistic strangulation. Unlike BDSM practitioners, professional fighters are trained to inflict maximal damage. And there is a high probability that a fighter will have been injured before strangulation occurs, increasing the hazards of the act.

28. Professional American football players are three times more likely to die of neurodegenerative disease than are members of the general population. Everett J. Lehman, Misty J. Hein, Sherry L. Baron, and Christine M. Gersic, "Neurodegenerative Causes of Death among Retired National Football League Players," *Neurology* 79, no. 19 (2012): 1970–1974. American football poses many other risks to physical and mental health as well.

29. The right to human dignity appears in international law in the Preamble of the Universal Declaration of Human Rights of 1948, where it is distinguished from other rights, considered subsidiary: "The recognition of the inherent dignity and of the equal and inalienable rights of all members of the human family is the foundation of freedom, justice and peace in the world." United Nations, https://www .un.org/en/about-us/universal-declaration-of-human-rights. In French law, the right to human dignity has been included in the Code civil since one of the country's "bioethics laws" was adopted in 1994: "The law ensures the primacy of the

person, prohibits any infringement to dignity of the person, and guarantees respect for the human being from the beginning of his life." Code civil, art. 16, Légifrance, Government of France, https://www.legifrance.gouv.fr/codes/article_lc /LEGIARTI000006419320. My translation. That same year, the *Conseil constitutionnel* held that the French constitution safeguards human dignity. Decision no. 94–343/344 DC, July 27, 1994, https://www.conseil-constitutionnel.fr/decision /1994/94343_344DC.htm. In European law, the right to dignity is included in Title 1: Dignity, Article 1, of the *Charter of Fundamental Rights*, proclaimed in 2000, Agency for Fundamental Rights, European Union, http://fra.europa.eu/en/eu -charter.

30. Michela Marzano, *Je consens, donc je suis: Éthique de l'autonomie* (Paris: Presses universitaires de France, 2006), 59–60. See also Michael Rosen, *Dignity: Its History and Meaning* (Cambridge, MA: Harvard University Press, 2012).

31. "Dwarf-tossing" seems to have originated as a bar attraction in Australia. Little people are thrown onto padded surfaces.

32. Conseil d'État, October 27, 1995, Commune de Morsang-sur-Orge, https://www.conseil-etat.fr/decisions-de-justice/jurisprudence/les-grandes-decisions -depuis-1873/conseil-d-etat-27-octobre-1995-commune-de-morsang-sur-orge-et -ville-d-aix-en-provence.

33. See Pierre-Yves Quiviger, "Du droit au consentement"; Olivier Cayla, "Jeux de nains, jeux de vilains," in *Les Droits fondamentaux de la personne humaine en 1995 et 1996*, ed. Gilles Lebreton, 149–164 (Paris: L'Harmattan, 1998); Antonin Sopena, "La dignité à l'épreuve du sadomasochisme, et inversement," *Vacarme* 51 (2010), www.vacarme.org/article1887.html#nh5.

34. Communication No. 854/199, Human Rights Committee, July 26, 2002, CCPR/C/75/D/854/1999, International Covenant on Civil and Political Rights, United Nations, https://digitallibrary.un.org/record/1488341/files/CCPR_C_75_D _854_1999-EN.pdf.

35. *Laskey and Others v. the United Kingdom*, ECHR 21627/93; 21628/93; 21974/93 (1997), § 15, https://hudoc.echr.coe.int/app/conversion/docx/?library =ECHR&id=001-58021&filename=CASE%20OF%20LASKEY%2C%20 JAGGARD%20AND%20BROWN%20v.%20THE%20UNITED%20KINGDOM .docx.

36. Convention for the Protection of Human Rights and Fundamental Freedoms, Rome, November 4, 1950, Article 8, amended and supplemented, European Court of Human Rights, October 2, 2013, 7, https://www.echr.coe.int/documents /convention_eng.pdf.

37. *Laskey and Others v. the United Kingdom*, § 8.

38. *Laskey and Others v. the United Kingdom*, § 40.

39. *Pretty v. the United Kingdom*, ECHR 2346/02 (2002), § 62, https://hudoc .echr.coe.int/eng?i=001-60448.

40. The victim lost consciousness and was branded, leaving lasting marks. The court describes the victim "screaming in pain" as well as "the pain, anguish and humiliation inflicted on the victim." *K. A. and A. D. v. Belgium*, ECHR 42758/98; 45558/99 (2005), § 15–16, my translation.

41. *K. A. and A. D. v. Belgium*, § 85, my translation.

42. Muriel Fabre-Magnan, "Le sadisme n'est pas un droit de l'homme," *Recueil Dalloz* 43 (2005): 2973–2981, 2973. For a more moderate analysis, see Xavier Pin, "Le consentement à la lésion de soi-même en droit pénal: Vers la reconnaissance d'un fait justificatif?" *Revue Droits* 49, no. 1 (2009): 83–106.

43. The so-called Rotenburg cannibal case involved a man, Armin Meiwes, who published online classified advertisements seeking a person willing to be eaten. An individual eventually agreed, and Meiwes killed and ate him. The case, which had immense repercussions at the time, is a paradigmatic example of the impossibility of a criminal law based on consent. See Alicia-Dorothy Mornington, "Can We Consent to Everything? Germany and a Case of Consensual Cannibalism," in *Envers et revers du consentement: La sexualité, la famille et le corps, entre consentement, contraintes et autonomie*, ed. Manon Garcia, Julie Mazaleigue-Labaste, and Alicia-Dorothy Mornington (Paris: Mare et Martin, 2023).

44. Fabre-Magnan, "Le sadisme n'est pas un droit de l'homme," 2977.

45. Marzano, *Je consens, donc je suis*, ch. 6.

4. Sex Is Political

1. Recognizing the influence of social norms means also recognizing that gender constructs and their effects differ across cultures. For instance, as Audrey Ghali-Lachapelle notes in her review of the French version of this book, norms concerning women's sexual power in Maghreb cultures differ greatly from those of Western ones, suggesting that the analyses of this book may not be applicable in the Maghreb context. Audrey Ghali-Lachapelle, review of Manon Garcia, *La conversation des sexes*, *Philosophiques* 49, no. 2 (2022): 621–627. See also Fatima Mernissi, *Scheherazade Goes West: Different Cultures, Different Harems* (New York: Pocket Books, 2001).

2. In France, #MeToo was followed by #MeTooGay and #MeTooInceste, which targeted a wider range of sexual violence.

3. The writings of Gabriel Matzneff exemplify the defense, popular among certain French intellectuals of the 1970s, of certain pedocriminals—especially those who could afford to invest money and prestige in a discourse to legitimize their practices. For an account of this atmosphere of pedocriminal protection and its consequences, see, for example, Vanessa Springora, *Consent: A Memoir*, tr. Natasha Lehrer (New York: HarperCollins, 2021).

4. See for instance, Rose-Marie Lagrave, *Se ressaisir: Enquête autobiographique d'un transfuge de classe féministe* (Paris: La Découverte, 2021).

5. Michel Foucault's *History of Sexuality* appeared in French, one volume at a time. The first volume, *The Will to Knowledge,* was published in 1976, *The Use of Pleasure* and *The Care of the Self* were both published in 1984, and the fourth volume, *Confessions of the Flesh,* was published posthumously in 2018.

6. Michel Foucault, *The History of Sexuality,* vol. 1, *An Introduction,* tr. Robert Hurley (New York: Pantheon, 1978), 1:10. (This publication refers to the first volume of *The History of Sexuality* as an introduction, rather than use Foucault's title, *The Will to Knowledge.*)

7. Foucault, *History of Sexuality,* 1:4–5.

8. Foucault, *History of Sexuality,* 1:23.

9. Foucault rejects the idea of a theory of power and instead calls his project an "analytics of power." Foucault, *History of Sexuality,* 1:82.

10. Foucault, *History of Sexuality,* 1:48.

11. Michel Foucault, "The Confession of the Flesh" (1977), interview, in Foucault, *Power/Knowledge: Selected Interviews and Other Writings,* ed. and trans. Colin Gordon, 194–228 (Brighton, UK: Harvester Press, 1980).

12. "On the face of it at least, our civilization possesses no *ars erotica.* In return, it is undoubtedly the only civilization to practice a *scientia sexualis;* or rather, the only civilization to have developed over the centuries procedures for telling the truth of sex, which are geared to a form of knowledge-power strictly opposed to the art of initiations and the masterful secret: I have in mind the confession." Foucault, *History of Sexuality,* 1:58.

13. Foucault, *History of Sexuality,* 1:57.

14. Although confession existed well before the nineteenth century, Foucault argues that there is a specifically modern practice of confession as a means of discovering the truth about oneself.

15. "Domination does not reside in the one who speaks (for it is he who is constrained) but in the one who listens and says nothing." Foucault, *History of Sexuality,* 1:62.

16. "[Sex] was at the pivot of the two axes along which developed the entire political technology of life. On the one hand it was tied to the disciplines of the body: the harnessing, intensification, and distribution of forces, the adjustment and economy of energies. On the other hand, it was applied to the regulation of populations, through all the far-reaching effects of its activity." Foucault, *History of Sexuality,* 1:145.

17. Foucault, *History of Sexuality,* 1:140.

18. Foucault, *History of Sexuality,* 1:43.

19. "While *ars erotica* is organized around the framework of body-pleasure-intensification, *scientia sexualis* is organized around the axis of subject-desire-truth. It is as if one could say that the imposition of true discourses on the subject of sexuality leads to the centrality of a theory of sexual desire, while the discourse of

pleasure and the search for its intensification are exterior to a science of sexual desire. Just as Foucault wanted to divorce the psychoanalytic theory of the unconscious from the theory of sexuality, so he wants here to detach the experience of pleasure from a psychological theory of sexual desire, of sexual subjectivity." Arnold I. Davidson, *The Emergence of Sexuality: Historical Epistemology and the Formation of Concepts* (Cambridge, MA: Harvard University Press, 2001), 211.

20. Hubert L. Dreyfus and Paul Rabinow, *Michel Foucault: Beyond Structuralism and Hermeneutics*, 2nd ed. (Chicago: University of Chicago Press, 1983), 212.

21. Judith Butler, *The Psychic Life of Power: Theories in Subjection* (Stanford, CA: Stanford University Press, 1997), 2.

22. Foucault, *History of Sexuality*, 1:157.

23. On the emergence of sexology in the nineteenth century, see Sylvie Chaperon, *Les Origines de la sexologie, 1850–1900* (Paris: Payot-Rivages, 2012).

24. Jacob Gersen and Jeannie Suk, "The Sex Bureaucracy," *California Law Review* 104, no. 4 (2016): 881–948.

25. On Foucault's views of age-of-consent law and their uses, see Judith Butler, "Sexual Consent: Some Thoughts on Psychoanalysis and Law," *Columbia Journal of Gender and Law* 21, no. 2 (2011): 405–429.

26. The term "heteropatriarchy" underlines the inseparability of heterosexuality and patriarchy: heterosexuality is a system of social organization that generates dependencies, power relations, and exploitations foundational to patriarchy. See Colette Guillaumin, *Racism, Sexism, Power and Ideology* (London: Routledge, 1995); Monique Wittig, *The Straight Mind and Other Essays* (Boston: Beacon Press, 1992); and Nicole-Claude Mathieu, "Identité sexuelle/sexuée/de sexe? Trois modes de conceptualisation du rapport entre sexe et genre," in Mathieu, *L'Anatomie politique: catégorisations et idéologies du sexe* (Paris: Côté femmes, 1991).

27. On consciousness raising, see Catharine MacKinnon, "Consciousness Raising," in *Toward a Feminist Theory of the State*, 83–105 (Cambridge, MA: Harvard University Press, 1989). "Feminism is the first theory to emerge from those whose interest it affirms," MacKinnon writes. "Its method recapitulates as theory the reality it seeks to capture. . . . Feminist method is consciousness raising: the collective critical reconstitution of the meaning of women's social experience, as women live through it" (83).

28. MacKinnon, "Consciousness Raising," 94.

29. MacKinnon, "Consciousness Raising," 95.

30. Maria Bevacqua, *Rape on the Public Agenda: Feminism and the Politics of Sexual Assault* (Boston: Northeastern University Press, 2000); Nicola Gavey, *Just Sex? The Cultural Scaffolding of Rape*, 2nd ed. (New York: Routledge, 2019).

31. Key texts of the "sex wars" include, on the prosex side, Patrick Califia, *Sapphistry: The Book of Lesbian Sexuality* (Tallahassee, FL: Naiad Press, 1980);

Emma Healey, *Lesbian Sex Wars* (London: Virago, 1996); and the articles collected in Gayle Rubin, *Deviations: A Gayle Rubin Reader* (Durham, NC: Duke University Press, 2011). Opposing views can be found in Robin Linden, ed., *Against Sadomasochism: A Radical Feminist Analysis* (East Palo Alto, CA: Frog in the Well, 1982); and Catharine MacKinnon, *Toward a Feminist Theory of the State* (Cambridge, MA: Harvard University Press, 1989). The book considered to be the most representative of the prosex camp, all sexual orientations included, is Carole Vance, ed., *Pleasure and Danger: Exploring Female Sexuality* (Boston: Routledge and Kegan Paul, 1984), the proceedings of The Scholar and the Feminist IX conference, Barnard College, April 24, 1982.

32. bell hooks, "Total Bliss: Lesbianism and Feminism," in *Feminism Is for Everybody: Passionate Politics*, 2nd ed., 93–99 (New York: Routledge, 2015), 97–98.

33. See Andrea Dworkin, *Pornography: Men Possessing Women* (New York: Perigee, 1981); and Dworkin, *Intercourse* (New York: Free Press, 1987).

34. On the emancipatory power of lesbian S/M, see Gayle Rubin, "Thinking Sex: Notes for a Radical Theory of the Politics of Sexuality," in *Pleasure and Danger*, ed. Carol Vance, 267–319 (Boston: Routledge and Kegan Paul, 1984).

35. The link between the leather movement, gay culture, and BDSM was firmly established with the publication of Larry Townsend, *The Leatherman's Handbook* (Paris: Olympia Press, 1972), considered the bible of the BDSM leather subculture. More broadly, there was clear, which is not to say universal, interest in BDSM across the gay movement of the 1970s. As just one example, the cult rock group The Velvet Underground, fronted by an openly gay singer, named one of its songs "Venus in Furs," after Sacher-Masoch's novella.

36. See, for example, *Coming to Power: Writings and Graphics on Lesbian S/M* (San Francisco: SAMOIS, 1981), an anthology considered the starting point of the lesbian sadomasochist movement. Fifteen years later, a second volume made explicit reference to the link between lesbian S/M and leather culture: Pat Califia and Robin Sweeney, eds., *The Second Coming: A Leatherdyke Reader* (Los Angeles: Alyson, 1996).

37. For more on biopower, see Foucault, *History of Sexuality*, vol. 1, and Foucault's Collège de France lectures from 1975 onward, collected in English translation in the series "Michel Foucault Lectures at the Collège de France." See, for example, Michel Foucault, *Security, Territory, Population: Lectures at the Collège de France, 1977–1978* (London: Palgrave Macmillan, 2009); Foucault, *The Birth of Biopolitics: Lectures at the Collège de France, 1978–1979* (London: Palgrave Macmillan, 2008); Foucault, *On the Government of the Living: Lectures at the Collège de France, 1979–1980* (London: Palgrave Macmillan, 2014).

38. Michel Foucault, "Sex, Power and the Politics of Identity: An Interview" (1984), in Foucault, *Ethics: Subjectivity and Truth,* ed. Paul Rabinow, 163–173 (New York: New Press, 1997), 165.

39. Lorna Bracewell, *Why We Lost the Sex Wars: Sexual Freedom in the #MeToo Era* (Minneapolis: University of Minnesota Press, 2021). The formula of "compulsory heterosexuality" is borrowed from Adrienne Rich. Adrienne Rich, "Compulsory Heterosexuality and Lesbian Existence," *Signs* 5, no. 4 (1980): 631–660. For a detailed overview of the critique of heterosexuality built by feminist, lesbian, queer, and trans thinkers, see Stéphanie Mayer, "Des critiques féministes de l'hétérosexualité: contributions et limites des théorisations lesbiennes et queer," *Recherches féministes* 33, no. 2 (2020): 25–43.

40. Think of the T-shirt worn by the model Cara Delevingne at the 2021 Emmys stating, "Peg the Patriarchy" in blood-red letters.

41. Alys Harte, "A Man Tried to Choke Me during Sex without Warning," BBC News, November 28, 2019, www.bbc.com/news/uk-50546184.

42. On the pretext of "erotic asphyxiation" as justification for strangulation, see Karen Busby, "Every Breath You Take: Erotic Asphyxiation, Vengeful Wives, and Other Enduring Myths in Spousal Sexual Assault Prosecutions," *Canadian Journal of Women and the Law* 24, no. 2 (2012): 328–358. A small amount of pressure (about eleven pounds) is enough to block the carotid artery, which can lead to fainting within seconds and brain death within minutes. It takes twice as much pressure to open a soda can. Kate Manne, *Down Girl: The Logic of Misogyny* (Oxford: Oxford University Press, 2017), 2.

43. Jane Mayer and Ronan Farrow, "Four Women Accuse New York's Attorney General of Physical Abuse," *New Yorker,* May 7, 2018; Sonja Moghe, "Former New York AG Eric Schneiderman's Law License Has Been Suspended for a Year over Allegations of Abuse," CNN, April 28, 2021, https://www.cnn.com/2021/04/28/politics/former-ny-ag-eric-schneiderman-law-license-suspended/index.html.

44. Janet Halley, *Split Decisions: How and Why to Take a Break from Feminism* (Princeton, NJ: Princeton University Press, 2008), 301.

45. "Nonbinding Bondage," *Harvard Law Review* 128, no. 2 (2014): 713–734, 724.

46. Anne McClintock, "Maid to Order: Commercial Fetishism and Gender Power," *Social Text* 37 (1993): 87–116, 87.

47. Damien Lagauzère, *Le Masochisme: Du sadomasochisme au sacré* (Paris: L'Harmattan, 2010), 9.

48. As one example, world-renowned dominatrix Catherine Robbe-Grillet explains that all the scenes she organizes are the result of requests from submissives. She is never the one asking; she chooses her partners according to their requests and organizes what she calls "ceremonies" based on the fantasies they express. Jeanne de Berg, *Cérémonies de femmes* (Paris: Grasset, 1985).

49. Andreas Wismeijer and Marcel Assen, "Psychological Characteristics of BDSM Practitioners," *Journal of Sexual Medicine* 10, no. 8 (2013): 1943–1952. The most comprehensive demographic and psychosexual work conducted on BDSM is an Australian telephone survey covering a representative sample of 19,307 people. This study establishes the psychosocial "normality" of BDSM practitioners but does not report on the gender distribution of practices. Juliet Richters et al., "Demographic and Psychosocial Features of Participants in Bondage and Discipline, 'Sadomasochism' or Dominance and Submission (BDSM): Data from a National Survey," *Journal of Sexual Medicine* 5, no. 7 (2008): 1660–1668.

50. For a sociological analysis of the role of the dominatrix, see Danielle Lindemann, *Dominatrix: Gender, Eroticism, and Control in the Dungeon* (Chicago: University of Chicago Press, 2012).

51. Benevolent in the sense of the "benevolent master" in Philip Pettit, *Republicanism: A Theory of Freedom and Government* (Oxford: Oxford University Press, 1997), 64.

52. See, for instance, "Contracts and Rules," Scarlet Dahlia, March 8, 2013, http://scarletdahlia.wordpress.com/2013/03/08/contract-and-rules.

53. "Will the Court now hold, on the same model [of consent], that the State has no right to interfere when women are beaten in the private home (it is well known that, in such cases, the women most often refuse to lodge a complaint and are apparently 'consenting'), and that prohibiting such practices would be contrary to human rights?" Muriel Fabre-Magnan, "Le sadisme n'est pas un droit de l'homme," *Recueil Dalloz* 43 (2005): 2973–2981, 2980.

54. For details about rape within BDSM, see Meg Barker, "Consent Is a Grey Area? A Comparison of Understandings of Consent in *Fifty Shades of Grey* and on the BDSM Blogosphere," *Sexualities* 16, no. 8 (2013): 896–914.

55. Jay Wiseman, "Are We Men a Bunch of Lying Pricks?" Livejournal blog post, January 26, 2008, http://jay-wiseman.livejournal.com/12634.html.

56. Catharine MacKinnon, "Sexuality, Pornography, and Method: Pleasure under Patriarchy," *Ethics* 99, no. 2 (1989): 314–346.

57. On women's supposed desire for sexual submission, see John Forrester, "Rape, Seduction and Psychoanalysis," in *Rape*, ed. Sylvana Tomaselli and Roy Porter, 57–93 (Oxford: Basil Blackwell, 1986).

5. Is Consent a Woman's Problem?

1. Alan Wertheimer, *Consent to Sexual Relations* (Cambridge: Cambridge University Press, 2003).

2. Samuel Freeman uses the term "high liberalism" to characterize the social branch of liberalism of which Rawls is the key exponent. The distinction from

classical liberalism lies in the status given to economic rights, which, under high liberalism, are not absolute. See Samuel Freeman, "Capitalism in the Classical and High Liberal Traditions," *Social Philosophy and Policy* 28, no. 2 (2011): 19–55. I am grateful to Raphaëlle Théry for introducing me to this analysis.

3. Anne Phillips, "Free to Decide for Oneself," in *Illusion of Consent: Engaging with Carole Pateman,* ed. Daniel I. O'Neill, Mary Lyndon Shanley, and Iris Marion Young, 99–117 (University Park: Pennsylvania State University Press, 2008).

4. See Natalie Stoljar, "Feminist Perspectives on Autonomy," in *Stanford Encyclopedia of Philosophy,* ed. Edward N. Zalta, rev. December 11, 2018, https://plato.stanford.edu/archives/win2018/entries/feminism-autonomy.

5. Susan M. Okin, *Justice, Gender, and the Family* (New York: Basic Books, 1989).

6. Okin, *Justice, Gender, and the Family,* 22–23.

7. Not all liberal feminists believe that Rawlsian theory is incompatible with the struggle for gender equality. Gina Schouten, for example, argues that it is possible to justify feminist policies on the basis of Rawlsian criteria of justice. Gina Schouten, *Liberalism, Neutrality, and the Gendered Division of Labor* (Oxford: Oxford University Press, 2019).

8. This rereading process started with Susan Moller Okin, *Women and Western Political Thought* (Princeton, NJ: Princeton University Press, 1979), and was followed by, among others, Jean Elshtain, *Public Man, Private Woman* (Princeton, NJ: Princeton University Press, 1981); Lorenne M. G. Clark and Lynda Lange, eds., *The Sexism of Social and Political Theory* (Toronto: University of Toronto Press, 1979); Carole Pateman, *The Sexual Contract* (Cambridge: Polity Press, 1988); and Mary Lyndon Shanley and Carole Pateman, eds., *Feminist Interpretations and Political Theory* (Cambridge: Polity Press, 1991).

9. John Locke, *Two Treatises of Government,* ed. Peter Laslett, 2nd ed. (Cambridge: Cambridge University Press, 1970), §48, 174.

10. "The patriarchal understanding of citizenship means that the two demands are incompatible because it allows two alternatives only: either women become (like) men, and so full citizens; or they continue at women's work, which is of no value for citizenship. Moreover, within a patriarchal welfare state neither demand can be met. To demand that citizenship, as it now exists, should be fully extended to women accepts the patriarchal meaning of 'citizen,' which is constructed from men's attributes, capacities, and activities. Women cannot be full citizens in the present meaning of the term; at best, citizenship can be extended to women only as lesser men. At the same time, within the patriarchal welfare state, to demand proper social recognition and support for women's responsibilities is to condemn women to less than full citizenship and to continued incorporation into public life

238

as 'women,' that is, as members of another sphere who cannot, therefore, earn the respect of fellow (male) citizens." Carole Pateman, *The Disorder of Women* (Cambridge: Polity Press, 1989), 197.

11. "'Consent' as discussed in democratic theory is about the manner in which (it is held) agreement is given through various (public) indicators of explicit or tacitly given consent, such as voting, the receipt of benefits from the state and participating in fair institutions. Democratic theorists do not pay attention to the fact that consent is also held to constitute the relation between the sexes. For women, consent is something which is at least as, if not more, important in private as in public life. The problem . . . is whether, given the patriarchal construction of what it means to be men and women and the present structure of relations between the sexes, 'consent' can have any genuine meaning in private or public life." Pateman, *The Disorder of Women*, 12.

12. Pateman, *The Sexual Contract*, 117.

13. Pateman, *The Sexual Contract*, 119–120. The legal doctrine of coverture was in force in the United Kingdom and other common law countries until the end of the nineteenth century.

14. Claude Lévi-Strauss, *The Elementary Structures of Kinship*, rev. ed. (Boston: Beacon Press, 1969), 61, 483, cited in Pateman, *The Sexual Contract*, 59.

15. "The contracts that have a prominent place in classic social contract theory are not only about material goods, but property in the peculiar sense of property in the person, and they involve an exchange of obedience for protection. . . . Contract theory is primarily about a way of creating social relationships constituted by subordination, not about exchange." Pateman, *The Sexual Contract*, 58.

16. In French law, the possibility of rape between spouses was recognized by the Criminal Division of the Court of Cassation in 1984 for divorcing spouses (Crim. 17 juil. 1984, Bull. no. 260) and in 1990 for all spouses (Crim. 5 sept. 1990, no. 90-83.786, Bull. Crim. no. 313). In the United States, marital rape progressively became illegal between 1970 and 1993, at which point it was illegal in all fifty states. Also in 1993, the UN High Commissioner for Human Rights recognized marital rape as a human rights violation.

17. Economic exploitation of women in marriage, and by extension in sexuality, is the subject of an important feminist literature. One can refer to the works of Christine Delphy, Paola Tabet, Colette Guillaumin, Danièle Kergoat, and Silvia Federici.

18. Carole Pateman, "Women and Consent," *Political Theory* 8, no. 2 (1980): 149–168, 153.

19. Pateman, quoting Rousseau, in "Women and Consent," 154–155. Emphasis in original.

20. I should take a moment to distinguish subordination from submission. Subordination refers to the objective fact of group inferiority and says nothing about the reasons for it or about the experience of those subordinated. Submission, in contrast, refers to the subjective experience of those subordinated and assumes that this subordination is not actively resisted.

21. Claude Habib, *Le Consentement amoureux: Rousseau, les femmes et la cité* (Paris: Hachette, 2001), 11. All quotations from this book are based on my translations.

22. Habib, *Le Consentement amoureux*, 14, 24.

23. Habib, *Le Consentement amoureux*, 49.

24. Habib, *Le Consentement amoureux*, 56.

25. See Claude Habib, *Galanterie française* (Paris: Gallimard, 2006); and the critique in Laure Murat, *Une révolution sexuelle? Réflexions sur l'après-Weinstein* (Paris: Stock, 2018).

26. Maurice Godelier, "La part idéelle du réel. Essai sur l'idéologique," *L'Homme* 18, no. 3–4 (1978): 155–188, 176. Emphasis in original. A part of this passage is quoted in Nicole-Claude Mathieu, "Quand céder n'est pas consentir. Des déterminants matériels et psychiques de la conscience dominée des femmes et de quelques de leurs interprétations en ethnologie," in *L'Arraisonnement des femmes. Essais en anthropologie des sexes,* ed. Nicole-Claude Mathieu, 169–245 (Paris: Éditions de l'EHESS, 1985).

27. Mathieu, "Quand céder n'est pas consentir," 177. Emphasis in original.

28. Nicole-Claude Mathieu, *L'Anatomie politique. Catégorisations et idéologies du sexe* (Paris: Côté femmes, 1991), 11.

29. Mathieu, "Quand céder n'est pas consentir," 187. Emphasis in original.

30. Mathieu, "Quand céder n'est pas consentir," 210. Emphasis in original.

31. This does not mean that these values cannot be transformed for emancipatory purposes, "but it is not at all the same thing to take up a general notion for your own benefit *after* you have realized that it serves you . . . in which case it is only an instrument of mystification." Mathieu, "Quand céder n'est pas consentir," 216. Emphasis in original.

32. Nicole-Claude Mathieu, "Introduction," in *L'Arraisonnement des femmes. Essais en anthropologie des sexes,* ed. Mathieu (Paris: Éditions de l'EHESS, 1985).

33. Mathieu, "Quand céder n'est pas consentir," 227.

34. Mathieu, "Quand céder n'est pas consentir," 230. Emphasis in original.

35. Mathieu, "Quand céder n'est pas consentir," 232.

36. Mathieu, "Quand céder n'est pas consentir," 233. Emphasis in original.

37. On the question of what male domination does to the psyche of women, see Sandra Bartky, *Femininity and Domination: Studies in the Phenomenology of Oppression* (New York: Routledge, 1990), which offers, among other things, a

phenomenological analysis of what happens to women when they become aware of male domination.

38. As noted in Chapter 4, I don't think MacKinnon and the other women of this movement are against sex. I refer to them here as "antisex" only to situate MacKinnon in the intellectual history I have drawn.

39. I developed this idea of consent to submission in Manon Garcia, *We Are Not Born Submissive: How Patriarchy Shapes Women's Lives* (Princeton, NJ: Princeton University Press, 2021).

40. See Catharine MacKinnon, *Women's Lives, Men's Laws* (Cambridge, MA: Belknap Press of Harvard University Press, 2005).

41. Catharine MacKinnon, "Sexuality, Pornography, and Method: Pleasure under Patriarchy," *Ethics* 99, no. 2 (1989): 314–346, 343.

42. MacKinnon, "Sexuality, Pornography, and Method," 322.

43. MacKinnon, "Sexuality, Pornography, and Method," 329–330.

44. On female masochism, see John Forrester, "Rape, Seduction and Psychoanalysis," in *Rape,* ed. Sylvana Tomaselli and Roy Porter, 57–93 (Oxford: Basil Blackwell, 1986); and Paula Caplan, *The Myth of Women's Masochism* (New York: Dutton, 1985).

45. MacKinnon, "Sexuality, Pornography, and Method," 340.

46. In order to secure a rape conviction despite the high standard of guilt beyond a reasonable doubt, prosecutors must typically be able to show that the victim refused sex—not just that she did not agree to it. This is true even in jurisdictions that define rape in terms of consent rather than use of force. See, for example, Michelle Anderson, "Negotiating Sex," *Southern California Law Review* 78, no. 6 (2005): 1401–1438.

47. Catharine MacKinnon, "Rape Redefined," *Harvard Law & Policy Review* 10, no. 2 (2016): 431–477, 442.

48. MacKinnon, "Rape Redefined," 440.

49. See, for instance, the definition of consent defended in Peter Westen, *The Logic of Consent: The Diversity and Deceptiveness of Consent as a Defense to Criminal Conduct* (Aldershot, UK: Ashgate, 2004), 3.

50. MacKinnon, "Rape Redefined," 442.

51. On the link between male domination and knowledge production, see Sally Haslanger, "On Being Objective and Being Objectified," in *A Mind of One's Own: Feminist Essays on Reason and Objectivity,* ed. Louise Antony and Charlotte Witt, 2nd ed., 209–253 (Boulder: Westview Press, 2002); and Sandra Harding, "Rethinking Standpoint Epistemology: What Is 'Strong Objectivity'?" in *Feminist Epistemologies,* ed. Linda Alcoff and Elizabeth Potter (New York: Routledge, 1993).

52. MacKinnon, "Sexuality, Pornography, and Method," 343.

6. Rape Is Not Sex Minus Consent

1. R. W. Connell, *Masculinities,* 2nd ed. (Berkeley: University of California Press, 2005), 76–80.

2. Catharine MacKinnon, *Toward a Feminist Theory of the State* (Cambridge, MA: Harvard University Press, 1989), 149.

3. See, for example, Marcel Rufo, *Élever son enfant: 0–6 ans* (Paris: Hachette, 2015), 88–89.

4. On men's desire in general, and in particular on the presentation of male desire as "irrepressible" and "awakened by sexual images," see Florian Vörös, *Désirer comme un homme: Enquête sur les fantasmes et les masculinités* (Paris: La Découverte, 2020), 44. My translation. The French figures quoted by Vörös are impressive: in 2006, three out of five men and three out of four women agreed that men have greater sexual needs than women. Nathalie Bajos, Michèle Ferrand, and Armelle Andro, "La sexualité à l'épreuve de l'égalité," in *Enquête sur la sexualité en France. Pratiques, genre et santé,* ed. Nathalie Bajos and Michel Bozon, 545–568 (Paris: La Découverte, 2008).

5. The term "incel" was popularized by Amia Srinivasan, "Does Anyone Have a Right to Sex?" *London Review of Books* 40, no. 6 (2018); and later by Srinivasan, *The Right to Sex* (London: Bloomsbury, 2021). There are incel women's groups—and the term itself was invented in 1990 by a Canadian woman who has since distanced herself from the meanings that have accrued to it—but their dynamics and demands are radically different from those of male incels. See also Isabelle Kohn, "Inside the World of 'Femcels,'" Mel Magazine, 2020, https://melmagazine.com/en-us/story/femcels-vs-incels-meaning-reddit-discord; Lois Beckett, "The Misogynist Incel Movement Is Spreading. Should It Be Classified as a Terror Threat?" *The Guardian,* May 3, 2021.

6. Besides Amia Srinivasan, see Kate Manne, *Down Girl: The Logic of Misogyny* (Oxford: Oxford University Press, 2017); and Manne, *Entitled: How Male Privilege Hurts Women* (New York: Penguin, 2020). In *Down Girl,* Manne defines misogyny as a form of policing women's behavior to keep them in their place in the patriarchy, hence the title.

7. See Massil Benbouriche, "Étude expérimentale des effets de l'alcool et de l'excitation sexuelle en matière de coercition sexuelle" (PhD diss., Université Rennes 2, 2016), 196.

8. Miranda Fricker, *Epistemic Injustice: Power and the Ethics of Knowing* (Oxford: Oxford University Press, 2007).

9. I rely here primarily on the work of Kristie Dotson and José Medina, but reference can also be made to Ian Kidd, José Medina, and Gaile Pohlhaus, eds., *The Routledge Handbook of Epistemic Injustice* (New York: Routledge, 2017);

Ishani Maitra, "The Nature of Epistemic Injustice," *Philosophical Books* 51, no. 4 (2010): 195–211; Elizabeth Anderson, "Epistemic Justice as a Virtue of Social Institutions," *Social Epistemology* 26, no. 2 (2012): 163–173; Emmalon Davis, "Typecasts, Tokens, and Spokespersons: A Case for Credibility Excess as Testimonial Injustice," *Hypatia* 31, no. 3 (2016): 485–501; and Briana Toole, "From Standpoint Epistemology to Epistemic Oppression," *Hypatia* 34, no. 4 (2019): 598–618.

10. Kristie Dotson, "A Cautionary Tale: On Limiting Epistemic Oppression," *Frontiers* 33, no. 2 (2012): 24–47.

11. See also, for example, María C. Lugones and Elizabeth V. Spelman, "Have We Got a Theory for You! Feminist Theory, Cultural Imperialism, and the Demand for 'The Woman's Voice,'" *Women's Studies International Forum* 6, no. 6 (1983): 573–581.

12. Patricia Hill Collins, *Black Feminist Thought: Knowledge, Consciousness, and the Politics of Empowerment*, 2nd ed. (New York: Routledge, 2000), vii–viii.

13. José Medina, *The Epistemology of Resistance: Gender and Racial Oppression, Epistemic Injustice, and the Social Imagination* (New York: Oxford University Press, 2013), 7–9.

14. Justin R. Garcia, Elisabeth A. Lloyd, Kim Wallen, and Helen E. Fisher, "Variation in Orgasm Occurrence by Sexual Orientation in a Sample of U.S. Singles," *Journal of Sexual Medicine* 11, no. 11 (2014): 2645–2652.

15. Note the discomfort of heterosexual men interviewed by Florian Vörös when Vörös evokes the erotic potentialities of prostate stimulation: Vörös, *Désirer comme un homme*, 46.

16. "Les femmes et l'orgasme," Enquête de l'Ifop pour Cam4, press release, December 2015, www.ifop.com/wp-content/uploads/2018/03/3243-1-study_file .pdf. This study shows that, contrary to myths about French sexual prowess, French women on average experience less sexual pleasure than do many of their European neighbors.

17. Debby Herbenick, V. Schick, S. Sanders, M. Reece, and J. Fortenberry, "Pain Experienced during Vaginal and Anal Intercourse with Other-Sex Partners: Findings from a Nationally Representative Probability Study in the United States," *Journal of Sexual Medicine* 12, no. 4 (2015): 1040–1051.

18. "The free so-called speech of men . . . silences the free speech of women." MacKinnon, *Toward a Feminist Theory of the State*, 205.

19. Rae Langton, *Sexual Solipsism: Philosophical Essays on Pornography and Objectification* (Oxford: Oxford University Press, 2009).

20. See Amia Srinivasan, "Talking to My Students about Porn," in Srinivasan, *The Right to Sex*, 33–73; Nancy Bauer, *How to Do Things with Pornography* (Cambridge, MA: Harvard University Press, 2015); and Mari Mikkola, *Pornography: A Philosophical Introduction* (Oxford: Oxford University Press, 2019).

21. F. Vera-Gray, C. McGlynn, I. Kureshi, and K. Butterby, "Sexual Violence as a Sexual Script in Mainstream Online Pornography," *British Journal of Criminology* 61, no. 5 (2021): 1243–1260.

22. Amartya Sen, *Inequality Reexamined* (New York: Russell Sage Foundation; Cambridge, MA: Harvard University Press, 1995), 55. Emphasis in original.

23. Martha Nussbaum, in her work with Sen, insists on the Aristotelian dimension of his approach. See also Pierre Aubenque, *La Prudence chez Aristote* (Paris: Presses universitaires de France, 1963).

24. Serene Khader, *Adaptive Preferences and Women's Empowerment* (New York: Oxford University Press, 2011), 5.

25. Khader, *Adaptive Preferences,* 30.

26. The January 2021 issue of the philosophy journal *Ethics* discusses consent and coercion in ideal and nonideal settings. "Symposium: Coercion and Consent," *Ethics* 131, no. 2 (2021): 207–368.

27. Quill R. Kukla, "A Nonideal Theory of Sexual Consent," *Ethics* 131, no. 2 (2021): 270–292, 270.

28. Linda Alcoff, "Introduction," in Alcoff, *Rape and Resistance: Understanding the Complexities of Sexual Violation* (Cambridge: Polity Press, 2018).

29. Ann Cahill, *Rethinking Rape* (Ithaca, NY: Cornell University Press, 2001), 158–161.

30. Susan Brison, *Aftermath: Violence and the Remaking of a Self* (Princeton, NJ: Princeton University Press, 2002).

31. Katie Way, "I Went on a Date with Aziz Ansari. It Turned into the Worst Night of My Life," *Babe,* January 13, 2018, http://babe.net/2018/01/13/aziz-ansari -28355.

32. Tom Dougherty, *The Scope of Consent* (Oxford: Oxford University Press, 2021), 11. In this and other work, Dougherty provides a detailed analysis of the philosophical issues around the scope of consent.

33. Tom Dougherty, "Sex, Lies, and Consent," *Ethics* 123, no. 4 (2013): 717–744.

34. Tom Dougherty, "Yes Means Yes: Consent as Communication," *Philosophy and Public Affairs* 43, no. 3 (2015): 224–253.

35. Dougherty, *The Scope of Consent,* Introduction.

36. Roseanna Sommers, "Commonsense Consent," *Yale Law Journal* 129, no. 8 (2020): 2232–2324, establishes that consent cannot be only a mental attitude.

37. Tom Dougherty, *The Scope of Consent,* Introduction. See also Aya Gruber, "Consent Confusion," *Cardozo Law Review* 38, no. 2 (2016): 415–458, which usefully distinguishes the various stages of the communicative process of consent.

38. See also Vanina Mozziconacci and Cécile Thomé, "Penser la sexualité pour penser l'éducation à la sexualité. Corps, utilisation du préservatif et conceptions du consentement," in *Ce qu'incorporer veut dire,* ed. S. Fleuriel, J.-F. Goubet, S.

Mierzejewski, and M. Schotté, 81–102 (Villeneuve-d'Ascq: Presses universitaires du Septentrion, 2021).

39. Kasia Kozlowska, Peter Walker, Loyola McLean, and Pascal Carrive, "Fear and the Defense Cascade: Clinical Implications and Management," *Harvard Review of Psychiatry* 23, no. 4 (2015): 263–287; Brian Marx et al., "Tonic Immobility as an Evolved Predator Defense: Implications for Sexual Assault Survivors," *Clinical Psychology* 15, no. 1 (2008): 74–90; and Anna Möller, Hans Sondergaard, and Lotti Helstrom, "Tonic Immobility during Sexual Assault: A Common Reaction Predicting Post-Traumatic Stress Disorder and Severe Depression," *Acta Obstetricia et Gynecologica Scandinavica* 96, no. 8 (2017): 932–938.

40. "Thus women in general (and especially heterosexual women) confront the fact that their sexuality and sexual opportunities are conditioned by the realistic possibility that a man or men will use force or violence to impose themselves sexually on them." Scott Anderson, "Conceptualizing Rape as Coerced Sex," *Ethics* 127, no. 1 (2016): 50–87, 72.

41. Nicola Gavey, *Just Sex? The Cultural Scaffolding of Rape*, 2nd ed. (New York: Routledge, 2019), 135.

42. Celia Kitzinger and Hannah Frith, "Just Say No? The Use of Conversation Analysis in Developing a Feminist Perspective on Sexual Refusal," *Discourse and Society* 10, no. 3 (1999): 293–316.

43. See, for example, Nicola Gavey and Kathryn McPhilipps, "Subject to Romance: Heterosexual Passivity as an Obstacle to Women Initiating Condom Use," *Psychology of Women Quarterly* 23, no. 2 (1999): 349–367.

44. See, for example, Michelle Anderson, "Negotiating Sex," *Southern California Law Review* 78, no. 6 (2005): 1401–1438, esp. 1417–1420.

45. See Kitzinger and Frith, "Just Say No?"; and the work of Melanie Beres, in particular Beres, "Sexual Miscommunication? Untangling Assumptions about Sexual Communication between Casual Sex Partners," *Culture, Health & Sexuality* 12, no. 1 (2010): 1–14.

46. David Lisak and Paul Miller, "Repeat Rape and Multiple Offending among Undetected Rapists," *Violence and Victims* 17, no. 1 (2002): 73–84.

47. See Massil Benbouriche, Benoit Testé, Jean-Pierre Guay, and Marc E. Lavoie, "The Role of Rape-Supportive Attitudes, Alcohol, and Sexual Arousal in Sexual (Mis)Perception: An Experimental Study," *Journal of Sex Research* 56, no. 6 (2019): 766–777.

48. Georges Vigarello, *A History of Rape: Sexual Violence in France from the 16th to the 20th Century*, op. cit.

49. On the understanding of rape victims as permanently damaged and lost to men, see Virginie Despentes, *King Kong Theory*, trans. Stephanie Benson (New York: Feminist Press, 2010).

50. For the charge of puritanism, see, for example, Laura Kipnis, *Unwanted Advances: Sexual Paranoia Comes to Campus* (New York: Harper, 2017).

51. Scott Anderson and Tom Dougherty have argued for two different versions of the idea that morally bad sex should be assessed along a continuum of severity, rather than viewed as being in a binary relation with morally permissible sex: Scott Anderson, "Conceptualizing Rape as Coerced Sex"; Tom Dougherty, "Sexual Misconduct on a Scale: Gravity, Coercion, and Consent," *Ethics* 131, no. 2 (2021): 319–344.

52. Ann J. Cahill, "Unjust Sex vs. Rape," *Hypatia* 31, no. 4 (2016): 746–761, 746.

53. Gavey, *Just Sex?* 128.

54. A considerable literature demonstrates that women frequently accept unwanted sexual relationships. See Charlene Muehlenhard, Terry Humphreys, Kristen Jozkowski, and Zoe Peterson, "The Complexities of Sexual Consent among College Students: A Conceptual and Empirical Review," *Journal of Sex Research* 53, no. 4–5 (2016): 457–487; and Breanne Fahs and Jax Gonzalez, "The Front Lines of the 'Back Door': Navigating (Dis)engagement, Coercion, and Pleasure in Women's Anal Sex Experiences," *Feminism & Psychology* 24, no. 4 (2014): 500–520.

55. Robin West, "The Harms of Consensual Sex," *American Philosophical Association Newsletters* 94, no. 2 (1995): 52–55.

56. See Alexia Boucherie, *Troubles dans le consentement: Du désir partagé au viol, ouvrir la boîte noire des relations sexuelles* (Paris: Éditions François Bourin, 2019).

7. Sex as a Conversation

1. "Big Think Interview with Gloria Steinem" (online video), *Big Think*, November 2010, https://bigthink.com/videos/big-think-interview-with-gloria-steinem.

2. A 2006 survey finds that one-fifth of French men aged eighteen to twenty-four have no interest in sex or relationships. Michel Bozon and Charlotte Le Van, "Orientations en matière de sexualité et cours de la vie. Diversification et recomposition," in *Enquête sur la sexualité en France. Pratiques, genre et santé*, ed. Nathalie Bajos and Michel Bozon (Paris: La Découverte, 2008), 539.

3. Charlene Muehlenhard and Stephen Cook, "Men's Self-Reports of Unwanted Sexual Activity," *Journal of Sex Research* 24, no. 1 (1998): 58–72.

4. An example of these manuals is the US bestseller Ellen Fein and Sherrie Schneider, *The Rules: Time-Tested Secrets for Capturing the Heart of Mr. Right* (New York: Warner Books, 1995).

5. Philosopher Ellie Anderson also recently developed an idea of consent as feeling-with. See Ellie Anderson, "A Phenomenological Approach to Sexual Consent," *Feminist Philosophy Quarterly* 8, no. 2 (2022), article 1.

6. On the challenge to feminism posed by women who experience submissive sexual desires, see Claire Richard, *Les Chemins de désir* (Paris: Le Seuil, 2019), as well as her radio documentary, *Soumission impossible,* Arte Radio, 2019.

7. Jennifer Hirsch and Shamus Khan, *Sexual Citizens: A Landmark Study of Sex, Power, and Assault on Campus* (New York: W. W. Norton, 2020), 15.

8. California Senate Bill No. 967, "Student Safety: Sexual Assault," Section 1, 67386(a), 1, September 28, 2014, https://leginfo.legislature.ca.gov/faces /billTextClient.xhtml?bill_id=201320140SB967.

9. Vanina Mozziconacci and Cécile Thomé, "Penser la sexualité pour penser l'éducation à la sexualité. Corps, utilisation du préservatif et conceptions du consentement," in *Ce qu'incorporer veut dire,* ed. S. Fleuriel, J.-F. Goubet, S. Mierzejewski, and M. Schotté, 81–102 (Villeneuve-d'Ascq: Presses universitaires du Septentrion, 2021).

10. Ann Cahill, "Recognition, Desire, and Unjust Sex," *Hypatia* 29, no. 2 (2014): 303–319.

11. Linda Martín Alcoff, *Rape and Resistance: Understanding the Complexities of Sexual Violation* (Cambridge: Polity Press, 2018), 94–95.

12. Alcoff, *Rape and Resistance,* 70.

13. Simone de Beauvoir, *The Second Sex,* trans. Constance Borde and Sheila Malovany-Chevallier (New York: Vintage Books, 2011), 416, translation modified.

14. On harms of masculinity, see Filipa Melo-Lopes, "What Do Incels Want? Explaining Incel Violence Using Beauvoirian Otherness," *Hypatia,* 2023, 1–23, https://www.doi:10.1017/hyp.2023.3; and Manon Garcia, "Masculinity as an Impasse: Beauvoir's Understanding of Men's Situation in *The Second Sex,*" *Simone de Beauvoir Studies* 32, no. 2 (2022): 187–206.

15. See Manon Garcia, *We Are Not Born Submissive: How Patriarchy Shapes Women's Lives* (Princeton, NJ: Princeton University Press, 2021), ch. 3.

16. Beauvoir, *The Second Sex,* 415.

17. Rosemary Basson quoted in Ann Cahill, "The Female Sexual Response: A Different Model," *Journal of Sex and Marital Therapy* 26, no. 1 (2000): 51–65, 53.

18. Quill R. Kukla, "'That's What She Said': The Language of Sexual Negotiation," *Ethics* 129, no. 1 (2018): 70–97. While the analogy between propositioning sex and inviting someone to an event is useful, it should not be taken too far. For instance, if someone does not show up at an event for which they have accepted an invitation, this would clearly be ungracious and could justifiably provoke offense. But Kukla does not suggest the same of sex: one cannot permissibly hold against a person their withdrawal from sex after consenting.

19. I am grateful to Maxime Tremblay for helping me pinpoint this hermeneutical dimension of the erotic conversation.

20. Roseanna Sommers, "Commonsense Consent," *Yale Law Journal* 129, no. 8 (2020): 2232–2324.

21. See also Jed Rubenfeld, "The Riddle of Rape-by-Deception and the Myth of Sexual Autonomy," *Yale Law Journal* 122, no. 6 (2013): 1372–1443.

22. According to data compiled by the Rape, Abuse & Incest National Network, out of every 1,000 sexual assaults, 310 are reported to the police, and 28 lead to a felony conviction. "The Criminal Justice System: Statistics," Rape, Abuse & Incest National Network, https://www.rainn.org/statistics/criminal-justice-system, accessed March 3, 2023.

23. Jacob Gersen and Jeannie Suk, "Sex Bureaucracy," *California Law Review* 104, no. 4 (2016): 881–948, 891–896.

24. I take this distinction between statutory and situational nonconsent from Marie Romero, "Le traitement pénal des violences sexuelles sur mineurs: controverses et débats autour des âges et du consentement. Une enquête au sein de quatre tribunaux français correctionnels et pour enfants" (2010), in *Envers et revers du consentement*, ed. M. Garcia, J. Mazaleigue-Labaste, and A.-D. Mornington, 95–116 (Paris: Mare et Martin, 2023).

25. See Quill Kukla's fascinating analysis of the problem of prohibiting sex among people with dementia. Quill R. Kukla, "A Nonideal Theory of Sexual Consent," *Ethics* 131, no. 2 (2021): 270–292, 274–277.

26. Lisa Wallin, Sara Uhnoo, Asa Wettergren, and Moa Bladini, "Capricious Credibility: Legal Assessments of Voluntariness in Swedish Negligent Rape Judgements," *Nordic Journal of Criminology* 22, no. 1 (2021): 3–22.

27. See Stephen Schulhofer, *Unwanted Sex: The Culture of Intimidation and the Failure of Law* (Cambridge, MA: Harvard University Press, 1998).

28. Obtaining figures on rape complaints versus convictions requires cross-referencing data sources that are themselves incomplete, so the numbers are never exact. But we can obtain illustrative estimates. For instance, the Cadre de vie et sécurité population-based survey finds about 93,000 French women reported being victims of rape or attempted rape in 2018. Compare this to the French Ministry of the Interior's figures on the number of rape complaints by women in 2018 (16,554) and the rape convictions handed down in the same year (1,269). This suggests a conviction rate of about 1.3 percent for the 93,000 experienced and attempted rapes. Again, this figure is not exact, but it is robust enough to demonstrate that very few instances of rape and attempted rape lead to criminal findings.

29. Aya Gruber, *The Feminist War on Crime: The Unexpected Role of Women's Liberation in Mass Incarceration* (Oakland: University of California Press, 2020).

30. Imogen Halstead, "Does the Custody Based Intensive Treatment (CUBIT) Program for Sex Offenders Reduce Re-Offending?" *Crime and Justice Bulletin,*

New South Wales Bureau of Crime Statistics and Research (Sydney), no. 193, July 2016.

31. Joyce E. Williams, "Secondary Victimization: Confronting Public Attitudes about Rape," *Victimology* 9, no. 1 (1984): 66–81.

32. Claire Saas, "L'appréhension des violences sexuelles par le droit ou la reproduction des stéréotypes de genre par les acteurs pénaux," *La Revue des droits de l'homme,* no. 8 (2015).

33. Gersen and Suk, "Sex Bureaucracy."

34. According to the Rape, Abuse & Incest National Network calculations based on Department of Justice statistics for 2015–2019, there are, on average, 463,634 victims, aged twelve or older, of rape and sexual assault each year in the United States. There are no reasons to believe these assaults are mostly committed by repeat offenders. "Victims of Sexual Violence: Statistics," Rape, Abuse & Incest National Network, https://www.rainn.org/statistics/victims-sexual-violence, accessed March 3, 2023. For US incarceration figures, see Wendy Sawyer and Peter Wagner, "Mass Incarceration: The Whole Pie 2022," press release, Prison Policy Initiative, March 14, 2022, https://www.prisonpolicy.org/reports/pie2022.html.

35. See the work of Julie Mazaleigue-Labaste and in particular Julie Mazaleigue-Labaste and David Simard, "Le consentement peut-il constituer un critère psychiatrique? Le critère du consentement dans les classifications psycho-pathologiques des déviances sexuelles," in *Envers et revers du consentement,* ed. M. Garcia, J. Mazaleigue-Labaste, and A.-D. Mornington, 27–59 (Paris: Mare et Martin, 2023).

36. See Joseph Fischel, *Sex and Harm in the Age of Consent* (Minneapolis: University of Minnesota Press, 2016); Sarah Stillman, "The List," *New Yorker,* March 14, 2016.

37. See Angela Y. Davis, *Are Prisons Obsolete?* (New York: Seven Stories Press, 2003); Chloë Taylor, "Anti-Carceral Feminism and Sexual Assault—A Defense: A Critique of the Critique of the Critique of Carceral Feminism," *Social Philosophy Today* 34 (2018): 29–49; Anna Terwiel, "What Is Carceral Feminism?" *Political Theory* 48, no. 4 (2020): 421–442; and Gruber, *The Feminist War on Crime.*

38. On the effects of incarceration on relatives of incarcerated people, see, for example, Gwénola Ricordeau, *Les Détenus et leurs proches. Solidarités et sentiments à l'ombre des murs* (Paris: Autrement, 2008).

39. Mimi Kim, "From Carceral Feminism to Transformative Justice: Women-of-Color Feminism and Alternatives to Incarceration," *Journal of Ethnic and Cultural Diversity in Social Work* 27, no. 3 (2018): 219–233.

40. See, for instance, the influence of money on plea bargains in rape cases. "Gender Justice," *Hi-Phi Nation* (podcast), May 23, 2020, https://hiphination.org/season-4-episodes/s4-episode-4/.

41. See Michelle J. Anderson, "Sex Education and Rape," *Michigan Journal of Gender and Law* 17, no. 1 (2010): 83–110.

42. Hirsch and Khan, *Sexual Citizens*, 9.

43. See the work of Vanina Mozziconacci, in particular *Qu'est-ce qu'une education féministe? Égalité, emancipation, utopie* (Paris: Éditions de la Sorbonne, 2022). See also discussion of obstacles to good sex education in Amia Srinivasan, *The Right to Sex* (London: Bloomsbury, 2021), 62–65; and Gabrielle Richard, *Hétéro, l'école? Plaidoyer pour une éducation antioppressive à la sexualité* (Montréal: Les Éditions du Remue-Ménage, 2020).

44. See Boston Women's Health Book Collective, *Our Bodies, Ourselves* (Boston: New England Free Press, 1970), and the more than forty different editions—in thirty-three languages and often with local variations—published in its wake. Dossie Easton and Janet Hardy, *The Ethical Slut: A Practical Guide to Polyamory, Open Relationships, and Other Freedoms in Sex and Love*, 2nd ed. (Berkeley, CA: Clarkson Potter/Ten Speed Press, 2017).

45. Beth Lown, "Difficult Conversations: Anger in the Clinician-Patient/Family Relationship," *Southern Medical Journal* 100, no. 1 (2007): 34–39. See, for example, the conversation script for delivering bad news: "Serious News: Breaking Bad News Using the GUIDE Tool," VitalTalk, 2019, www.vitaltalk.org/guides /serious-news. See also The Conversation Project, https://theconversationproject .org.

46. Sally Haslanger, "How to Change a Social Structure," unpublished manuscript, January 8, 2022, https://www.ucl.ac.uk/laws/sites/laws/files/haslanger_how _to_change_a_social_structure_ucl.pdf.

47. See Meg Barker, "Consent Is a Grey Area? A Comparison of Understandings of Consent in Fifty Shades of Grey and on the BDSM Blogosphere," *Sexualities* 16, no. 8 (2013): 896–914.

Conclusion

1. Sally Haslanger, "Gender and Race: (What) Are They? (What) Do We Want Them to Be?" *Noûs* 34, no. 1 (2000): 31–55, 33.

Acknowledgments

Many feminists before me have shown that the myth of the genius thinker, sole producer of his thought and his work, is based on an androcentric and erroneous conception of the construction of knowledge. I am responsible for the weaknesses in this book, but I credit its strengths, whatever they may be, to others who have made its existence possible. The research underlying this book came together over the course of years, and I thank Sandra Laugier for her support and encouragement throughout. I would also like to thank those who have helped me on my path as a philosopher and who have trusted me and given me confidence, notably Nancy Bauer, Sean Kelly, Susan Brison, Sally Haslanger, Gary Herrigel, Dimitri El Murr, and Verity Harte.

Not only this book, but my entire life, would be very different had I not met Maxime Catroux, publisher extraordinaire, through the wonderful Cécile Daumas. Maxime and Caroline Psyroukis, my publicist, each in her own way supported, helped, and encouraged me with a constancy, benevolence, and efficiency that amaze me every day. May they be infinitely thanked.

I thank the Harvard Society of Fellows and its senior fellows for giving me the opportunity to write this book in the best possible conditions despite the pandemic. Many conversations with junior and senior fellows, especially Noah Feldman, have enriched this book. I am also grateful to Dunster House, its deans, tutors, and students for providing the best environment for the development of my ideas. In particular, the conversations I had as part of my responsibilities as a tutor dealing with issues of sexuality and consent were very important to the development of this book.

This book is also the result of years of conversations and exchanges of ideas with a great many people, among them Christopher Lewis, Kate Kirkpatrick, Filipa Melo Lopes, Mathias Chichportich, Deborah Mühlebach, Simon Bertin, Marie Cazaban-Mazerolles, and Itaï Kovacs. I thank Raphaëlle Théry, Michael Della Rocca, Paola Nicolas, Pauline Trouillard, Julien Jeanneney, Daniele Lorenzini, and Mélanie Jaoul for their comments on various iterations of the manuscript. None of the errors in this book is attributable to them, but my analyses have undoubtedly benefited from their insights.

I thank Sharmila Sen for having trusted me to write an English version of this very French book for Harvard University Press. The whole team at the press helped me through this process, which felt at times like writing a whole new book. Anne McGuire's help navigating citation systems was a godsend, and I am beyond grateful for the incredible editing work of Simon Waxman. The English edition is deeply enriched by feedback I received on its French predecessor, especially at a conference organized by Naïma Hamrouni at the Université du Québec à Trois-Rivières. I am grateful to Lila Braunschweig, Amandine Catala, Marie-Hélène Desmeules, Cécile Gagnon, Audrey Ghali-Lachapelle, Anne Iavarone-Turcotte, Marie-Pier Lemay, Sabrina Maiorano, Audrey Paquet, Marie-Anne Perreault, Laurence Ricard, and Maxime Tremblay for their comments. I am also grateful to Emanuele Coccia for his friendship, his encouragement, and the exchanges we had around this book. Finally, I cannot thank enough my beloved Yale students, Ursula Hardianto, Charlotte Hughes, Solenne Jackson, Nathaniel Rosenberg, Lara Yellin, Emily Xin, and particularly Anne Gross and Oliver Guinan for discussions that helped me adapt this book for an English-speaking audience. I feel incredibly lucky for our reading group.

The people who love me and whom I love know what I owe them, but I would like to thank my family—in particular my mother, Claire Simon—for their moral support. I thank Stéphane Pouyaud for her unfailing friendship and for all the ways in which she contributed to making this book happen. I thank Katie and Jordan Anderson, Rahima Bensaid and Gabriel Koehler-Derrick, and especially Izzy O'Connell for the care they took of my children while I was writing this book. I am eternally grateful that I was able to read, write, and reflect knowing my daughters were loved and safe in my absence. I thank the Tracys for being our family away from home; this book benefited more than I can say from our Sundays together.

Finally, I thank Tamer Teker, who not only supports me but also bears with me. My words cannot do justice to his patience, love, and kindness. And Norah and Éliane, who, with their father, make my life sparkle with a thousand lights.

Index

Note: The letter *n* following a page number and followed by a note number refers to material appearing in the endnotes.